The Trick of Singularity

STUDIES IN THEATRE HISTORY AND CULTURE

· · · · · ·

# *The* TRICK *of* SINGULARITY

## *Twelfth Night*
and the
Performance
Editions

· · · · · ·

Laurie E. Osborne

University of Iowa Press

 *Iowa City*

University of Iowa Press, Iowa City 52242
Copyright © 1996 by the University of Iowa Press
All rights reserved
Printed in the United States of America

Design by Omega Clay

Printed on acid-free paper

Library of Congress Cataloging-in-Publication Data
Osborne, Laurie E.
   The trick of singularity: Twelfth night and the
performance editions / by Laurie E. Osborne.
      p.      cm.—(Studies in theatre history and culture)
   Includes bibliographical references and index.
   ISBN 0-87745-544-9
   1. Shakespeare, William, 1564–1616. Twelfth night—
Criticism, textual.   2. Shakespeare, William, 1564–1616—
Dramatic production.   3. Shakespeare, William,
1564–1616—Stage history.   4. Comedy.   I. Title.
II. Series.
PR2837.O83   1996
822.3′3—dc20                                        95-49374
                                                              CIP

01   00   99   98   97   96   C   5   4   3   2   1

*For John, Jenny, and Andrew,*
*whose encouragement, generosity, and exuberance*
*make my multiple texts possible*

# Contents

# Acknowledgments

My institutional and personal debts are numerous. Both Oakland University and Colby College have been generous in support of this project through a summer research grant and a sabbatical extension grant, respectively. Beyond my college's support, I must also thank the National Endowment for the Humanities for the 1990 summer research grant that allowed my early investigations of the performance editions and the Folger Shakespeare Library for a short-term research grant which enabled me to finish my research. Some of the materials in this book have appeared, often in very different form, in other places. Chapters 2, 3, and 4 elaborate arguments I first made in "The Texts of *Twelfth Night*" (*ELH* 57 [1990]: 37–61), reprinted here with the permission of the Johns Hopkins University Press. The theoretical issues raised in chapter 2 appear in different form in "Rethinking the Performance Editions: Textual and Theatrical Reproductions of Shakespeare," in *Shakespeare, Theory and Performance*, edited by James Bulman. My work on the additions to Antonio's role was first published as "Antonio's Pardon," in *Shakespeare Quarterly* 45 (1994): 108–14. Chapter 6 offers a revised version of "Letters, Lovers, Lacan: Or, Malvolio's Not-So-Purloined Letter," which first appeared in *Assays: Critical Approaches to Medieval and Renaissance Texts* 5 (1989): 63–81. I am grateful to all these journals, Jim Bulman, and Routledge for permission to reprint these materials here in revised form.

Many people have commented helpfully and critically about this manuscript. I have appreciated advice about particular chapters from Valerie Traub, Peter Donaldson, Jean Howard, David Suchoff, Bernice Kliman, Barbara Hodgdon, Michael Warren, Heather Dubrow, and Stephen Orgel. They encouraged me to push the argument and myself. I reserve special thanks for those hardy souls who have read the whole manuscript in the course of its multiple versions: Kent Cartwright for braving a very early draft, Mike Bristol for commentary and encouragement through early frustrations, Simon Joyce for painstaking editing and brutal cutting, my research assistant Charles Prescott for endless proofreading, and, last but most industrious, my indefatigable editor Tom Postlewait for driving me productively crazy in the final preparation of the manuscript.

Along with those who supported the work, I want to thank those who preserved my sanity. My parents, who have been through it themselves, assured me that I would finish the book. My colleagues at Oakland and Colby, especially Kevin Grimm, Laurie Evans, David Suchoff, Elizabeth Sagaser, and Stephanie Foote, encouraged and endured me in the process. Finally I owe more than I can say to John, Jenny, and Andrew, two of whom have lived with this project for almost their entire lives. To dedicate it to them hardly seems enough.

# Introduction

On the humid July afternoon in Washington when I sat shivering in the Folger reading room, all I expected to do was look at a few promptbooks. However, when I opened *Twelfth Night* promptbook no. 2, what fascinated me more than the penciled-in prompter's notes was the text itself, Cumberland's 1830 edition of *Twelfth Night*. After its flowery introduction praising the comedy as Shakespeare's last play, the text itself presented the scenes in a different order than the one I knew and omitted great sections of dialogue.[1] I opened another promptbook only to discover that its text, David West's 1794 edition of the play, left out act 4, scene 3 in its entirety. I was well aware that theatrical productions always rewrite Shakespeare's plays in substantial ways, but I had never before encountered published texts including those revisions. I looked for promptbooks but found performance editions.

Whereas a promptbook records blocking, stage business, cuts, and additions for a particular production, a performance edition is an actual published text which promises that it appears as "printed under the authority of the managers from the prompt book" (Inchbald [1808], title page). The promptbook serves a specific and limited readership—the producers, actors, and others mounting the play—but the performance edition appeals to a wider audience. These texts proclaim their allegiance to performance and offer versions of the plays far removed from the Folio. Unlike the promptbook, which is a private, hand-marked theatrical document, the per-

formance edition is a printed text for public sale and advertises its relationship to the theatre.[2] Consequently, performance editions may include the
prompter's markings but also offer cast lists and introductions that clearly
exceed a promptbook's needs. General readers may buy the text to remem-
ber an enjoyable performance; they do not typically use it to stage their own
production. Because of these alternative purposes and audiences, performance editions differ in important ways from promptbooks.

Such distinctions become all the more intriguing because of the textual
symbiosis between performance editions and promptbooks. Sometimes the
promptbooks supply the basic text and staging details for performance editions like *Oxberry's New English Drama* (1821) and *Lacy's Acting Plays* (1855).
In turn, these published texts are often themselves taken up in the theatre
and marked again as promptbooks. John Philip Kemble typically used his
own performance editions for promptbooks, marking additional cuts and
stage business in his already altered text. In many of those same Kemble
texts, Samuel Phelps restored materials for his Sadler's Wells productions of
the 1840s and 1850s. Together promptbooks and performance editions preserve the development of acting traditions because they record performance
choices. Yet because the boundaries between the two are so blurred, they
have been effectively merged and confused by theatre scholars.

This intermingling has placed Shakespearean performance editions in an
anomalous position. Because they vary wildly from the sixteenth- and seventeenth-century texts, textual scholars ignore them. For instance, the editors
of the Oxford Shakespeare attend closely to performance issues, but performance editions do not figure in their evaluations of Shakespeare's textual
history.[3] Even Gary Taylor, who insists so fruitfully that Shakespeare's texts
are constantly reinvented, mentions the performance editions only briefly
before returning to his principal interest: the scholarly reinventions of
Shakespeare.[4] All in all, current textual scholars acknowledge the multiplicity, collaboration, and constant reworking of Shakespeare's texts—but only
within the scholarly textual history. They implicitly agree with an early de-
tractor of the performance editions, J. P. Genest, who deplored the "mutilated state" of the plays in *Bell's Shakspeare* (1774). Genest suggested that the
edition was only useful because "it is copied from the Prompter's book, and
gives the names of the performers who acted the characters, as near the time
of publication as Bell could procure them."[5] Performance editions belong to
theatre history, not to textual studies. Or so the logic goes.

However, because of the features which performance editions share with
promptbooks, theatre historians typically treat these texts as the equivalent
of promptbooks. William P. Halstead, whose fourteen-volume *Shakespeare*

*as Spoken* offers an invaluable compilation of cuts and rearrangements that the plays have experienced in performance, treats promptbooks and performance editions as completely interchangeable resources. He only singles out the performance editions in brief, useful editorial histories for each play in the appendix volumes.[6] Charles Shattuck's multivolume *John Philip Kemble Promptbooks* privileges the promptbook in both its title and introductions, even though most of the texts that Kemble marked are also performance editions which he had published previously.[7] Both strategies efface the performance edition's distinctive position at the intersection of textual and theatrical production.

I take a different perspective. Intertwined with both theatrical traditions and scholarly editing, performance editions contribute significantly to the cultural history of Shakespeare's plays, in ways detailed in chapter 2. Because these texts blend editorial and performance materials, they require an innovative blend of textual studies and performance criticism. The reward is the uncovering of an editorial tradition based in performance. This tradition starts with the quartos and Folios, flares into enormous activity in the eighteenth- and nineteenth-century "acting texts," and flourishes now in the radically new form of film and video editions.

In this range of textual enactments, *Twelfth Night* appears in multiple forms: all different, all historically contingent, none the play itself. Because *Twelfth Night* offers an apparently stable text and a relatively consistent history of performance linked with performance editions, the comedy offers textual and theatrical histories which intersect usefully with important issues for performance editing. *Twelfth Night*'s textual history is deceptively simple. The play was first published in 1623, so there are no early quartos offering alternative texts. Unlike *All's Well That Ends Well*, typeset at about the same time, *Twelfth Night*'s text presents few problems. Editors typically find the Folio text to be very clean, aside from a few mistitled speech headings and a dropped line of Sir Andrew Aguecheek's. Nevertheless, a few changes of plan—like Viola's abandonment of her intention to sing before the Duke—have led critics like J. Dover Wilson to suggest that the play's text was revised.[8] And indeed some later performance editions enact alternative versions of *Twelfth Night* signaled in the Folio text.

A wide variety of performance editions is available because of *Twelfth Night*'s consistent popularity in the theatre. Although not performed during the Restoration, the play was revived in 1741 and later gained prominence with David Garrick's Drury Lane revival in 1770, a production which probably formed the basis of the text in *Bell's Shakspeare* (1774).[9] After that, it played intermittently throughout the late eighteenth and nineteenth

centuries. This return to the theatre coincided with the series of performance editions that I investigate in chapters 3 and 4.

The changes introduced in *Twelfth Night*'s performance editions are not
so extreme that the texts constitute obvious variants. Unlike Charles Burnaby's *Love Betray'd* (1703), which uses only about fifty lines of the Folio text,
the performance editions are *not* adaptations. Their titles and texts announce that they are William Shakespeare's *Twelfth Night*. Nonetheless, the
alterations made to the Folio text include not just cuts but also significant
rearrangements and additions, as performance editors seek to record theatrical practice. Typical changes include the inversion of the first two scenes
and more complicated cuts and additions to the two scenes involving Antonio and Sebastian. Eighteenth-century theatrical revisions to the play in-
augurate an acting tradition that extends through the nineteenth century
and well into the twentieth. Recently, new media for reproducing performance on record, film, audiotape, videotape, CD-ROM, and Laserdisk augment the possible forms performance editing can take. The video editions,
my focus in chapter 5, introduce radically new technology for representing
performance but nonetheless continue many of the characteristic nineteenth-
century changes.

The thematic issues within *Twelfth Night* are also pertinent to its textual
variations. For example, the play's ambiguous presentation of gender roles
provokes performance editors to rework aspects of the female leads, particularly Viola's disguise and Olivia's aggressive courtship. The performance editors rework *Twelfth Night*'s representations of gender in response to changing gender ideologies and revise homoerotic attractions because of new
perceptions of desire in the nineteenth and twentieth centuries. Changes in
theatrical practice, like the radical shift away from the sixteenth-century
convention of boys taking the parts of Viola, Olivia, and Maria, influence
the suitable portrayal of women. In the eighteenth and nineteenth centuries,
actresses played the female roles; more recently, technological innovations in
film have allowed a single actress to play both Viola and Sebastian, inverting
the crossdressing common on the Renaissance stage. These revolutionary
changes in the performance of women's roles materially influence the performance editions of the play.

Likewise, the opposition between order and misrule within the play, best
exemplified in the fool roles of Malvolio, Feste, and Aguecheek, surfaces in
the performance editions' reordering of scenes. Proper order and the acceptable place and time for misrule concern both the characters within *Twelfth
Night* and the performance editors and theatrical professionals who reproduce the play. Early-nineteenth-century theatrical managers, like John Philip

Kemble, felt compelled to sort out *Twelfth Night*'s scenes in order to produce unity of action. The apparent unruliness of Shakespeare's scenic structure, from the nineteenth-century perspective, authorized rearrangements
of the play that are reminiscent of Malvolio's torturous reworking of
"M.O.A.I." in the discovered letter. At the same time, letters of love and
challenge which circulate within *Twelfth Night* also script new versions of
the characters, as the texts within the comedy generate patterns of displacement which I analyze in chapter 6.

Thus, *Twelfth Night* proves an expansive history of textual multiplicity,
from the eighteenth-century performance editions to our recent video texts.
And even the identity of the supposedly stable Folio text has undergone
significant changes. For example, in the early 1800s scholars radically revised
their understanding of when the play was written. Instead of perceiving it as
Shakespeare's last play, a farewell to the theatre, they came to see it as a play
from his middle period. Consequently, even the Folio's identity shifts with
the change in date, as I show in chapter 1, and shifts again once the now-
cherished seventeenth-century texts participate only in scholarly recuperations rather than in the traditions of performance editing it helped to initiate. Thus the multiple performance editions that follow the Folio are crucial
to our understanding of both later scholarly editions and the complex material effects of performance. With the arrival of films and especially video, the
performance editions themselves begin to adopt multiple forms, extending
to incorporate performance into textual reproducibility.

As a result, I advocate a necessary convergence of textual studies and performance theory, a collaboration that represents a significant innovation in
both fields. When Stephen Urkowitz, Randall MacLeod, and Stephen Orgel
direct close attention to textual features that have performance implications,
they concentrate on the early published texts.[10] They do not concern themselves with the series of editions that follows the quartos and Folios. Margreta de Grazia and Gary Taylor do take up later texts, but only treat the
scholarly editions.[11] Because textual scholars ignore their textual status, the
performance editions serve only as collections of theatrical signifiers. However, when performance critics turn to semiotics to study the theatre, they
treat the staged event as the only pertinent collection of signs.[12] In fact,
Marco De Marinis ultimately defines "performance text" as the material
semiotic event that occurs in the theatre and leaves no place for the performance edition in his schema beyond the category of "script."[13] However,
the attentiveness of textual scholars to the physical attributes of the text is a
necessary counterpart to the semiotic interpretations offered by performance
critics: both are crucial to the study of performance editions. By attending to

individual textual features as well as the influence and semiotics of performance, I want to show that a blending of these approaches yields the richest reading of *Twelfth Night*'s cultural history.

The comedy performed on the Renaissance stage only acquires its apparently singular identity as *Twelfth Night* because a variety of alternate textual and theatrical productions affirm the play's currency within each new historical moment. Performances, artwork, adaptations, variorums, school texts, breviates, performance editions—the list includes incredibly varied *Twelfth Nights*. Ultimately, no version of the play stands alone, unaffected by other texts or performances which compete with or complement its historically specific production. Thus I favor an unusual kind of intertextual analysis. My approach differs from the important work of Stephen Greenblatt, who also brings together different texts in order to read *Twelfth Night*'s inscriptions of gender and desire. Unlike Greenblatt's combination of medical discourses, Michel de Montaigne's histories, and the playtext, my analysis intermingles the multiple productions of a single Renaissance play.[14] I explore how a comedy about twins becomes the canonical *Twelfth Night*, developing an identity that is itself constantly being revised.

For Shakespeare, as for other writers and dramatists, the first texts or performances initiate literary identity. As one age's popular culture becomes another age's canonical work, the first texts often participate in editorial traditions far removed from the scholarly editions which follow. For example, Charles Dickens's novels, now published as exhaustive volumes that daunt students with their length, were first published serially. The scholarly recuperation of Dickens's *Nicholas Nickleby*, in one text (with notes, etc.), acknowledges the book's initial serial production but, self-evidently, does not participate in that tradition of editing.[15] Nor do the readers enjoy the narrative suspense of receiving the novel in sections. The elaborate multinight Broadway production or PBS reproduction may capture some of that suspense, but now *Nicholas Nickleby* appears in several forms, all of which combine to create what Dickens's novel is in the late twentieth century.

Similarly Shakespeare's Folios and quartos are also a starting place for scholarly editions. However, the early texts have more in common with the editions which so startled me on that hot July afternoon than with the variorum Shakespeare texts that resided on the shelves behind me in the Folger Reading Room. The first published texts of Shakespeare's works are poised at the juncture of performance and text. Their editors, like later performance editors, alternate between reproducing specific performance attributes—the text, the speakers, the entrances and exits—and offering "readerly" features, like Ben Jonson's dedication and John Heminge and Henry

Condell's preface. The Folio initiates the tradition of Shakespearean performance editing. As I explore the wildly varying texts of the nineteenth-century performance editions, I emphasize the negotiations between textuality and performance that mark all drama as a genre on the edge of two distinct material enactments.

The texts of Shakespeare's plays are always subject to historically specific tastes, to available conditions of theatrical and textual reproduction and to ideological pressures on representations of gender and desire. As a result they change in material form as well as cultural significance. From the seventeenth century to the twentieth, these varied texts are consistently imagined to be his original creation when they are in fact culturally and historically bounded creations. My inquiry into *Twelfth Night*'s multiple texts proves how usefully the performance editions reflect the interactions of a particular play with the different historical and cultural contexts that rewrite and renew its identity as a work.

The case of *Twelfth Night* suggests to me that the multiple versions of texts which in some way *claim* a common identity produce the effect of a singular text, though that singularity is an obvious impossibility. Thus, it is possible for me to talk about *Twelfth Night*, at least with my contemporaries who occupy the same intertextual space, and assume provisionally that the play has one identity for all. However, my work throughout this book complicates that singular identity by displaying how very differently the play is constructed at other times and in multiple texts. Shakespeare's works occupy their important and ever-changing cultural place because of their intertextuality. We must learn from Malvolio's mistakes and avoid "the trick of singularity" (2.5.151).

# 1

· · · · · ·

# Double Dating

S imultaneity and coincidence are the essential features which connect Viola and Sebastian in *Twelfth Night.* Twins, after all, are born
at the same time and coincide in one womb. Indeed, Sebastian identifies himself as Viola's twin, rather than merely her brother: "He [Sebastian
of Messaline] left behind him myself and a sister, both born in an hour: if
the heavens had been pleased, would we had so ended!"[1] Though Viola
never reveals that her brother is her twin until she is mistaken for him, Sebastian begins his existence in the play as a twin and, just as importantly, as
a displaced twin. His lament for lost simultaneity is followed in the next
scene by Viola's response to her own emotional quandary: "O time, thou
must untangle this, not I, / It is too hard a knot for me t'untie" (2.2.39–40).
For both twins, time is the deciding factor: Sebastian regrets the failure of simultaneity in his experience while Viola commits herself to time, both when
she adopts her male disguise and when she discovers the situation which that
disguise has provoked.[2] By rescuing Sebastian, Antonio has, from Sebastian's
perspective, disrupted the simultaneity of the twins' experience, which arose
from their birth at the same time and was reflected in their crucial similarity
of feature. What was once a twinned existence in brother and sister becomes
a string of coincidences in Illyria. Whereas before they experienced life at the
same time (and would have died at the same time), when the play begins
their lives are only coincidentally the same. Both are rescued and befriended
by a ship's captain; both set down in Illyria; both decide to serve Duke

Orsino; and both are caught in the interplay between Olivia's household and the Duke's. The events which occur to them are similar but no longer identical.

In consequence, a minor but fascinating textual problem develops in *Twelfth Night*. As Dennis Huston succinctly puts it, "Sebastian and Viola collide spatially when they are temporally almost three months apart."[3] The doubled time experienced by the twins arises from two unnecessarily specific temporal references, one which precedes the sequence of scenes which causes the problem and one which follows those scenes. Before Viola leaves the Duke to woo Olivia on his behalf, Valentine, noting how fond the Duke has become of his new page, draws her attention to the fact that "he [the Duke] hath known you but three days" (1.4.2–3). In the middle of the conversation between Viola and Olivia which immediately follows, after she parts company with Olivia in act 1, scene 5 and before she receives from Malvolio the ring Olivia has sent after her in act 2, scene 2, Sebastian lands in Illyria with Antonio. His first appearance in act 2, scene 1 would cause no controversy except that in act 5 Antonio insists that Sebastian has just arrived that day and has been with Antonio "for three months before" (5.1.92). During the three days in which Orsino has come to trust Cesario, Sebastian has passed three months with Antonio. Sebastian's lament for lost simultaneity is made literal in the context of the major differences between the twins' experiences: Viola becomes enamored of Orsino in three days, and Sebastian becomes the beloved of Antonio in three months.

This temporal disjunction provokes interesting responses from both critics and producers of the play. The standard critical explanation is that the incongruity is not noticeable to a spectator watching the action. As John Dover Wilson puts it, "It is only evident to the careful *reader*; the spectator would notice nothing wrong."[4] When *Twelfth Night* becomes a text to be read rather than a performance which has a promptbook, the discrepancy becomes noticeable; the reader facing the text recognizes the references to time. Perhaps because *Twelfth Night* is so thoroughly a text as well as a play by the early 1700s, a number of productions, as presented in both promptbooks and performance editions, appear to resolve the problem anyway. They either omit all or part of Viola's conversation with Valentine in act 1, scene 4 or, more drastically, move the first scene between Sebastian and Antonio so that it does not intrude between Olivia sending the ring and Viola receiving it. Both resolutions of the double date within *Twelfth Night* are quite revealing, but the ease with which Valentine's reference to three days can be dropped shows how arbitrary the reference is from the start.

*Twelfth Night* shows an attention to time which rivals that in *As You Like It*, ranging from the sea captain's assertion that he was "bred and born / Not three hours' travel from this very place" (1.2.22–23) to the priest who has married Olivia and Sebastian "since when, my watch hath told me, toward my grave / I have travell'd but two hours" (5.1.160–61). Most often, however, periods of time define the relationships in this play, as if emotional distance or proximity were a temporal consideration. Orsino responds to Olivia's plan to mourn for seven years by imagining how great her love for him will be if she will "pay this debt of love but to a brother" (1.1.34). When Valentine marvels at the three-day bond between Orsino and Cesario, he seems to suggest an instant attraction. Even Malvolio articulates his imagined relationship with Olivia in a specific time frame and plans his life, "Having been three months married to her" (2.5.44). These measures of affection have all the consistency of Cecily and Gwendolen in *The Importance of Being Earnest* when each stakes her claim as Ernest's fiancée by asserting, respectively, the most recent proposal or the first.[5] In the same way, strength of affection in *Twelfth Night* can be measured in one scene by seven year's mourning and in another by three day's acquaintance.

Yet the force of time as a measure of emotional ties most vividly appears in Sebastian's assertions of his feeling for his sister and in Antonio's response to the apparent betrayal of Sebastian. Sebastian's claim of being born within an hour of Viola first introduces simultaneity as a principle of closeness. Their separation in the course of the play, first introduced by Viola and then intensified in Sebastian's claim of twinning, signals a failure of congruent experience. This loss of simultaneity is set against the way relationships in Illyria are figured in terms of varying, and even sometimes contradictory, time frames.

Antonio brings together these two models in response to the twins he perceives as one. He represents "Sebastian's" inexplicable coldness to him by describing how Sebastian "grew a twenty years' removed thing / While one would wink; denied me mine own purse, / Which I had recommended to his use / Not half an hour before" (5.1.87–90). He offers this description in almost the same breath in which he affirms that he and Sebastian have spent the last three months together; the proof of the intensity of their former closeness is that *he* has acted as Sebastian's twin: "No int'rim, not a minute's vacancy, / Both day and night did we keep company" (5.1.93–94). The measure of Sebastian's betrayal is the disjointedness of a half hour transfigured into twenty years' remove. Antonio's claim of his own former simultaneity with Sebastian establishes the twins' newly disparate existences;

their relationship and their identities, both temporally defined, have been temporarily suspended. Cesario can only recover her identity as Viola, and Sebastian, first disguised as Roderigo and then taken as Cesario, can only publicly resume his identity as Sebastian when Viola and he once again occupy the same place at the same time.

When Antonio first invokes the model of simultaneity, his claim is dismissed as lunacy. Even so, Orsino's response to him extends the three days of Valentine's remark to three months: "fellow, thy words are madness. / Three months this youth hath tended upon me" (5.1.96–97). Thus begins the process in the final scene whereby the coincidences in *Twelfth Night* begin to produce simultaneity. The odd congruence of Orsino's and Antonio's three-month connection with Cesario, the similar claims on her loyalty from Olivia and Orsino, and the identical grievances of Sir Toby and Sir Andrew are concurrent demands on Viola which build to the ultimate coincidence: "One face, one voice, one habit, and two persons!" (5.1.214). This final coincidence, which cannot be explained away as Antonio's madness or Viola's duplicity, leads the twins to their dance of mutual recognition. They survey what proofs, what coincidences, link them. Each had a father named Sebastian; the father of each had a mole upon his brow. The final and deciding coincidence is, suitably, temporal—both recall the father who "died that day when Viola from her birth / Had number'd thirteen years" (5.1.242–43).

The most unusual aspect of this proof is frequently overshadowed by Sebastian's inexplicable failure to identify himself as Viola's twin: he does not acknowledge that his father also died on his thirteenth birthday but says, "He finished indeed his mortal act / That day that made my sister thirteen years" (5.1.245–46). His answer apparently violates the parallelism of their mutual catechism ("My father had a mole upon his brow." / "And so had mine" [5.1.240–41]), but actually follows Viola's impulse to identify herself. After all, Sebastian has external verification when he recognizes Antonio and Antonio names him; Viola's identity is the issue, as Sebastian's questions indicate: "what kin are you to me? / What countryman? What name? What parentage?" (5.1.228–29). Her self-identification depends on the internal evidence of memory. The proof she offers is remarkable indeed—the date of her thirteenth birthday is the date of her father's death. Olivia reinforces this return to simultaneity and restored relationships when she offers to be Orsino's sister and asserts that "one day shall crown th'alliance on't" (5.1.317); the twins will marry simultaneously, and Orsino and Olivia will become brother and sister in amity at the same time. The "whirligig of time" (5.1.375) may bring its revenges to Malvolio, but "golden time convents"

(5.1.381) to sort out most of the other relationships in Illyria—once the twins are restored to the same time.

Similar concerns for simultaneity and identity, time and connection, are the very principles at work in the determinations of two very different dates for the play in the late eighteenth and early nineteenth centuries. In the late 1700s when Edmond Malone first argued that a chronology of Shakespeare's plays would be useful, texts like *Twelfth Night* which appear only in the Folio posed special problems. In the absence of quartos or other early references, scholars relied on internal evidence to ascertain a play's date. Horace Howard Furness points out in the Variorum edition that a scholar named Thomas Tyrwhitt discovered an apparent topical reference to undertakers; as a result, the play was dated at 1614 when there was considerable parliamentary furor about undertaking, "although this date involved the undesirable conclusion that *Twelfth Night* was the last play that Shakespeare had written." [6] Published references to the 1614 origin of *Twelfth Night* actually begin with Malone's "An Attempt to Ascertain the Order in Which the Plays Attributed to Shakspeare Were Written," which is included as part of the introductory material in the George Steevens edition of Shakespeare's works in 1778. [7] In discussing the chronology he offers, Malone affirms the 1614 date by challenging readers to discover "among the plays produced before 1600, compositions of equal merit with *Othello, King Lear, Macbeth, The Tempest,* and *Twelfth Night* which we have reason to believe were all written in the latter period" (p. 271). For the next fifty years, most experts considered *Twelfth Night* to be one of the later, if not the last, of Shakespeare's works.

References to the 1614 date of *Twelfth Night*'s composition occur in a variety of places besides Malone's scholarly essay. Perhaps the most pervasive case is *The Life of WILLIAM SHAKSPEARE: Collected and Arranged from Numerous Rare and Authentic Documents. Containing EVERY FACT OF IMPORTANCE from the Birth of This Eminent Poet to the Close of His Brilliant Career,* written by Joseph Graves in the 1820s. Though Graves acknowledges that all efforts to establish which of Shakespeare's plays was written first have failed, he feels confident enough about some of the sequence to assert that: "we may not hesitate . . . to station 'Pericles, the three parts of Henry VI., Love's Labour lost; The Comedy of Errors; The Taming of the Shrew; King John; and Richard II.,' among his earliest productions, we may with equal confidence, arrange 'Macbeth; Lear; Othello; Twelfth Night; and the Tempest;' with his latest, assigning them to that season of life, when his mind exulted in the conscious plenitude of power." [8] The cover of this *Life of Shakespeare* announces that it is "adapted and printed, for the purpose of binding up with any edition of Shakspeare's Plays." Some editions, particularly *Cumberland's British Theatre* (1830), did indeed bind up Graves's version of Shakespeare's life with the plays. Moreover, others who were producing biographies of Shakespeare echoed Graves, like Charles Symmons, who in 1837 also assumed that Shakespeare wrote *Twelfth Night* "when his mind exulted in the conscious plenitude of power."[9]

Even *The Dramatic Souvenir: Being Literary and Graphical Illustrations of SHAKESPEARE and Other Celebrated English Dramatists*, published in 1833, devotes fully half of its "literary illustration" of the play to discussing its composition: "Malone considered *Twelfth-Night* was written at leisure, in 1614, when the author had retired from the Theatre, the very last of his plays, and about three years before his death."[10] These ideas about the date of the play were also accepted by Shakespeare enthusiasts, as John William Cole's intensely annotated edition of Shakespeariana indicates. His copious notes on the available editions and documents associated with Shakespeare testify to his interest in the plays and their author, while he lists in his own hand *Twelfth Night*'s date of composition as 1614.[11]

However, in 1831 John P. Collier completely revised the date of *Twelfth Night*'s composition by publishing his discovery of John Manningham's 1601–2 diary entry, which alludes explicitly to a production of the comedy: "Feb 2, 1601[–2] At our feast we had a play called *Twelve Night or what you will*, much like the comedy of errors, or Menechmi in Plautus, but most like & neere to that in Italian called Inganni. A good practise in it to make the steward believe his lady widdowe was in love with him by counterfayting a letter."[12] This reference seems indeed, as Collier says, "a striking, and at the same time a rarely occurring, and convincing proof" (p. 327). This determination also completely revises the date promoted by Malone and others.

This nominally "absolute" determination of the comedy's date dislocates the text; as a result, later editions had to explain the change. Burton's Theatre Edition, published in 1852, quotes the Oxberry introduction but carefully rectifies the date by offering Collier's discovery, evidently common knowledge by that time (p. v). Other editors, like those of *Chambers's Household Shakespeare* (1840), felt obligated to justify the earlier error: "The dramatic art evinced in *Twelfth Night*, and its general excellence, led to a belief that it was one of the poet's latest productions" (p. 1).[13] Far from rendering the comedy more firmly established, the diary entry actually exposes the ways in which even identical texts can vary because of "extratextual" considerations such as their date of composition.

The Tyrwhitt *Twelfth Night* (1614) differs from the post-Manningham *Twelfth Night* (1602) established by Collier because Tyrwhitt depended on the way the playwright's imagination supposedly transformed and reflected the events of his day within the play. Collier, on the other hand, derived his date for the play from the physical evidence of the play's production. Both versions of *Twelfth Night*'s date depend on the crucial mutuality which the play itself considers—coincidence and simultaneity. For Tyrwhitt, and Malone as well, the mention of undertakers in act 3, scene 4 and the furor over "undertaking" in Parliament in 1614 were too great a coincidence for the reference not to be deliberate: "Mr. Tyrwhitt, with great probability, conjectures, that *Twelfth Night* was written in 1614: grounding his opinion on an allusion, which it seems to contain, to those parliamentary *undertakers*, of whom frequent mention is made in the Journals of the House of Commons for that year" (Malone, p. 344). Toby's jesting about undertaking reflected Shakespeare's creative rendering of a topical issue particularly hot in 1614—the two must have occurred simultaneously.

When Collier discovered the Manningham diary, Toby's comment was revealed as an irrelevant coincidence rather than one which denotes simultaneity. The many features which define the comedy Manningham saw—the title *Twelve Night, Or what you will*, the plot's similarity to *The Comedy of Errors*, the trick on a steward involving a letter—coincide in the diary entry dated 1601. Although there is a play by John Marston called *What You Will*, all the circumstances in Manningham's diary combined constitute an even greater coincidence than a single reference to undertakers. Thus the occurrence of Manningham writing in his diary and Shakespeare's company producing *Twelfth Night* must be mutually determinant—the date attached to one can also be attached to the other.

Like the twins, two texts of *Twelfth Night*, one dated 1614 and another dated 1601, look the same but participate in different relationships. These doubled texts enact the situation imagined in Jorge Luis Borges's short story "Pierre Menard, Author of *Don Quixote*." The narrator claims that Menard's "work, possibly the most significant of our time, consists of the ninth and thirty-eighth chapters of Part One of *Don Quixote* and a fragment of the twenty-second chapter."[14] Menard does not copy the novel; he does not produce a contemporary version or a transcription; he does not write it by reenacting Cervantes's life. He takes up a different challenge—to write *Don Quixote* as Pierre Menard. As a result, the narrator tells us, "The text of Cervantes and that of Menard are verbally identical, but the second is almost infinitely richer" (p. 52). In this story, Borges displays the inherent contradiction between, on the one hand, attempting to anchor the text historically in relation to its author and, on the other hand, claiming that a text transcends its time. By insisting that the second *Don Quixote* is "infinitely richer," Borges imagines that the temporal displacement enriches and changes the text, even though the later version is "verbally identical." The second *Twelfth Night*, dated at 1601, may not necessarily be "infinitely richer" but it has certainly occasioned many more readings of the play, including some analyses explicitly based on the 1601 date, like Leslie Hotson's *The First Night of Twelfth Night*.[15]

For the readers of the early nineteenth century, *Twelfth Night* is a comedy self-evidently from the close of Shakespeare's career. Yet, for the twentieth-century reader, with the benefit of 150 years of scholarship based on the 1601 date, *Twelfth Night* is obviously a middle comedy with connections to *Hamlet* and to the tragedies. Like the two versions of *Don Quixote* in Borges's story—one from the sixteenth century and one from the twentieth—the Folio text of *Twelfth Night* before 1831 and after are typographically identical, but utterly different.

Although *Twelfth Night* seems one of the least problematic works in the Shakespearean canon because we can now establish its date so confidently, the achievement of that fixed date actually reveals the text's multiplicity rather than its singularity. Moreover, the real purpose of dating *Twelfth Night* or any Shakespearean play is not so much absolute as relational. The shift of *Twelfth Night*'s date not only exposes the doubled nature of that play, but also calls into question the status of *The Tempest*. The speculation on *The Tempest* as Shakespeare's last play (and final statement) originated at the time when *Twelfth Night*'s date shifted. Malone corrected his own chronology in 1821 to give the date as 1607, and, as Gary Taylor notes, Thomas Campbell at around the same time first put forward the attractive theory about *The Tempest*'s valedictory quality.[16]

When Malone initially published his attempt to discover the order of Shakespeare's plays, he laid out the potential importance of such knowledge: "While it has been the endeavour of all his editors and commentators, to illustrate his obscurities, and to regulate and correct his text, no attempt has been made to trace the progress and order of his plays. Yet surely it is no incurious speculation, to mark the gradations by which he rose from mediocrity to the summit of excellence; from artless and uninteresting dialogues, to those unparalleled compositions, which have rendered him the delight and wonder of successive ages" (pp. 270–71). Malone implied that the idea of giving a chronology to Shakespeare's works had not occurred to anyone before him, even though Nicholas Rowe indicated his own curiosity concerning the dating of the plays as early as 1709 (Taylor, p. 157). Malone also linked chronology to the evolution of Shakespeare's art. Indeed the readers and critics of Malone's day were interested in his chronology and fashioned

their own theories of Shakespeare's development. Joseph Graves gave a typical view: "It is probable that such as were founded on the works of preceding authors, were the first essays of his dramatic talent: and such as were
more perfectly his own, and are of the first sparkle of excellence, were among
his last" (pp. 9–10). Graves, like Malone and others, carried his point by
inviting the reader to compare the earlier works with the superior later ones.

The significance of dates, then, is twofold. The comedy's date of composition determines its connections with the other plays, and those connections anchor the text to the author's evolving psyche. As Margreta de
Grazia has argued, Malone's purpose in determining the sequence of plays
was little more than a small part of his overarching aim to establish Shakespeare as an individual. She further suggests that this treatment of Shakespeare's artistic development becomes a model for the emerging bourgeois
subject.[17] That model hinged on the idea that his development registered
ever-greater perfection.

Comments on *Twelfth Night* found in performance editions before 1831
underscore this notion. George Daniel's 1830 introduction to the play is particularly fulsome: "It is, therefore, not without emotion that we approach
this last work of Shakspeare's mighty genius. . . . That Shakspeare parted
with the world on terms of friendship, this legacy of his love sufficiently
demonstrates; though, in the Epilogue Song (the last lines that he ever
wrote,) we think we can discover something that savours of transient bitter-
ness" (Cumberland, p. 5). Daniel even goes so far as to praise John Fawcett's
acting of Feste by commenting that "he sang the Epilogue Song with true
comic spirit; and with a harmony and *feeling* as if conscious that the *last
words of Shakspeare* were trembling on his lips" (Cumberland, p. 7). While
asserting *Twelfth Night*'s privileged position as the last play, these statements
also raise several problems.

Most striking, perhaps, is the reference to the Epilogue Song, which we
are asked to take as Shakespeare's last words. After all, Malone himself notes
that the song appears "earlier" in Shakespeare's career, in a slightly different
form as one of the Fool's songs in *Lear*.[18] If Feste's cryptic song is Shakespeare's final statement, the various attempts to decipher or dismiss the song
which begin as early as 1774 with Bell's edition take on new significance:
"The epilogue song gives spirit to the conclusion, tho' there is very little
meaning in it, except a trifling address to the audience in the last line" (Bell,
vol. 5, p. 329).[19] The song troubled Leigh Hunt as well, who praised Fawcett's presentation of the Clown's role but disliked the song: "Yet we do not
like to think that this was the last song which Shakespeare wrote. It has too
much of the scorn of the world and all he has seen in it."[20]

There are also more subtle problems revealed in the assumptions expressed by Daniel. For example, it is now common knowledge (with all the uncertainty the phrase should imply) that Shakespeare left the theatre well before he left the world. Yet placing the date of *Twelfth Night* at 1614 suggests that Shakespeare wrote the play after retiring from London. *Twelfth Night* is thus not only the last of his plays but also a work written after he left the playhouse. Malone goes to some lengths to explore this most unusual aspect of Tyrwhitt's date. He develops an elaborate explanation of why Shakespeare would take up the pen again after he had abandoned the theatre: "When Shakspeare quitted London and his profession, for the tranquillity of a rural retirement, it is improbable that such an excursive genius should have been immediately reconciled to a state of mental inactivity. . . . To the necessity, therefore, of literary amusement to every cultivated mind, or to the dictates of friendship, or to both these incentives, we are perhaps indebted for the comedy of *Twelfth Night*; which bears evident marks of having been composed at leisure, as most of the characters that it contains, are finished to a higher degree of dramatick perfection, than is discoverable in our author's earlier comick performances" (Malone, p. 344). Malone perceived a greater perfection in Shakespeare's characterization in his "last" comedy, underscoring his notions of Shakespeare's developmental improvement. Daniel concurred and reinforced this sentiment in the opening of his introduction: "We have now come to the last production of the Divine Shakspeare. Having followed his genius through its bright path of glory, we arrive at the point where it sets, with a splendour worthy of its highest meridian" (Cumberland, p. 5).

These comments may seem like little more than amusing, if antiquated, examples of previous misconceptions about Shakespeare, which we can safely ignore. Nevertheless, the readers of Shakespeare in the late eighteenth and early nineteenth centuries knew a different *Twelfth Night* from the 1601 text we read now, whether they subscribed to the bardolatrous view of the comedy which Daniel offers or thought, as the Oxberry edition tells us, that "it is not a little singular that this play should be one of the last of Shakespeare's productions, a play that has all the joyousness and revelry of youth about it" (Oxberry, p. ii).

Even though explanations of Shakespeare's developing art have changed considerably, Malone was more prophetic than he knew. While perhaps no longer a subject as hotly debated as it was when Malone and George Chalmers argued about whether Shakespeare wrote *Twelfth Night* "in 1614 or in 1613" (*Souvenir*, p. v), the dating of his plays still functions as the unacknowledged foundation for many critical arguments. Our readings depend upon the coincidences recorded in Manningham's diary as thoroughly as Malone and Tyrwhitt relied on a coincidental reference to undertakers. However, as the twins' experiences in the play and Malone's error point out, coincidences do not necessarily indicate simultaneity. Current criticism may take a different model of development, but it derives comparably from the interconnections between chronologically linked plays and their presumed reflections of an author's individual evolving psyche.

For example, many psychoanalytic approaches to *Twelfth Night* rely on its position in Shakespeare's development. Leonard Manheim argues that the play is a wish-fulfillment fantasy restoring the playwright's son Hamnet, twin to Judith, who died in 1596.[21] In turn, Thomas MacCary discovers in the plays a model of male sexual development through homoerotic attraction which he sees most fully expressed in the mature comedies like *Twelfth Night*: "The late romances do not share that fervour and obsession so characteristic in the mature comedies like *Twelfth Night*."[22] Joel Fineman, in his argument about the shifting uses of doubling at the crucial shift in Shakespeare's career from comedy to tragedy, implicitly depends on the contemporaneity of the four plays he considers, *As You Like It, Hamlet, Troilus and Cressida*, and, of course, *Twelfth Night*.[23] Likewise, C. L. Barber and Richard Wheeler explicitly rely on canon chronology for their study of Shakespeare's psychology, *The Whole Journey*.[24] For these critics, involved in considering Shakespeare's development, the status of *Twelfth Night* as mature comedy is essential and unquestioned.

Even critics less overtly concerned with Shakespeare's overall psychological development also assume the fixed placement of *Twelfth Night* in the canon. Nowhere in his essay about the problem of identity in the play does Dennis Huston specify the play's date as a concern, yet he opens the essay by explicitly linking the comedy to *Hamlet* and brackets the comedy's treatment of sexuality as "an idea that Shakespeare used twice before as a starting point for comedy—in *Love's Labour's Lost* and *The Taming of the Shrew*—and would use again with more serious overtones in *Measure for Measure*" (p. 283). Matthew Wikander, who juxtaposes psychological and anthropological readings of adolescent experience in *Twelfth Night* with the experiences of the boy-actress in Shakespeare's company, also calls upon *Hamlet* in support of the ambivalence toward the theatre which he reads in the boy-actress facing his uncertain future in the company.[25]

In contrast to the central and sometimes invisible role of the 1601 date in these studies, the 1614 date figures in current criticism only as a curiosity. Both Margreta de Grazia and Gary Taylor mention it in passing, but both are more concerned with the developing uses of Shakespeare as an icon rather than with the development of a particular set of texts. Taylor, for example, dismisses Leigh Hunt's praise of *Twelfth Night* as Shakespeare's last play with the conclusion that, given modern scholarship, Hunt is wrong (p. 157). The 1614 date is simply incorrect and therefore irrelevant. Or is it? After all, Taylor catalogs successive generations of scholars and readers who all discover their own versions of Shakespearean authenticity, and de Grazia explores late-eighteenth- and early-nineteenth-century scholarly recuperations in terms of the emergence of bourgeois subjectivity. Similarly, because revisions of the date relocate and duplicate a text like *Twelfth Night*, the text's relationships to the rest of the canon are more historical constructs than transparent reflections of Shakespeare's development.

The shift in *Twelfth Night*'s date implicitly challenges any absolute assumptions, including our own, about the comedy's position in the Shakespearean canon. The historical contingency of our ideas about Shakespeare's chronology, based on the evidence available now, suggests that the suppositions in our current criticism and the analyses themselves are only provisional. However, the resulting loss of transcendent truth does not negate the value of their readings and assumptions or of ours. Instead the significance of successive understandings of the Shakespearean text derives from their historical specificity, that is, from their placement within a particular cultural situation and historical moment. Consequently, the 1614 date of *Twelfth Night* is more than a mistake or an oddity; it is one of those historical moments which reveals the multiplicity of Shakespearean plays in general and of *Twelfth Night* in particular. Collier's discovery changed the *Twelfth Night* texts as it changed the comedy's date of composition because the physical texts of the play, which we think of as permanent and limited, always exist only within a multiplicity of contexts, including their several selves.

For some scholars, this multiplicity may seem easily resolved. After all, doesn't the problem disappear if what is "really" changing is the interpretation and not the material text itself? This question raises the implicit issue of the material text and its boundaries. The narrative of *Twelfth Night*'s changing date actually reveals three distinct texts, all of which are (at least potentially) typographically the same. The first is the *Twelfth Night* for which the date of composition is irrelevant and unknowable, mere speculation according to Nicholas Rowe. When Malone introduces the importance of recovering the chronology of Shakespeare's plays, not only does he initiate the creation of the Shakespearean subject, as de Grazia argues, he also creates a second *Twelfth Night*, composed around 1614. With the chronology, what was outside the text and unnoted becomes part of the text and inseparable from its interpretation. As the 1601 date gradually became well known, altering the comedy's position among Shakespeare's plays, the change yielded yet a third *Twelfth Night*. The very typographical sameness of these *Twelfth Night* texts points to the real issue: what is inside and what is outside the text? The uncertainty of the text's limits, which this chapter explores in terms of date, the rest of this book examines in terms of the many physical texts associated with Shakespeare's comedy.

Thus double dating offers my first negotiations between "inside" and "outside" the text. When Jacques Derrida argues that the text is "henceforth no longer a finished corpus of writing, some content enclosed in a book or its margins, but a differential network, a fabric of traces referring endlessly to something other than itself," he suggests that texts endlessly overrun their apparent boundaries.[26] Nonetheless, we assume an inside and an outside to texts like *Twelfth Night*. On the one hand, the shifting grounds of *Twelfth Night*'s date implies that dating is somehow outside the text, changeable, subject to constant revision, victim to chance, coincidence, and time. The double date is an aberration; our current date is correct. On the other hand, the changes that *Twelfth Night* underwent between the early nineteenth century and now, merely because of the dating, suggest that the changeability of *Twelfth Night*'s date is part of the multiple traces which break open the notion of the singular text.

In the shift of dates, the texts of *Twelfth Night* experience a temporal dislocation similar to that the twins experience in Illyria; the 1614 *Twelfth Night* exists in a different time with different connections than the 1601 *Twelfth Night*, even though they both occur in one place—the Folio text. When the coincidences overwhelmingly support the 1602 date, *Twelfth Night* apparently takes on a fixed, determinant date. Comparably, when coincidence supports Sebastian's version of time, identity is restored, as Viola redefines herself in terms of father/author and twin. The mysterious other time which Viola/Cesario occupied during the comedy vanishes, just as the 1614 date of the Tyrwhitt *Twelfth Night* becomes irrelevant and has, in essence, vanished. Perhaps the spectators watching the play, like the critics now discussing the date, would not notice the double time of the twins' experience, yet it is that separation and reunion of the twins in time which underscores the metaphoric force of relative time in many relationships within the play.

As a result, the end of *Twelfth Night* gives a truer picture than the current critical perception of a single *Twelfth Night* fashioned around 1600: Viola and Sebastian are twins, the same in appearance but involved in different relationships. The Tyrwhitt *Twelfth Night*, associated with the late plays and implicated in an early-nineteenth-century theory of Shakespeare's development, and the Manningham *Twelfth Night*, associated with the end of

Shakespeare's comic writing and implicated in his psychological development, are the same but different. The existence of the second does not
negate or dissolve the experience of the first, any more than the dominance
of Sebastian's time and the resulting coincidences negate Viola's earlier experiences in the play. *Twelfth Night* leaves us with both twins, and I argue that
this history of double dating leaves us with multiple texts. The odd congruence of the history of *Twelfth Night*'s dating and the stories of the twins
within the play is, of course, just coincidence.

For my reading, that coincidence demonstrates that the multiplicity of
texts, generated materially through history as Jerome McGann suggests, constantly reworks the boundaries of "the text." [27] The permeable, provisional
edges, the Derridean "folds" where suddenly the outside edge touches the
inside of the form, open a space which is somehow neither inside nor outside.[28] Reading the "outside" history of Shakespearean texts, as this book
does, does not and cannot avoid reading the "inside" of those texts as well.
This continuing transgression of the textual edges, which are themselves
constantly under construction and erasure, is an essential feature of my
critical project. The apparently exterior history of performance editions—
considered to be outside proper textual history, irrelevant to reading the
play, tangential in critical scholarship—also offers an "interior" history of
the comedy: a repetition of loss and return, impossible desire and shifting
sexual identity, displacement and continuity, and, inevitably, simultaneity
and coincidence.

# Performance Editions
# and the Quest for the Original
# *Twelfth Night*

D espite a textual history which is apparently as unproblematic as its date, the 1623 *Twelfth Night* text is inherently multiple, as speculations about its construction reveal. When textual critics debate its source text and examine its history of textual emendation, they unintentionally reveal that several texts of the comedy probably circulated in the Renaissance playhouse and certainly several appeared thereafter. Even with only the playhouse copies and the printed Folio, the seventeenth-century *Twelfth Night* encodes complex textual interactions.

From the late eighteenth century on, the play began to appear in new forms as well. By the mid-nineteenth century, scholarly editions, performance editions, and reading editions presented versions of the play that differ strikingly from each other. In each of these categories, editors established their criteria for editing in part by defining their products in relationship to the other versions. The Folio text has connections to each of these new textual forms; however, it is most closely allied to the performance editions in status and purposes.

That alliance is evident in the editorial self-presentation of the two most influential performance editions of the period: *Bell's Shakspeare* (1774), the first eighteenth-century performance edition, which was edited by Francis Gentleman from David Garrick's promptbooks, and *A Select British Theatre* (1815), the final collection of John Philip Kemble's individually published

performance editions. Their introductions, prefatory materials, and treatment of the text echo those of the 1623 Folio. In all three, editors register
considerable anxiety and ambivalence about their project as they market
their texts in competition with the theatre while claiming staged productions as the source of their texts' authenticity. As a result, all the editors express problematic views of the stage, focus attention on Shakespeare's genius,
and disguise the editing process and its difficulties.

My analysis of this editorial tradition also extends to include four more
collective editions: *Inchbald's British Theatre* (1808), *Oxberry's New English
Drama* (1821), *Cumberland's British Theatre* (1830), and *Lacy's Acting Plays*
(1855). Together with *Bell's Shakspeare* and *A Select British Theatre*, these editions develop bibliographic materials that reflect ongoing efforts to solve the
problem of representing performance as text. While they possess common
features—like the invocation of nineteenth-century theatrical personnel as
editors and the inclusion of stage directions and cast lists—these texts also
present the evolution of performance editing strategies.

The tradition of performance editing develops in response to changing
conditions of theatrical and textual production. In part because of competition with other texts, nineteenth-century performance editions cultivate textual apparatus of several types: elaborate stage directions, increasingly decorative title pages, introductions, and specific small touches, like Lacy's list of
entrances for characters. These textual additions appeal to a variety of audiences ranging from theatrical personnel to critical readers; more importantly, many of these features mark the version's currency. The performance
edition offers the play as it is performed *now*, that is, in a specific historical
context. As a result, performance editions do not mediate between past and
present, but between a theatrical present and immediate recollection.

The 1623 Folio initiates an editorial tradition which the nineteenth-
century performance editions develop. Critics who insist on a return to the
Folio text by using facsimile editions ignore the fact that these editions participate in scholarly editing rather than performance editing. In order to un-
dertand both the Folio's editorial situation and the historical contingencies
that have allied texts and performance since the sixteenth century, we must
explore the long-ignored performance editions of Shakespeare.

### "Diverse stolne, and surreptitious copies"

*Twelfth Night* first appears in print in the 1623 Folio. Unlike other early texts
like *King Lear* and *Hamlet*, the Folio text has no quarto rivals to challenge its
textual integrity.[1] In fact, its text is remarkably clean and free of error and,
consequently, appears particularly stable.[2] The few minor changes that the

second Folio records hardly constitute an alternative version; its replacement "Violenta" with "Viola" in a stage direction, for example, presents a simple correction to an obvious error. All in all, the Folio presents a singularly unproblematic text for the comedy, as secure and well defined as its date of composition.

However, even in texts which appear only in the Folio, later editors have subtly altered meaning. In terms of *Twelfth Night*, for example, Barry Adams discusses Rowe's emendations of lines nine through fourteen of the first scene, which include changes in capitalization, spelling, and punctuation. Adams argues that, while the words are identical to the Folio edition, Rowe's typographical changes, which are frequently copied in later editions without comment, diminish Orsino's rhetorical power.[3] Similarly, the combined editorial efforts of the second Folio editor and William Warburton produce amendments in Viola's soliloquy which implicate her thoroughly in an assertion of feminine weakness. The 1623 Folio lines "Alas, O frailtie is the cause, not wee, / For such as we are made, if such we bee" (p. 260) appear in editions from the early nineteenth century on as "Alas, our frailty is the cause, not we, / For such as we are made of, such we be" (2.2.30–31).[4] As these minor variations from the Folio in later editions demonstrate, editors can revise characters in subtle, but distinctive ways which affect both text and performance. Because of the work by Gary Taylor, Randall MacLeod, and Michael Warren, critics now attend closely to such editing of Shakespearean texts and, as a result, often call for the return to the original Folio and/or quartos.

Yet the Folio *Twelfth Night*, which Adams claims as "uniquely authoritative" (p. 52), is an edited copy as well. Most obviously, the *Twelfth Night* of the Folio is at the mercy of a compositor who typeset "Violenta" in the place of "Viola," perhaps recalling a name he had just set in *All's Well That Ends Well*. Also, the origin of the version which the compositor used to set the play is in doubt: was *Twelfth Night* typeset from a promptbook, foul papers, or a transcription of foul papers? As the critics cast back for an original which will authorize the Folio text, they encounter a series of texts, each with characteristics which mark it as a copy and distinguish it from other copies.

The debate over the source of the Folio *Twelfth Night* exemplifies how the quest for an original leads only to more copies. Unsatisfied with J. Dover Wilson's assertions of the promptbook as the comedy's source text, Robert K. Turner argues that "the text contains signs of changes of plan and a few loose ends of composition as well as a generally adequate but in some particulars incomplete array of stage directions. Because these characteristics of foul papers occur in conjunction with evidence of transcription, we may conclude that F1 *TN* was printed from a scribal copy of Shakespeare's working draft of the play."[5] By examining the characteristics of transcribed foul papers and those of promptbooks, Turner discovers that the flaws in the Folio *Twelfth Night* coincide more with the former than with the latter. All these features are documented not from actual foul papers or promptbook transcriptions, but from editions in which those materials are already typeset.[6] Moreover, in the case of transcription and promptbook versions, their distinctive characteristics establish their own status as copies. Then why doesn't William Jaggard typeset the Folio of 1623 from the foul papers which are presumably the original version? Turner's best guess is that "Jaggard, having just had a dose of foul papers in composing *AWW*, declined similar copy for the remaining comedies and insisted that *TN* (and *WT*) be put into better shape" (p. 137). Even the foul papers must "be put into better shape" (i.e., edited) before they can be published. In essence, what Turner does in his quest for the origins of the Folio *Twelfth Night* is to compare copies.

Both Turner's and Adams's analyses register the desire to return to the original. That same desire motivates Michael Warren and Gary Taylor when they insist that the quarto and Folio of *Lear* are equally valid and deserve individual consideration. However, the success of their work and the resulting editorial acknowledgment of multiple early texts have implications beyond the narrow result of a new examination of quartos and Folios. When textual bibliographers reveal that we have only edited versions of Shakespeare's works and ask us to accept a range of copies as authentic texts, they open up not only *Lear* but also the rest of Shakespeare's plays to new consideration.

Both the typographical signs of Folio *Twelfth Night*'s status as a copy and the marks of later editing establish that historically specific conditions determine the physical text and inevitably reveal that text as a copy. As Jonathan Goldberg puts it, "The historicity of the text means that there is no text itself; it means that a text cannot be fixed in terms of original or final intentions."[7] To frame this another way, the material existence of texts within history means that there is no singular text which establishes the playwright's initial or final intentions. If we accept this argument, we have two options. On the one hand, we can take the Folio edition alone or in connection with any available quartos as the earliest and therefore most authentic text. This procedure implies that an original exists that the first published version(s) can approximate more accurately than later editions. On the other hand, if we fully accept the inaccessibility and indeed the impossibility of an original, then we must turn our attention to the series of copies and their relationships to one another.

Clearly, textual bibliographers take up the first option. When laying down the principals of bibliographic research, Fredson Bowers explicitly insists that determining the original source of an edition, Folio or quarto, is crucial to establishing the editorial procedures used in approaching that material (Bowers, *On Editing*, p. 4). In a later essay, Bowers suggests that "ultimately we shall know more about the characteristics of these compositors so that something may be attempted in the way of lifting the veil of print that hides the underlying copy."[8] In Bowers's view, "the peeling off of the veneer of print" will reveal a more authentic text ("Search," p. 37). Recent textual critics have urged a return to the earliest texts in order to study "not the author's 'original' perhaps, but what he hath left us."[9] Even Grace Ioppolo, who argues that Shakespeare's texts are inherently multiple because of his own revising, begins and ends her claim with the Folios and quartos.[10]

However, to trace the sources or analyze the revision of these texts, textual critics must compare copies. Warren, Taylor, and others contrast Folios and quartos to assert the original validity of both *Lears*. Ioppolo studies Shakespearean revision in part by comparing Folios and quartos but also by extending her examination to alternate texts—the manuscripts and printed texts of other playwrights. She reveals that sixteenth-century written texts were constantly emended and altered in ways which typesetters often did not treat as alternate versions. The concept of the "original" persists, but Shakespearean textual bibliography, both old and new, reveals that only copies exist. Comparisons, not origins, authorize any text.

In effect, the first option I have offered turns out to *be* the second; that is, when we treat Folios and quartos as the originals, we inevitably compare copies whether we recognize it or not. Even an early single text—*Twelfth Night*—contains implicit copies. Some characteristics indicate possible revisions for different actors, like a Viola who could not sing, or for removal of references to God in order to accommodate the Licensing Act (Ioppolo, pp. 80–84). However valuable textual comparisons are in exploring how Shakespeare's plays were published and circulated in the sixteenth and seventeenth centuries, they also implicitly confine the play historically to the presumed period of conception and publication. I therefore take the second position and argue that we should deal with the series of copies without concern for an imagined original.[11] In fact, all the copies are pertinent in our consideration of the play. This series of texts, including, but not limited to, the Folio *Twelfth Night*, offers a rich resource for understanding the material production and historicity of the Shakespearean play.

In presenting this argument, I draw on three related ways of conceiving literary creations that Jerome McGann posits: the actual physical texts, the play that enables the production of those texts, and the work—that is, the "global set" of the texts and plays arising in the history of the production of *Twelfth Night*.[12] I suspect, however, that my interest in the "global set" of all texts and plays extends beyond McGann's practical attentions to texts which he perceives as contributing to the "literary" production of the work. Nonetheless, his insistence on the necessarily collaborative nature of texts and the "immutable law" of change in the textual condition contributes valuably to my study of the "complex (and open-ended) histories of textual change and variance" in *Twelfth Night* (McGann, p. 9).

My approach also complicates McGann's partially metaphoric statement that "*this text*, every text, is unique and original to itself when we consider it not as an object but as an action" (p. 183). He makes that equation in order to insist on the historical specificity of particular texts, that is, their physical features and the historically contingent factors which have encouraged and resisted the production of the poem or play as a physical, lexical object. Since a play is always produced doubly as text and performance, the playtext relates more literally to action. Consequently, I see the edited texts of the plays as more closely akin to performance than critics normally think.[13] The texts of *Twelfth Night* as well as the individual productions of the play participate in their immediate context of enactment.

Thus, the similarities between text and performance are as crucial as their differences, as both interact in producing the work. Current arguments about the variations in the *King Lear* texts support this contention. For example, Michael Warren and others suggest that the Folio *Lear* is a version substantially revised for publication, whereas Stephen Urkowitz argues forcefully for performance alternatives marked out in quarto and Folio *Lear*s.[14] When Gary Taylor and Stanley Wells decided to include two versions of *Lear* in the Oxford Shakespeare, they proved, almost despite themselves, that there are no final or originary Shakespearean texts.[15] Just as importantly, they also suggested a new way of considering the marks of history on the "text," particularly the traces of performance. In fact, their most striking (and to some annoying) editorial choice, beyond including both the history and the tragedy of *Lear*, was to interpolate numerous stage directions. When these critics push textual bibliographers to consider the theatrical context of possible Shakespearean revision, they also reveal interconnections between publication and performance. Their research reinforces what performance critics have long maintained: there is no perfect, authorially sanctioned text of a script for performance. Theatrical productions underscore the flaw in affirming a fixed and immutable Shakespearean canon, since every presentation, whether in text or performance, represents a version, not the play itself.

In effect, theatrical producers, actors, and managers also edit Shake-speare's plays, by cutting, rearranging, and otherwise altering a play in important ways. Nor are their amendments limited to the actual performance, since the producers and directors work first with a text, modifying it into a promptbook and often returning to it and reworking it for later revivals. Many of these performance choices also find their way into printed editions of the play. In the case of *Twelfth Night*, one of the few debates about the Folio text concerns whether or not it was taken from a promptbook of the play. However, editions that register the theatrical alterations also appear long after the quartos or Folio of any Shakespearean play.

These performance editions are not authoritative in any sense that the textual bibliographers would accept. Even eighteenth-century critics often deplore texts like *Bell's Shakspeare* (1774) for their editing practices, as John P. Genest's comments attest: "In 1773 and 1774 Bell, a bookseller in the Strand, published an edition of Shakspeare in numbers, each number containing a play—this has been censured as the worst edition of Shakspeare ever published; which *strictly* speaking is true, as it presents the plays in a mutilated state."[16] However, these texts are interesting and even significant precisely because they acknowledge and celebrate their relationship to staged productions. Even Genest is willing to concede their importance as theatrical documents: "in another point of view, this edition is very useful, as it is copied from the Prompter's book, and gives the names of the performers who acted the characters, as near the time of publication as Bell could procure them" (p. 439).

These editions both generate and display the multiplicity of the play's material existence in a historical continuum. For example, specific performance editions often present radical revisions of a play and, considered in relation to other editions, can offer fascinating revelations into alternate versions, including the Folio.[17] Because these texts are so strongly linked to stage popularity, performance editions generally respond more noticeably to ideological pressures than do scholarly productions of Shakespeare's "timeless" texts. In fact, their structure, aims, and editorial self-presentation establish the distinctiveness and importance of performance editing as a set of material practices. For these reasons, the performance editions are especially interesting and useful in the history of Shakespeare's plays.

Consequently I examine *Twelfth Night* as a series of texts rather than a single text grounded only in the Folio "original." In the next few chapters, I acknowledge a multiplicity of texts and allow the free play of copies in order to explore the issues raised by performance editing.[18] *Twelfth Night*'s flexibility as an enactable property and its textual variety are fashioned always within the context of critical, social, and theatrical practices. In short, performance editions reveal how a play becomes a work, and how multiple texts affect and interact with culturally and historically specific conditions.

### Alternative Editing Traditions

If the texts of a Shakespearean play have no original and are in fact a series of copies which exist only in relationship to one another, we have a number of different possible models for organizing these materials. Like the creators of computer software and some nineteenth-century editors, we could take up the later texts as increasingly perfected versions which supersede all previous copies. Following the textual bibliographers, we could treat the earliest text as the Platonic original, degraded in its subsequent reproductions. We could even separate these texts into logical categories according to editorial purposes. I open with this last strategy in order to explore what distinguishes performance editions from other texts.

The late eighteenth century and nineteenth century offer a proliferation of *Twelfth Night* texts, including several different categories of textual production. By the late eighteenth century, Steevens, Johnson, and Malone have largely established their textual structures and aims within a tradition of scholarly editing. Despite some important differences in content, they structure their texts similarly, including extensive annotations for obscure passages and introductions to each play. Later scholarly editions also add supplemental essays on topics ranging from catalogs of spurious or disputed texts to Malone's essay on dating the composition of the plays.[19] Scholarly editions typically present all texts the editors consider to be Shakespeare's; *Twelfth Night* thus appears as one among many.

Inspired by *Twelfth Night*'s return to the stage in 1741 and the extremely popular run staged by Garrick in 1771, performance editions of the comedy also flourish. These editions present additions, cuts, and rearrangements which apparently derive from the promptbook copy. Although their title pages may announce that the text is "conformable to the Prompter's book," the editors normally do not call attention to any variations from the full scholarly text. In effect, the changes recorded in the performance editions appear without any explanation or explicit acknowledgment of differences from the early texts. Such editions also incorporate a range of texual features from cast lists to introductions.

In addition, some new and relatively short-lived types of editions appear around this time, capitalizing on the renewed popularity of Shakespeare and his growing status as the national playwright. The most notable of these are the texts for those who wish to read Shakespeare's plays aloud. These editions frequently present the "normal" theatrical variations by typographically marking excised passages and giving headnotes to scenes which explain where they have been moved. For example, the Bathurst *Twelfth Night* (1786) asserts that "the Parts distinguished by inverted Commas are omitted in the Representation" (Bathurst, p. A3), and the *Memorial Theatre* edition (1882) promises that "the alterations are noted in each place where they occur. The passages omitted in representation are indicated by the smaller type" (*Memorial Theatre*, p. vi).[20] Whereas the Bathurst edition does not specify its purpose, the *Memorial Theatre* text explicitly states that "for the convenience of the frequenters of the theatre, these plays will present the stage arrangement, and yet give the original text in its entirety, so that they may be useful to families and circles where the delightful practice of reading aloud occupies a part of the winter evenings" (*Memorial Theatre*, p. iii).

The most extreme versions of this editorial strategy offer only the design for curtailing the play. In the late nineteenth century, Samuel Ferguson published *Shakespearean Breviates: An Adjustment of Twenty-four of the Longer Plays of Shakespeare to Convenient Reading Limits*, in which *Twelfth Night* is only three pages long. Ferguson lists only the changes to be made and supplies summarizing speeches in rhymed couplets for the material that he urges readers to omit. For example, he leaves out Viola's first appearance and paraphrases the premise of the play in somewhat ponderous couplets, introducing both twins at the same time as do some nineteenth-century performance editions: "Conceive a shipwreck; and imagine two / Of the passengers, with fractions of the crew, / At several, ventures on the Illyrian coast / Escaped, each deeming that the other's lost. / Twins are they, Greeks, a sister and a brother / So like you'd scarce know either from the other."[21] At the end of this speech Ferguson instructs his readers to "Read scenes 3,4." Apparently he did not care which text of *Twelfth Night* they used when enacting his cuts.

In their display of textual fragments, the breviates are related to the collections of individual passages which also come to prominence in the nineteenth century. The isolated presentation of passages translates the plays into poems, the playtexts into "Shakespeare's most beautiful passages." Along with these verse collections, prose versions like the Lambs' *Tales from Shakespeare* offer texts like *Twelfth Night* translated into different genres. Excerpts of the verse from the plays as poetry and revisions of the plot as narrative both support the tacit assumption, held by both Samuel Taylor Coleridge and William Hazlitt, that Shakespeare's plays are better read than acted.[22]

These verse and prose texts, like the breviates, were designed for private performances, including the most private performance of reading. Few speeches from *Twelfth Night* appear in the verse collections beyond Viola's "Patience on a monument," but the Lambs' version of *Twelfth Night*, like Ferguson's introduction, opens with both Viola's and Sebastian's shipwreck and presents Viola's scene first as the natural start of the story.[23] The breviate, verse, and prose *Twelfth Night*s are texts which flourish temporarily; they are useful in this study primarily for the attitudes that they adopt toward the play.

The scholarly, performance, and reading editions of *Twelfth Night*, on the other hand, are significantly interconnected. When the scholarly editors present elaborate textual introductions and offer copious explanations of quibbles and topical references long out of date, they implicitly foreground their historical distance from the Folio and quartos. The textual differences between the early published versions and current idiom provoke the scholarly editors' multiple explanations and justify the structure they adopt. Editors who take theatrical productions as their source are less interested in such distinctions. While editing *Bell's Shakspeare*, Francis Gentleman even asserts in the general introduction "that multiplying conjectural verbal criticisms tends to perplex rather than inform readers" (Bell, vol. 1, p. 8). In both individual performance editions and multivolume sets like *A Select British Theatre* (1815), performance editors insist that their texts are companions to the theatre rather than exhaustive scholarly volumes.

The editors of reading editions often stake out a territory somewhere between the scholarly and performance editions. In effect, these editions juxtapose the fuller text of the scholarly edition with the altered text and limited footnotes of the performance edition. After asserting the usefulness of the *Memorial Theatre* edition of *Twelfth Night* (1882) for reading aloud, C. E. Flower argues that "this edition . . . shows at a glance the difference between the plays as written and now acted, and a reference to it between the acts may even be of use to those familiar with the full text. This may, indeed, serve as a substitute for the traditional acting editions, which were often most carelessly 'cut' and which have been entirely discarded in the admirable revivals of late years" (*Memorial Theatre*, p. iv). As the performance editors affirm the differences between their texts and scholarly editions, so the editors of reading editions correct the performance editions' flaws in order to promote their own versions.

This wide variety of texts in the late eighteenth and early nineteenth centuries reminds us that there are several distinct traditions of editing, each with its own history and characteristics. The editors of each category treat each other's texts as both the context and the contrast for their own editorial projects. By comparing their apparatuses and purposes to those of other playtexts, these editors mark out and market their own publications. Thus, at issue in the performance editions is more than their record of theatrical variations or their implicit and explicit claims to authenticity.[24] These editions are important as part of a Shakespearean editorial tradition that starts with the Folio and interacts with several alternative editorial traditions.

The 1623 Folio in some ways resembles the drawing room editions of the mid to late 1800s. Like the texts designed for reading aloud, the Folio was a relatively new kind of text—the collected dramatic works of an author. It had an uncertain future—witness Ben Jonson's difficulties in publishing his 1616 Folio of playtexts.[25] The Folio also interacts with the scholarly editions, but principally as their point of origin. Edmond Malone and George Steevens devised strategies and encountered problems in editing because they aimed to bridge historical difference in language, incident, or customs—a concern obviously not shared by the Folio editors. In fact, the Folio editors faced a task more closely resembling the work of nineteenth-century performance editors as they transform performance to text and tempt audiences to become readers.

Renewed attention to Shakespeare in the nineteenth-century theatre inspired many performance editions. After the Restoration, *Twelfth Night* played at the Drury Lane Theatre for the first time in 1741. Thereafter the play was revived periodically at both Drury Lane and Covent Garden well into the nineteenth century. During this period, several presses offered individual copies of the play "now published as it is performed at the Theatres Royal" (Kemble [1815]) or even based on the performance of a specific actor or actress—"as performed by Madame Helena Modjeska (Countess Bozenta)" (Modjeska [1883]). When nineteenth-century performance editors note theatres and performances prominently in their titles or front pages, they mount an appeal to the theatre audience that resembles the interest held by the quartos and hinted at in the Folio when Heminge and Condell claim: "*so much were your L L. likings of the severall parts, when they were acted, as before they were published, the Volume ask'd to be yours*" (Folio, "Epistle Dedactorie").

The Folio's acknowledged origin of interest, like that of these later editions, lies in the performances which preceded the publication. Theatrical production made the 1623 Folio a viable financial undertaking. This premise concurs with textual evidence that the Folio editors probably considered the promptbooks the most authoritative documents available to them (Turner, pp. 130–37). Ultimately the strategies and concerns expressed in the quartos and Folios link them with later performance editions. Together they illuminate a distinct editorial tradition based in performance.

### Performance Editing Anxiety

The links between the Folio and later performance editions become obvious in the context of the late-eighteenth- and nineteenth-century collections of performance editions. These bound sets of plays most closely resemble the Folio's structure and retrospective gathering of playtexts. Their editors, like the Folio editors, responded to idiosyncratic individual performance editions by marking off their collected "works" as both different and better. In the process, both seventeenth- and nineteenth-century performance editors revealed anxieties about taking their texts from the protean theatre and presented their own projects in provocatively contradictory terms.

Two collected editions exercised the most influence on performance editions throughout the period: *Bell's Shakspeare*, based on Garrick's promptbooks and edited by Francis Gentleman, and *A Select British Theatre*, based on John Philip Kemble's versions of the plays. These collections echo the Folio as it sets itself in opposition to the quartos, the "diverse stolne, and surreptitious copies, maimed, and deformed by the frauds and stealthes of injurious impostors" (Folio, p. A3). In *Bell's Shakspeare* (1774), Gentleman takes the "original" Folio as a maimed edition which must be cured of "those cobwebs, and that dust of depraved opinion, which Shakspeare was unfortunately forced to throw on them" (Bell, vol. 1, p. 6). Thus, the Folio must be put into order, much as Robert K. Turner suggests that the foul papers of *Twelfth Night* had to be put into order before Jaggard would publish the play. Resembling even more closely Heminge and Condell's claims that readers have hitherto been abused with flawed copies, the introduction to *A Select British Theatre* asserts: "Whoever has cast his eye over a few pages of the plays in common use, will have seen that AUTHORITY they have none; they are printed from copies of copies, corrupted and uncorrected; or what is still worse, corrected into apparent meaning, but not that of the Author" (*Select*, vol. 1, p. v). Bell's introduction suggests that the Folio copy requires examination and correction; *A Select British Theatre* posits a series of marred copies which John Philip Kemble must cure by consulting "the copy printed either by the Author, or his earliest Editor" (*Select*, vol. 1, p. vi).

Despite these assertions that textual difficulties mar the copies and the promise of textual strategies for amending them, both Francis Gentleman and John Philip Kemble turned to the stage for *their* authority in editing the texts. In *Bell's Shakspeare*, Gentleman recorded the stage alterations because "the THEATRES, especially of late, have been generally right in their omissions, of this author particularly, we have printed our *text* after their regulations; and from this part of our design, an evident use will arise; that those who take books to the THEATRE, will not be so puzzled themselves to accompany the speaker; nor so apt to condemn the performers of being imperfect, when they pass over what is designedly omitted" (Bell, vol. 1, pp. 6–7). He claims both that the theatres have appropriately corrected Shakespeare's text and that their amendments produce texts that can aid those who attend the theatre. The stage supplies not just appropriate revision, but also the intended readers of the volume.

Nonetheless, this dependence on the stage was not as straightforward as Gentleman's comments suggest. For example, he also sought to impose these texts on the theatre: "we would hope, that a reasonable standard being thus laid down, professors of drama [that is, actors] will not be so forward, as capriciously and arbitrarily to deviate from it; it is commendable to consult the extent of expression, but through idleness to retrench what is beautiful and necessary, or through vanity to retain what is heavy and uneffential [*sic*] to action, we deem an affront to the public, and a disgrace to the performer" (Bell, vol. 1, p. 7). This odd assertion of the text's ascendancy over the stage is not unique. In *A Select British Theatre*, the publishers use a similar strategy in their introduction: "our Provincial Theatres have, in this publication, the means of making our great Bards speak their own language through the land they have ennobled by their writings. The Actor too can no longer have an apology for mistake—his negligence will be without excuse" (*Select*, vol. 1, p. vi). Part of the rhetoric here is that of a vendor affirming the value of a new product, but both editions express a disconcertingly aggressive attitude toward the theatre, especially since the theatre served as the text's source. This competition with the stage also has its parallel in Heminge's and Condell's plea to their readers: "But, what ever you do, Buy . . . though you be a Magistrate of wit, and sit on the Stage at *Black-Friers*, or the *Cock-pit*, to arraigne Playes dailie, know, these Playes have had their triall alreadie, and stood out all Appeales" (Folio, p. A3). Like the Folio editors, the later performance editors took their authority from the play's popularity onstage, but, because their reading audience also came from the theatre, they had to affirm the value of their texts as distinct from—and superior to—the staged productions.

By examining these collections in juxtaposition with the Folio, we can locate certain pressures and contradictions inherent in the performance edition. To justify such attention to these "trifles," as the Folio editors call the plays, the editors must affirm the value of the stage to the editing process. To transform the theatre audience into a reading public, they must allow and even assert the connection between text and performance. These editions are competing for readers, both with the flawed copies they claim to fix and with the theatre itself. Heminge and Condell make this conflict clear in their plea that the reader buy the Folio even if he or she is a constant playgoer. Competition became even more acute in the late eighteenth century when performance editions could appear almost coincidentally with stage productions.[26] As both situations show, performance editions must establish how different they are, not only from other editions but also from the theatrical productions which authorize their versions.

These conflicting purposes result in a distinctive editorial anxiety about the project, represented in problematic acknowledgments of the stage. For example, performance editors often assert a fixed text, which has passed the trials of public performance. From the 1623 Folio through the 1815 *Select Theatre*, performance editors make remarkably similar claims: the plays appear in *this* edition—the Folio, *Bell's Shakspeare, A Select British Theatre*—as finally "cur'd, and perfect in limbs" (Folio, p. A3), "restored to due proportion and natural lustre" (Bell, vol. 1, p. 6), and "preserved . . . by some man of letters, who has proper veneration for the Author, to lead him to seek for *purity*" (*Select*, vol. 1, p. v). They imply that the theatrical production or independent performance edition has tainted the play, but the current edition rectifies that problem and establishes the text in its purity. Thus the problematic relationship between text and performance leads performance editors to claim, paradoxically, that these editions offer a textual stability against which the stage itself should be measured.

Yet, however forceful their arguments for textual authenticity or regulation, performance editors continue to negotiate the relationship between their texts and the staged productions. The result is an odd combination of humility and hubris. In the Folio, the editorial double bind between acknowledging and rejecting (or ignoring) the theatre is explicitly framed as a paradox in the dedication: "we are falne upon the ill fortune, to mingle two the most diverse things that can bee, feare, and rashnesse; rashnesse in enterprize, and fear of the successe" (Folio, p. A2). Rashly publishing these trifles while fearing that their trivial collection will succeed, the Folio editors confess the humbleness of their subject matter, playtexts, at the same time that they insist on the value of publishing them.

The later editions of Bell and Kemble reproduce similarly revealing contradictions. Gentleman affirms that Bell's edition purifies Shakespeare's text, but he also mentions "a delicate fear" raised by Garrick that "the prunings, transpositions, or other alterations, which, in his province as a manager he had often found necessary to make, or adopt, with regard to the text, for the convenience of representation, or accommodation to the powers and capacities of his performers, might be misconstrued into a critical presumption of offering to the literati a reformed and more correct edition of our author's works" (Bell, vol. i, p. 8). Although Gentleman has suggested the greater purity of his text and its usefulness as a fixed standard for theatrical representation, he proves unexpectedly self-effacing in his retreat from competition with the scholarly "correct" editions. This disavowal of any competition with texts designed for the "literati" suggests that the scholarly editions exacerbated the anxiety associated with printing an edition which draws upon theatrical practice.

In *A Select British Theatre*'s introduction, the editors argue that they are offering actors a proper text at the same time that they note, "It is foreign to the object of this publication, to notice the Stage itself" (*Select*, vol. i, p. vii). They offer an equally interesting contradiction in their evaluations of Kemble's editing: "Where the play called for curtailment, [Kemble] omitted; where additions had been approved, he adopted;—but the basis must be the Author's, and should be preserved in its original state;—he therefore accurately copied the original text" (*Select*, vol. i, p. vi). Somehow Kemble accurately copied the original but still cut and added material. He was the humble transcriber of Shakespeare's original text, yet he nonetheless dared to alter the texts where they "called for curtailment."

Unable to resolve contradictions in their editing practices, many performance editors turn to the greater authority of the playwright as the grounds for the validity of their edition. By claiming their texts as the transparent presentation of the author's genius, they can obscure their process of editing along with its disturbing connections to the stage. The Folio editors, of course, have the greatest claim to Shakespeare as their authority. The obvious effort they make to present themselves as mere gatherers of papers seems perfectly logical: "His mind and hand went together: And what he thought, he uttered with that easinesse, that we have scarce received from him a blot in his papers. But it is not our province, who onely gather his works, and give them to you, to praise him" (Folio, p. A3). Their assertions have effectively diverted attention from editorial revisions, including Shakespeare's. As a result of the bard who scarcely blotted a line, textual scholars thought, until recently, that only one text of any Shakespearean play could be genuinely his.[27] Their claims for Shakespeare's authority and production of singular texts in the Folio's preface responded to Renaissance antitheatrical prejudice, which extends to the potential for counterfeiting and multiplicity in the production of playtexts.[28]

Eighteenth-century publishing constraints exacerbated editorial concerns about textual and theatrical multiplicity. Printing presses had to be kept in operation, accelerating the production of texts and placing even greater pressure on the problematic relationship between page and stage, a relationship that was already vexed in the Renaissance.[29] As a result, the introductions of both *Bell's Shakspeare* (1774) and *A Select British Theatre* (1815) claim to present Shakespeare's work in its purest form and cite him as the unique authority for their texts. However, the paradoxes inherent in claiming to present Shakespeare without intermediary become more obvious in these later editions, where sweeping alterations from the Folio and quarto texts accompany statements like those in the *Memorial Theatre* edition of *Twelfth Night* (1882): "It may be remarked that although the fun at times runs fast and furious, there is scarcely a sentence or word in this play which requires to be omitted or altered" (*Memorial Theatre*, p. vi). Even John Philip Kemble, whose talents gave *A Select British Theatre* a "pure" text, produced three distinct versions of *Twelfth Night* in 1810, 1811, and 1815, each with slightly different cuts and alterations, but all with significant variations from the Folio text.

The existence and profitability of performance editions inevitably depend upon theatrical performance; however, the process of editing a text by using theatrical materials creates significant editorial ambivalence. Consequently, eighteenth- and nineteenth-century publishers and editors promoted the connection to the stage at the same time that they rejected or offered to control the variability of the play as staged. In the process, the performance editors, often unnamed, downplayed their own editorial work. Their efforts produce an array of "authentic" texts which reveal vividly how an editorial approach based in performance creates as many textual choices as there are theatrical choices.

### Translating Performance to Text

Previous sections of this chapter suggest how closely the purposes and anxieties of the Folio editors are allied with those of later performance editors. My aim has been to argue the usefulness of studying later performance editions as they illuminate the tactics of the Folio editors when they faced the multiplicity of Shakespearean texts. This section and the next focus closely on the interrelationships among six performance editions published in collections from 1774 to 1855. In addition to the two collections already mentioned, I include *Inchbald's British Theatre* (1808); *Oxberry's New English Drama* (1821); *Cumberland's British Theatre* (1830); and *Lacy's Acting Plays* (1855). Spanning the late eighteenth through the mid-nineteenth century

fairly evenly, these six editions deserve serious attention because they develop textual materials and editorial strategies that reflect ongoing efforts to
negotiate the relationship between performance and text.

Though the structure of the collected editions associates them with the
Folio, several crucial features distinguish them from the earlier performance
edition. Most obviously, of these editions, only Bell's confines itself to presenting just Shakespeare's plays. In *Inchbald's British Theatre*, *Twelfth Night*
appears as the last Shakespearean play in volume 5, out of a set of twenty-five
volumes of plays. In *A Select British Theatre* (1815) the comedy appears in the
first volume; all in all Kemble presents twenty-six Shakespearean plays in the
first six volumes of nine in the series. Neither *Oxberry's New English Drama*
nor *Cumberland's British Theatre* bothers to set Shakespeare's works off in
any way; *Twelfth Night* appears in volumes 11 and 12, respectively, sand-
wiched between the plays of different dramatists. In *Lacy's Acting Plays*,
*Twelfth Night* appears in volume 36 between *Samuel in Search of Himself*
and *A Doubtful Victory*. The later nineteenth-century collections mix old
and new plays indiscriminately, reflecting the variable use of Shakespeare's
plays in a company's repertoire. Performance editors move toward a mélange
of different plays, deliberately *not* separating out the earlier plays or plays of
a given author.

The physical format of the texts also underscores the performance editions' changing strategies and purposes. Take, for example, the fact that all
these collected performance editions are multivolume works rather than
single-volume collections like the Folio. In fact, by the time John Stockdale
publishes his text of *Shakspeare's Plays* in 1784, the single-volume Shakespeare text is apparently unusual, or so his introduction suggests: "A new
edition of Shakspeare, and an edition of so singular a form as the present, in
which all his plays are comprehended in one volume, will, perhaps, appear
surprising to many readers; but, upon a little reflection, their surprize will,
the editor doubts not, be converted into approbation."[30] Stockdale insists
that his volume is a potential reference work, a cheap alternative for the
lower classes who need to be educated and entertained by Shakespeare. He
even offers it as a possible companion for long chaise rides. All of these purposes, according to his introduction, call for a single volume. The multivolume performance texts, on the other hand, cater to audiences who wish
to take small volumes to the theatre along with them. The editors also
fashion these collections in bound volumes which physically resemble the
scholarly editions. Moreover, the multivolume structure maintains a crucial
openendedness, so that as more plays are produced editors can publish them
and add them to the collected set.

Even such a small feature as pagination tells a story about the construction of eighteenth- and nineteenth-century performance editions. *Bell's Shakspeare* (1774) uses sequential pagination in each volume, so that the text of *Twelfth Night*, the last play in volume 5, starts on page 296. For all the other editions, each play starts fresh on page 1, even if it is placed next to last in a given volume, like Mrs. Inchbald's *Twelfth Night* (1808). As the pagination indicates, the plays gathered in these volumes (even including Bell's) were published individually and sold at the theatre before being bound in a collected edition. Kemble's *A Select British Theatre* (1815), with its long editorial introduction justifying the collection of these forty plays and Kemble's editorial prowess, offers further evidence; the front pages of his individual plays within the volume include at the bottom in brackets the theatre price—"[one shilling]." Whereas the Folio editors undertook a separate editorial process when they worked from quartos, promptbooks, and foul papers in order to gather disparate materials into a coherent whole, in the nineteenth century the same editorial work served both for the cheap version sold at the theatres and for the more extensive collective edition.

From the Restoration onward, most plays that were performed, even if only once, were published. This wholesale publication of plays in the theatres explains to some degree the many individual editions of *Twelfth Night* that are available. Even though the play was not a huge financial success in the nineteenth century, the nineteenth-century practice of publishing almost all plays performed insures that a reasonable variety of *Twelfth Night* texts reached print. One reason for this increasing publication of performance editions was the Copyright Act of 1710, which gave playwrights ownership of their own works, at least for fourteen years. As a consequence, plays were more often sold by their authors than pirated, as the quartos may have been. Moreover, the time between performance and publication began to decrease dramatically from 1660 to 1800. Although publishers in the early 1700s usually waited at least until the first run was over, by the turn of the century some playtexts were in print as early as the second day the play was performed (Kenny, pp. 314–15).

Since the authors selling the works often insisted that the complete play be published, most performance texts published prior to Bell's did not record the stage alterations of the playtext. As Shirley Strum Kenny notes, "Commonly printer's copy, while doubtless closely resembling the script sent to the playhouse, did not reflect the cuts and revisions made during the rehearsals in the early runs" (p. 316). The speed of publication was one factor as playwrights whose works had been purchased by publishers sometimes sent their texts to the booksellers even before rehearsals had started. Especially after the Copyright Act of 1710, authors had the right to sell their work to *both* the theatrical companies and booksellers, thus profiting from both material productions of their plays. During this period, the profitability and market of published individual performance editions were strongly allied with performances.

Shakespeare's plays, however, represented an unusual case in this history of performance editions. Since he was not a living author, his copyright, according to the act, was to remain with its current owner, publisher Jacob Tonson. In effect, as Taylor notes, the Tonson family held onto the copyright for Shakespeare's works until his nephew's death in 1772, when those rights were auctioned off (*Reinventing*, pp. 69–70). Once Tonson's hold was loosened, however, a variety of editions of Shakespeare's works began to proliferate. Historical changes in the copyright laws and printing press operation work together in the nineteenth century to produce multiple versions for *Twelfth Night* and for many other plays.

Shakespeare's performance editions entered the marketplace in 1773–74 with Bell's edition, which also inaugurated a new approach to publishing Shakespeare's texts. Bell addressed closer attention to the stage production, including cast lists and cuts from performance; his editions, like the *New English Drama* texts associated with Oxberry, offered "innovative popular editions which, for the most part, tried to reproduce both the reading and the acting texts, at least as far as stage cuts were concerned" (Kenny, p. 327). In the case of Shakespeare, performance editors were unhampered by any authorial insistence that the whole text be preserved. As a result, Shakespeare's performance editions came closer to the theatrical production than playtexts of living authors, who often demanded that the whole text be published.

Nineteenth-century editors also added a new layer of dramatic authority by introducing current theatrical professionals, often as part of the collections' titles and always at the head of the individual play. Whereas the quarto editors more commonly established the connections between their texts and performance by indicating the specific occasion of enactment before a specific, and always illustrious, audience, the nineteenth-century performance editors concentrated on the popular theatrical figures rather than the audiences. For example, *A Select British Theatre* (1815) offered on the title page: "**Shakspeare's TWELFTH NIGHT**; or WHAT YOU WILL: *A COMEDY.* Revised by **J. P. KEMBLE**; and now published as it is performed at THE THEATRES ROYAL." References to a variety of well-known people of the theatre complicate the identification of actual editors because theatrical figures actually participate in these editions in widely varying degrees. Mrs. Inchbald, for example, only wrote introductions for *Inchbald's British Theatre*, as she affirms in an open letter to critics in 1808: "One of the points of my agreement was, that I should have no control over the time or the order in which the prefaces were to be printed, but that I should merely produce them as they were called for, and resign all other interference to the proprietor or editor of the work."[31] In fact, she could not even influence which works were to be included, as S. R. Littlewood points out: "it cannot be too strongly emphasised that the plays were not chosen by her, and that, in many cases, one has only to turn to the prefaces to find out that, had she had her own way, this or that 'lamentable tragedy' would certainly not have found a place among the candidates for classical honours."[32] Mrs. Inchbald's limited participation in preparing the volumes which bear her name leaves open the question of who is actually editing these texts.

The "hands-off" editing of Mrs. Inchbald differs considerably from Kemble's role, as acknowledged by the publishers of *A Select British Theatre*: "When the Publisher undertook the present Work, he determined, that every care should be taken to render it perfect: but he confesses that the task would have been beyond his means, but for the able and most friendly aid of Mr. Kemble. The unwearied attention of that Gentleman to these volumes, while they were passing through the press, has given the confidence of presenting a correct Work to the Public" (*Select*, vol. 1, p. viii). Although Kemble participated closely in preparing the texts for publication, his texts nonetheless show signs of being taken from the individual copies of the plays rather than from any carefully gathered new collations. He sometimes published his individual performance editions before the actual performances, most obviously in the cases of *All's Well That Ends Well* (published in 1793, produced in 1794), *Julius Caesar* (published in 1811, produced in 1812), and *Twelfth Night* itself (published in 1810, produced in 1811). Thus when biographer James Boaden describes Kemble's treatment of the plays he chose for performance, he indicates as well Kemble's editorial practices: "Now this, in Mr. Kemble's notion of the business, was, not to order the prompter to write out the parts of some old mutilated promptcopy lingering on his shelves; but himself to consider it attentively in the author's genuine book: then to examine what corrections could be properly admitted into his text; and, finally, what could be cut out in the representation, not as disputing the judgment of the author, but as suiting the time of the representation to the habits of his audience, or a little favoring the power of his actors."[33] Kemble's "editing" of these plays took place in preparation not for publication, but for performance. Moreover, as Boaden's comments suggest, Kemble did not just defer to the author's intention, as *A Select British Theatre* claims, but conformed his texts to his audience's expectations and his own company's skills.

Because none of the editions after Kemble's offer publisher's acknowledgments, it is frequently difficult to tell to what extent the persons cited in the title have contributed to the work of editing. In *Oxberry's New English Drama*, each individual title page suggests that the play is "the only edition existing which is faithfully marked with the stage business, and stage directions, as it is performed at the Theatres Royal. by William Oxberry, Comedian," even though I have found no evidence that Oxberry acted in *Twelfth Night* aside from his appearance in the 1813 Shakespeare Jubilee as Andrew Aguecheek. We may assume that, like Mrs. Inchbald, Oxberry wrote the opening remarks, though neither of them is explicitly acknowledged in the introduction as the author. However, neither was involved in the specific productions that the editions mention. *Cumberland's British Theatre* includes George Daniel's remarks about *Twelfth Night* (signaled by D. ——G. at the end of the remarks) but offers no indication of what, if anything, Cumberland himself contributed beyond purchasing Thomas Dolby's stereoplates (Halstead, vol. 14, p. 9).

When publishers included contemporary theatrical personnel in the editing process, they achieved two goals. First, their theatrical connections implicitly linked the editions tightly with theatrical practice. The gesture openly marketed the edition by foregrounding the theatre, even if theatrical personnel contributed little to the actual editing. Second, by using the names of noted dramatists, actors, and managers without fully describing their participation, the publishers masked the identities of the editors who actually prepared these texts.

Both of these purposes are also at work in the quartos and Folios, but in very different ways. When nineteenth-century performance editors consistently present current theatrical figures in introductions, frontispiece engravings, and title page announcements, their strategies recall some of the textual features in Shakespeare's early editions: the introduction and dedication by Heminge and Condell, Ben Jonson's celebratory verses, and even the quartos' allusions to the theatrical company and occasion of performance. The editorial posture adopted by Heminge and Condell in their preface effectively hides the enormous responsibility taken on by publisher William Jaggard in editing the texts. For both of these strategies, the difference in the later performance editions is mostly one of degree. Since Heminge and Condell were Shakespeare's contemporaries and the textual bibliographers have unveiled Jaggard's role in editing the Folio, the ways that their introduction exploits the Folio's proximity to performance are less obvious than the use of actors and managers in nineteenth-century performance editions. Because the Folio editors competed only with "diverse stolne" copies already associated with the theatres, they had no need to assert the self-evident proximity between Shakespeare's plays and their performances in the seventeenth century.

However, nineteenth-century editors and publishers competed with an enormous variety of available Shakespearean editions. They self-consciously advertised their editions in connection to the theatre in order to carve out a reading audience. In effect the publishers presented the plays as at least doubly authored, by Shakespeare and by the producer of the performance. Thus nineteenth-century title pages and introductions emphasize the collaborative nature of the performance edition. But such partnerships between theatrical practitioners were not new to the eighteenth and nineteenth centuries; as both Stephen Orgel and Timothy Murray suggest, collaboration also figured in the sixteenth- and seventeenth-century publication of Shakespeare's texts. All performance editions tend to present the plays as collaborative productions, associated with and created by both author and theatrical companies.

### The Changing Preface of *Twelfth Night*

Nineteenth-century performance editors presented more than a vigorously altered playtext; they added a variety of textual features as they tried to incorporate stage performance into the linguistic text. As performance editors endeavored to make this alliance of page and stage as specific as possible, they turned not only to promptbooks but also to other editions. To recall particular performances, they included an array of materials—Oxberry's engraving of a specific actor; the cast lists, single and multiple, from Kemble on; commentary on particular performances in some of the introductions; and ever more detailed stage directions. The increasingly elaborate prefatory materials serve to establish the editions' connections to theatrical productions, a connection which the Folio had no need to enforce. These features also register the performance edition's competition with other kinds of texts.

Successive nineteenth-century performance editions use ever more aggressive strategies to ally their texts with stage productions, beginning with their treatment of the cast of characters. Both Bell (1774) and Inchbald (1808) list only *Dramatis Personae*—Orsino, Sebastian, Antonio, Valentine, Sir Toby Belch, Sir Andrew Aguecheek, A sea captain, Fabian, Malvolio, Clown, Olivia, Viola, Maria (Bell).[34] *A Select British Theatre* (1815) changes the order of the characters somewhat, retitles the list "Persons Represented," and, most noticeably, adds cast lists for Drury Lane and Covent Garden. Though no production dates are given, the cast lists fit seven Covent Garden productions of the play in the 1810–11 season and a single Drury Lane production on January 13, 1813. *Oxberry's New English Drama* (1821) and *Cumberland's British Theatre* (1830) include not just cast lists but also descriptions of costumes for each character; Cumberland's are most vivid:

> SIR ANDREW AGUECHEEK—Orange-coloured doublet and trunks, trimmed in yellow; yellow cloak, trimmed in orange; hat and stockings to match
> SEBASTIAN—Deep amber tunic, with short sleeves; white body and pantaloons, trimmed with sky blue and black galloon; short russet boots, black cap, with blue and black feathers.
> ANTONIO—Yellow body and pantaloons, and blue fly, trimmed with scarlet and buttons. (Cumberland, p. 8)

In addition, Oxberry's text announces the time that presentation takes. Lacy's *Twelfth Night* (1855) gives cast lists, costume descriptions, an introduction, a glossary of unfamiliar terms, and even a list of page numbers for each character's entrances. Each new edition provides more and more textual features linking its text to performance.

Only Bell's edition draws specific attention to the differences between performance and text. Building on his initial claim that "action must render [*Twelfth Night*] more pleasing than perusal" (Bell, vol. 4, p. 295), Gentleman continues throughout his text to include footnotes which lament the stage's removal of certain passages and which occasionally offer the full text. He also concludes each act with brief commentaries which often touch upon staging, as at the end of act 1: "when performed with abilities, we find this Act open the characters and the story very pleasingly" (Bell, vol. 4, p. 313). These constant allusions invoke stage practice but have the paradoxical effect of distancing the text from the stage, presenting the edition almost as a commentary on performance.

As the century progressed, performance editors elaborated more on the stage business, particularly actors' movement. Whereas Bell (1774), Inchbald (1808), and Kemble (1815) all recorded exits and entrances, the last two often indicated exits within scenes as well as at the end.[35] Oxberry (1821) and Cumberland (1830) offered exit directions as well, while Lacy (1855) went even further in offering other stage actions and their relative positions, such as noting that Olivia "sits, R.C. right center," in order to hear Orsino's messenger in act 1, scene 5. This increasing attention to stage placement is

matched by greater and greater detail in stage directions themselves, particularly within complicated scenes. For example, the enactment of Malvolio's
gulling is recorded in ever more thorough stage directions throughout
the series of editions. Both Bell and Inchbald augmented the entrances and
exits in act 2, scene 5 by including directions that Maria "throws down a Letter, and exit," and Malvolio is seen "taking up the Letter" (Inchbald, pp. 34,
36). Possibly because Kemble himself played Malvolio in 1789, he added several stage directions to the scene in his 1815 edition. Not only does Maria
"enter . . . with a Letter," but also "the Men hide themselves." Later in scene,
Malvolio both takes up and "opens the Letter." After the conspirators see
Malvolio leave, "they advance from behind the Trees" (Kemble, pp. 31–35).
All in all, Kemble's edition gives almost twice as many stage directions for
the same scene as Inchbald's edition does. The important point is not that
these actions take place—most of them are self-evident within the language
of the scene—but that these editions offer more and more clues to where
these actions occur in the text as well as on the stage.

Other added stage directions differ from text to text or offer variant information. In Kemble's text, the stage directions sometimes go beyond indicating just the action. When the officers come to break up the duel between
Antonio and Sir Toby, "Sir Andrew hides himself behind the trees.—[and]
Viola retires a little," but "Antonio shows great alarm.—[and] Sir Toby
sheathes his sword" (Kemble, p. 51). Thus this edition introduces directions
not only for the action but for the emotions behind the action. Lacy's
*Twelfth Night* carries this strategy still further in the same scene but during
the fight between Aguecheek and Viola: "They fight; VIOLA, very timid, and
SIR ANDREW tremulously parrying her blows. SIR TOBY and FABIAN urg-
ing them on each other" (Lacy, p. 48). Once these texts begin to register
emotions accompanying actions, they move from supplying a promptbook
blueprint for performance to describing the performance and narrating the
event.

Just as textual critics take stage directions in so-called Bad quartos of
Shakespeare's plays for strong evidence of their connection to performance,
so the stage directions published in these performance editions suggest a
move closer and closer to the theatrical promptbook, with its notations of
actions, props, and stage positions. When the strategies for marking the
promptbook are brought explicitly into the editorial project, promptbook
notations become part of the bibliographic code of the performance editions
(McGann, p. 66). But the incorporation of some promptbook notations
does not make these texts the equivalent of promptbooks, even though they

are often treated as such.[36] Instead the publication of promptbook mark-ings—especially the descriptive stage directions mentioned above—empha-sizes the textuality of theatrical production as managers and actors mark texts to fashion performances.

The increase in performance materials also records the rivalries between successive editions. The Bell, Inchbald, and Kemble editions basically limit themselves to promising to present the play "as performed at the Theatres-Royal, Regulated from the prompt-book, with the permission of the man-agers, by Mr. Hopkins, Prompter" (Bell, vol. 4, p. 293). Both Bell and Inch-bald give notice as well that there is an introduction or remarks before the play and, for Bell, "notes critical and illustrative." *Oxberry's New English Drama* (1821) announces itself to be "the only edition existing which is faith-fully marked with the stage business and stage directions." In *Cumberland's British Theatre* (1830), Daniel then goes so far as to list all the other materi-als on the title page: "a description of the costume,—cast of characters,—Exits and Entrances, relative positions of the performers on stage, and the whole of the stage business." In the individual Cumberland texts, this infor-mation also appears on the cover in the midst of an elaborate pillared en-graving in which Shakespeare's name is printed on a luminous lamp at the bottom center.

The visual impressions created by elaborate title pages are augmented by title page engravings, which all of these editions except Kemble's use. Unlike the Folio, with its engraving of Shakespeare, or the quartos, with their small decorative woodblock designs, these editions include a full-page engraving of a specific character, scene, or actor at the front of the individual play, thus adding imagery to their representation of the play. For example, in Mrs. Inchbald's *Twelfth Night* (1808), the opening engraving represents Olivia un-veiling before Viola with the caption, "Look, sir, such a one I wear," depict-ing the moment of the play which is the most illustrated of all scenes in the comedies (fig. 1).[37] Such images were an innovation, as Bell's spirited defense of English engraving suggests (Bell, vol. 1, advertisement). Jonathan Bate points out that the late eighteenth century used Shakespearean engravings extensively, appropriating the plays for political and social commentary.[38] Though most engravings appeared in what Bell calls six-penny magazines, the performance editors demonstrated a growing interest in representing Shakespearean scenes, both visually and textually.

The increasing insistence upon theatrical materials marks these editions as copies, even as the details become more specific. Throughout the nine-teenth century, performance editors drew in more and more apparatus; as a

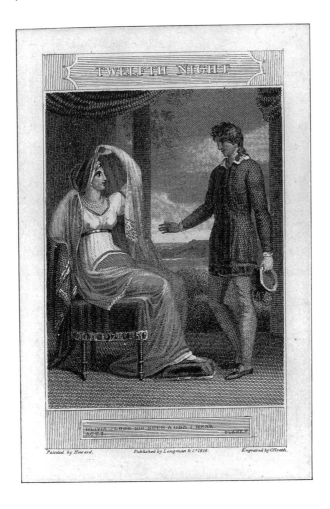

**Figure 1.** Olivia's unveiling, act 1, scene 5. Courtesy of the
Folger Shakespeare Library.

result, their texts expose the performance edition's nature as one version but
not the play. The popular theatrical authorities on the title page of a performance edition assured its purchasers that they were buying a copy of the
play as performed *now*, different from earlier performance editions and
allied with a specific, and transitory, historical moment of theatrical production. As these six nineteenth-century collections of Shakespeare's plays
demonstrate, performance editions did not mediate between a Renaissance
past and a Victorian present as scholarly editions seemed inevitably to do.

Instead, performance editors negotiated the relationship between near-simultaneous reproductions on stage and in print. When these texts were sold in the theatres or in bound volumes, they provided their readers with the latest Shakespearean text, not the first.

To present the most up-to-date text, some editors whose lexical texts of *Twelfth Night* are practically identical—Kemble, Oxberry, and Cumberland—offered enormously different textual apparatus. The choices of extra materials differentiated these editions from each other. Just as importantly, these new materials made the performance editions attractive to multiple audiences. For example, some features seemed aimed particularly at actors and directors who might buy the text, like Lacy's inclusion of page numbers for every character's entrances. By implying the text's usefulness for actors as one of its marketable features, Lacy extended the textual appurtenances of the performance edition to reflect a varied readership of these texts beyond playgoers. When actors and managers purchased these performance editions, they often transformed the text back into performance. Most prompters in the nineteenth century took these editions as their base texts and then added their own markings or, as in the case of Samuel Phelps, restored missing materials.[39] Kemble reproduced all of his promptbooks in his own performance editions after the devastating fires which destroyed the theatrical libraries at Drury Lane and Covent Garden. Thus performance editions could readily become working texts in the theatre.

Yet other innovations—the costume descriptions, the description of stage movements, the more generalized engravings which draw attention to characters in a scene rather than actors who have portrayed those characters—favor a reader imagining a performance. For such readers, the performance edition is a blueprint for the imagined performance, complete with exits, entrances, and elaborate stage directions. These strategies encourage "reading" the theatre.

The introductions to these editions appeal to several audiences. Most often, form seems to dictate content; that is, introductions, as a textual feature borrowed from scholarly texts, frequently take up scholarly issues ranging from the date of composition to character analysis. True, Mrs. Inchbald counters Charles I's well-known preference for Malvolio by commenting, "Had His Majesty seen Mrs. Jordan perform in it, he no doubt would have called it 'Viola'" (Inchbald, p. 3), and, in *Cumberland's British Theatre* (1830), Daniel devotes his entire last paragraph to analyzing the performances of Feste, Sir Andrew, Sir Toby, Malvolio, and Viola, in that order. However, more than any other single feature of the performance editions, their introductions anticipate readers with scholarly as well as theatrical

interests. The "readerly" appeal of these introductions becomes most obvious in veiled (and not-so-veiled) defenses against Dr. Johnson's criticism of
*Twelfth Night*: "This play is in the graver part elegant and easy, and in some
of the lighter scenes exquisitely humorous. Ague-cheek is drawn with great
propriety, but his character is, in a great measure, that of natural fatuity, and
is therefore not the proper prey of the satirist. The soliloquy of Malvolio is
truly comick; he is betrayed to ridicule merely by his pride. The marriage of
Olivia, the succeeding perplexity, though well enough contrived to divert on
the stage, wants credibility, and fails to produce the proper instruction required in drama, as it exhibits no just picture of life."[40] In their response
to his critique, these introductions acknowledge the importance of literary judgments of the plays even for texts prepared, at least in part, by theatrical professionals.[41]

Mrs. Inchbald's introduction, for example, takes up both issues that
Johnson raises in her extended discussion of the punishment meted out for
Malvolio's presumption in wishing to marry Olivia. She questions the
morality of *Olivia's* behavior as she tries to redeem Malvolio from ridicule:
"It might, nevertheless, be asked, by a partizan of Malvolio's, whether this
credulous steward was much deceived, in imputing a degraded taste, in the
sentiments of love, to his fair Lady Olivia? as she actually did fall in love with
a domestic; and one, who, from his extreme youth, was, perhaps, a greater
reproach to her discretion, than had she cast a tender regard upon her old
and faithful servant" (Inchbald, p. 4). Mrs. Inchbald goes on to draw a
moral about Olivia's attraction to Cesario from another part of the play,
Orsino's admonition that women take lovers older than themselves. She also
cites the text of Fabian's comment that "if this were played upon a stage now,
I could condemn it as an improbable fiction" for evidence which "ought to
mollify criticism upon some of the most extraordinary incidents contained
in this work" (Inchbald, p. 5). What may be most interesting about the two
quotations from *Twelfth Night* which she includes in her "Remarks" is that
neither appears in "her" edition of the play. Her literary defense of *Twelfth
Night* reaches beyond the text included in the performance edition which
she introduces.

Different characteristics in the performance editions' apparatus served to
broaden the audience for these texts. In the process, performance editors allied their editions with other kinds of texts: promptbooks, "reading" editions, and even scholarly editions. The arguments of the introductions, as
well as the increasing textual apparatus, signal that the performance editions
of this period are profoundly interconnected with other kinds of editions,
particularly the Johnson-Steevens scholarly edition.

### Just the Facsimile

Comparisons between the Folio and these later performance editions also illuminate our current version of transparent access to Shakespeare's genius,
the Folio facsimile. As Michael Warren puts it, "I wish to propose a new format for the scholarly study of individual plays, and possibly even for the
teaching of Shakespeare's plays, which would involve the encounter with the
earliest versions in photographic reproduction with their original confusions
and corruptions unobscured by the interferences of later sophistication"
("Textual Problems," p. 35). This is our claim to textual authenticity. However, despite many admittedly powerful readings of Shakespeare's work
which arise from looking at Folio and quarto facsimiles rather than later editions, the return to a facsimile of the Folio is not a return to the Folio. In
fact, I would argue that a return to the literal Folio texts is not a return to
the Folio.

To take up first the photographed Folio advocated by Warren as the appropriate text, what we have in the Folio facsimile is the illusion of a return
to the original "authentic" *Twelfth Night*; we can see the Folio's typographical features, but not without the intrusion of a twentieth-century version of
"transparent editing." The Folio facsimile is a picture of the Folio, created
by editors who have decided how much to reduce the page size, who give
their introductions, and who choose which particular Folio or Folios they
will photograph and present. The medium which *we* have decided can offer
an uncorrupted view of Shakespeare's text is just as much a historically
grounded intervention in the text as the nineteenth-century performance
editors' insistence that the stage alterations in Shakespeare's plays revealed
his true genius.

More to the point, the 1623 Folio participates in a tradition of performance editing not shared by a photographic reproduction of the Folio text.
Folio facsimiles arise from scholarly interest; they are not produced under
the same or even similar pressures created by the Folio's proximity to performance. In advocating a "return" to the Folio facsimile, we urge the use of a
copy, which participates in a different editorial situation than the Folio and
which is marked by the interferences of later sophistications in printing (i.e.,
photographic reproduction). Moreover, because of the technology involved,
the editorial task of producing a Folio facsimile creates its own distinctive
problems. Fredson Bowers suggests two different ways of producing a facsimile, by photographing a single copy of the Folio or by examining different copies to discover which pages are marred by inking or proof correction
as the text was printed. Since any individual early text is itself a collation of

different formes, or printings, "no especial textual virtue inheres to any given copy of a book."[42] Thus even the editors of Folio facsimiles must compare a range of copies to choose their text, taking pages from different Folios if necessary. Again there are copies, not a single authoritative text as editors draw from different texts and compare them in order to achieve textual authenticity.

Even typographical identity in a particular Folio text (also at the mercy of historical changes in the physical text) does not make for an identical text: its historicity makes the material text necessarily multiple. As Jerome McGann puts it, "texts vary from themselves (as it were) immediately, as soon as they engage the reader they anticipate. . . . Every text has variants of itself screaming to get out, or antithetical texts waiting to make themselves known. . . . Various readers and audiences are hidden in our texts, and the traces of their multiple presence are scripted at the most material levels" (pp. 9–10). The twentieth-century reader, visiting the Folger Shakespeare Library or the Huntington, can examine the same Folio text of *Twelfth Night* once perused by her nineteenth-century counterpart. However, the twentieth-century reader examines a rare book and reads a text framed by a hundred years' more scholarship than the nineteenth-century reader. Facing the 1623 Folio at different historical moments, these readers may assume that the text before them has an unchangeable identity. Yet each reads a different text, in terms of value, context, placement, or displacement from the order of Shakespearean production. We may "return" to the material text dated 1623, but what we find there, what exists there, cannot be confidently ascribed to be what was there for the 1623 reader, or for the 1790 reader who knew Malone's dating or the reader from 1830 who knew Collier's revised date of composition. Like those past readers, we cannot erase our historical moment, but "going back to the Folio" can create a dangerous illusion of getting back to origins. The important consequence for my argument is that, although changes that the nineteenth century enacted in the comedy, especially the rearrangements of scenes, seem aberrant and sometimes abhorrent today, such performance editing can offer significant revelations about the changing texts of *Twelfth Night*.

The comparison of the collected performance editions from 1770 to 1855 underscores several significant aspects of performance editing. First, the competition and interaction with other types of editions which arise in the nineteenth century enrich the performance edition's strategies for approaching theatrical practice through textual apparatus. However, these strategies are by no means straightforward in their results. The added introductions, cast lists, frontispiece engravings, and stage directions do not operate uniformly to invoke performance but create a complicated blend of discursive approaches to the play.

Second, this evolving mixture of the textual and the theatrical ultimately does not take its authority from any individual production—there is no defining original performance any more than there is an original text. The performance editions may list the casts from two or more runs of the play; they may even give the cast list for productions, like the 1820 operatic adaptation of *Twelfth Night*, when the text offered does not reflect the production. In fact, the quartos show far more interest in the place and exact occasion of enactment than the later performance editions do, as the frontispiece of the 1608 *King Lear* suggests: "*As it was played before the Kings Majestie at Whitehall upon S. Stephans night in Christmas Hollidayes. By his Majesties servants playing usually at the Gloabe on the Banck-side.*"[43] Later performance editions assert their proximity to performance through theatrical documents, those associated with production—playbills, reviews, and, most importantly, promptbooks—and those created specifically to reflect the theatre—introductions, engravings, and advertisements. To insist on the textual qualities of these materials does not necessarily detract from the performance editors' efforts to ally their texts with performances; it merely demonstrates that the later performance editors' approach to their materials encouraged the inclusion and creation of theatrical documents as more valuable and worthy of publication than the Folio editors did. The aim is the same, to interest the theatrical public in the drama as text, but more documents are available, acceptable, and easily publishable in the nineteenth century.

Third, the later performance editions, in part because they include so much in the way of theatrical material and introductions, reveal the conditions which underlie their editorial choices. The Folio gives little and the quartos scarcely more in terms of evaluating the textual oddities it records. We are forced to speculate about the sources of contradictions in Viola's behavior or odd variations in speech headings and references to Orsino for the Folio text, often implicitly discovering multiple versions of the play by judging such anomalies as alternatives. In their developing bibliographic codes, the nineteenth-century performance texts offer their own logic for our examination. Their concerns about specific characters and their interest in consistency and moral purpose provide my initial approach to the variations which they introduce into the Folio text and to the alternative texts of *Twelfth Night* which they present.

Unlike a Folio facsimile that seems to promise an original text, performance editions reveal the degree to which historical context determines what the text can be. Moreover, the purposes and unexpected effects of late-eighteenth-century and early-nineteenth-century changes in *Twelfth Night* show that their choices in providing scenic unity often disguised other crucial pressures which operated on the texts, such as concerns about consistency of identity, interest in the roles of women, and uneasiness about Sebastian's relationship with Antonio.

What the nineteenth century found improbable, indecorous, or outlandish about the play it attributed to Shakespeare's time; what was beautiful or socially and morally appropriate was evidence of Shakespeare's transcendent genius. While the nineteenth-century performance editions flaunt their status as copies linked to performance, they promote the "original" authority of Shakespeare. We can now see the contradictions between the insistent multiplicity of the performance editions and the assumption that Shakespeare is the authorizing original for these versions. The nineteenth-century performance editing of *Twelfth Night*'s texts reveals how the Shakespearean play enables the production of multiple texts and how thoroughly those texts—and ours—are embedded in history.

3

·······

# Rearranging the Texts from
# Bell to Lacy and Beyond

Patterns of performance editing, in both collected and individual editions, inscribe significant differences in the way *Twelfth Night* can
construct theatrical meaning. For example, the Globe Theater 1937
edition cuts the whole scene in which Viola receives the ring from Malvolio
(2.2), and the West edition (1794) omits entirely Olivia's proposal to Sebastian (4.3).[1] Without Viola's soliloquy, the only evidence that she understands
Olivia's passion occurs in the scenes between the two of them. Without
Olivia's proposal to Sebastian, Olivia's claim in the final scene that Cesario
is her husband is almost as big a surprise to the audience as it is to Viola. The
omission of either scene changes both the duration and balance of the
performance and alters the information presented to the audience, delaying
Viola's awareness of Olivia's passion and intensifying the surprise of the demands on Viola/Cesario in the last act. These are sweeping cuts, which remove an entire scene; there are less extensive omissions which occur more
frequently.[2]

The second type of alteration affecting the performance editions, the pervasive rearrangements of the Folio *Twelfth Night*'s scenic order, significantly
reworks the comedy's structure.[3] Nine performance editions between 1808
and 1900, including individual as well as collective editions, open *Twelfth
Night* with Viola's entrance (1.2) and thus substantially change the play's
initial emphasis. In terms of performance, this shift makes sense. The development of the proscenium stage and scenery meant that it was more

theatrically convenient to get the seashore scene out of the way and consoli-
date the interior scenes in Orsino's and Olivia's houses. These scenic features
in the nineteenth-century theatre materially change the texts and alter their
sense. When Viola appears first, the initial emphasis of a production is on
loss and mourning, not the melancholy of love. The sea captain's view of
Olivia, mourning and bereft, is our first impression of her, not the Duke's
invocation of what she will be like when she loves. Moreover, if the Duke
follows her onstage, Viola seems more firmly in charge of her fate. Instead of
entering a situation that already exists theatrically, she introduces Orsino
and Olivia and chooses between them.

Augustine Daly's production, whose text was privately published in 1893,
takes the inversion of the first two scenes and moves the scene of *Sebastian's*
shipwreck (2.1) to the beginning so that his shipwreck even precedes hers!
Staging both shipwrecks at the beginning, though theatrically and scenically
convenient, completely undercuts the sense of Viola's loss by introducing
the potential for mistaking the twins well before the plot has presented Viola
in two roles, lover of Orsino and beloved of Olivia. This variation draws
*Twelfth Night* very close to *The Comedy of Errors* and emphasizes the comic
rather than the melancholy possibilities of the situation.[4] Such rearrangements alter the texts not by cutting aspects of the play but by shifting emphasis to particular elements, like Viola's mourning or the comedy of mistaking twins.

Of course, performance critics often discuss the rearrangement of the first
few scenes, but nineteenth-century performance editions enact other major
redesigns in scenic structure, perhaps less obvious because of the well-known
inversion of the opening. All but one of the nine editions which change the
opening also move the scene introducing Sebastian and Antonio (2.1). As it
stands in the Folio, Sebastian's first appearance in the play intervenes between Olivia's discovery of her passion, which drives her to send Malvolio
after Cesario with the ring in act 1, scene 5, and Malvolio's "return" of the
ring to Cesario in act 2, scene 2. According to the most frequent changes in
nineteenth-century performances, the sequence runs 1.5, 2.2, 2.1: Olivia's
interview with Viola and request that Malvolio "return" the ring, then Viola's receipt of the ring and acknowledgment of Olivia's love, and only after
that Sebastian's first appearance in the comedy.

This second change in sequence also creates a new set of theatrical possibilities. In the Folio, no sooner does Olivia express her desire for the unat-
tainable Cesario than Viola's eminently suitable twin appears. The Folio text
seems to provide a substitute here, much as Orsino's desire for the unattain-
able Olivia in the Folio text's opening is followed immediately by the arrival

of another eligible young woman, also in mourning for *her* brother. In the order suggested by the performance editions, Sebastian's appearance, following Viola's assertion that the situation is a knot she cannot untie, seems a response to Viola's dilemma rather than Olivia's desire.[5] This sequence effectively underscores the sense that Sebastian appears as Viola's surrogate whenever the situation threatens to demand too much of her—when Olivia falls in love with her, when Sir Andrew and Sir Toby try to pursue the duel, and when Antonio, the Duke, and Olivia are all claiming her loyalty at the end of the comedy. The emphasis in act 2 moves from a pattern of desire and displacement in the Folio to one of demand and duplication in the performance editions.

These two rearrangements of the Folio order develop throughout the six main performance editions for *Twelfth Night*. Bell (1774) does not alter the sequence of the text at all. While Inchbald's edition (1808) takes the opening switch, that text keeps Malvolio's encounter with Viola (2.2) immediately after Antonio and Sebastian first appear (2.1) but removes the Folio act and scene breaks so that the two scenes appear to be one. With Kemble's editions (1810, 1815), however, Malvolio's brief scene is shifted so that it can be a separate scene, designated act 1, scene 6, just after Viola's interview with Olivia and preceding the audience's first glimpse of Antonio and Sebastian. Following Kemble's lead, Oxberry (1821), Cumberland (1830), and Lacy (1855) all make the switch. Possibly this adoption of Kemble's changes reflects the theatrical commonplace of having the prompter copy used promptbooks for the next set of performances. Whatever the case, the rearrangement in act 2 is adopted wholeheartedly by performance editors and persists throughout the nineteenth century, producing *Twelfth Night* texts with distinctive variations from the Folio text.

Even though Kemble supposedly went back to the original texts, his edition introduces yet a third change in sequence when he moves Antonio's and Sebastian's second meeting (3.3) forward in the play to follow the gulling of Malvolio (2.5). With this move, Antonio's second conversation with Sebastian (3.3) precedes Olivia's declaration of love to Viola (3.1) and Aguecheek's plan to duel with Viola (3.2). By shifting the scene, the performance editions let Maria's invitation to come see Malvolio cross-gartered (3.2) lead directly into the scene between Olivia and the besotted Malvolio (3.4). In the Folio order, Sebastian and Antonio once again appear in a sequence of scenes linked with Viola and Olivia; this time their appearance follows Olivia's open declaration of love and the threatened duel. The Folio displays the women's dilemmas and then presents Sebastian, potentially solving their problems. By shifting Sebastian's second appearance to early in act 3, the performance editions undo the problems facing Viola and Olivia before they occur. With this third change in scene order, Kemble actually introduced more rearrangements than the texts which preceded his and paved the way for later performance editions to do the same.

The explanation offered for such transpositions in the *Memorial Theatre* edition (1882), which records the standard 2.1 switch as well as some other changes in the order of scenes in the play, is novel, if unconvincing:

> It was stated in the introduction that the representation of some of Shake-speare's Plays upon the modern stage, with its extensive scenic accessories, requires, in many instances, a different arrangement in the order in which some of the scenes succeed each other. Moreover, in some of the plays as originally printed, the unity and continuous development of the plot ap-pears to be needlessly sacrificed by what was probably a carelessly-arranged sequence of scenes, or acts, that may have been suited to circumstances which no longer exist. This is peculiarly the case with "Twelfth Night," where, in the original form, the development of the various incidents in the plot intercept each another in a way that would now be most preplexing [*sic*] to an audience, and detrimental to effective scenic presentation.
>
> (*Memorial Theatre*, p. v)

The editor goes on to argue that "by these transpositions the 'unities' are more nearly approached and several changes of scenery avoided" (*Memorial Theatre*, p. vi). As this introduction indicates, the changes in the order of *Twelfth Night* have a double significance. First, they alter the play to suit nineteenth-century scenery and stage practice. Second, they conform to the taste of late-eighteenth-century and early-nineteenth-century spectators who supposedly valued the unities and would be confused by the apparently in-terrupted sequences which occur in the Folio text. The resulting alterations to the play actually emphasize how the Folio text incorporates the scenes with Antonio and Sebastian as interruptions in Orsino's courtship of Olivia and in Olivia's pursuit of the page. The efforts to stage particular actions as continuous, like Malvolio taking the ring from Olivia (1.5) and passing it on to Viola (2.2), actually underscore how insistently the Folio *Twelfth Night* breaks up such sequences.

My own bias toward the Folio text will be evident since I employ the Fo-lio's scene designations in this chapter and the next, even though there is good reason to suppose that the scene headings were, in fact, introduced by the Folio editors.[6] The performance editors' treatment of scenes in their rearrangements is as revealing as the Folio editors' decisions about scene breaks. Ultimately, the nineteenth-century performance editions of *Twelfth*

*Night* do not demonstrate "a carelessly-arranged sequence of scenes, or acts" (*Memorial Theatre*, p. v) but a play whose scenes—while interpenetrating one another—are sufficiently separated from one another that they can be "sorted out" in productions committed to unifying certain actions. When the comedy moved from the unlocalized Shakespearean stage to the nineteenth-century's proscenium stage and elaborate sets, the new consciousness of place as a defining factor influenced both the understanding and the treatment of the playtext. The performance editions thus register the requirements of later theatrical conditions, although the texts themselves do not include the groove number and property lists that Charles Shattuck finds so useful in promptbooks.[7]

This reordering often strikes current critics as blatant misreading of Shakespearean scenic structure, but such changes call into question the ways the text *can* be rearranged. "Making sense" of *Twelfth Night* in the nineteenth century reveals how the play is reconstructed by changing ideas about what "sense" is. Our own insistence on proper Folio order is just as much a historically determined taste as was the nineteenth century's commitment to scenic spectacle. Most importantly, both the nineteenth century's tendencies and our own have ideological as well structural implications for the study of *Twelfth Night*'s texts. The dramatic "sense" of certain unified actions and practical considerations of detailed sets and place clearly influence the performance editions' construction of the play. However, nineteenth-century performance editions also reflect other criteria of intelligibility: evaluations of character, expectations of gender roles, and awareness of sexuality. Both in the nineteenth century and now, theatrical taste influences the performance editions in ways which reveal the ideological pressure points of the play.

### Cutting for Character

Despite the *Memorial Theatre* claims, the changes these editions register do not merely simplify theatrical representation; many also work to create continuity in a character's identity and actions. As my brief discussion of substantial textual changes suggests, rearrangements in scenic order rework individual characters. Karen Greif even suggests that John Philip Kemble "realigned the scene order so that each act comprised a defined block of action, usually with strong opening and closing scenes that centered attention on Viola or Malvolio, the two leads."[8] In addition, many of the cuts underscore the importance of character, as performance editing often works to conform characters to nineteenth-century ideals of consistency.

The growing attention to character is a significant innovation in this period.[9] In 1785, Thomas Whatley published his influential *Remarks on Some of*

*the Characters of Shakspeare*, in which he hailed character as the most important attribute of drama. In the 1839 edition, he reiterates what he means by
character:

> But no assemblage of these [distinguishing features] will together form the
> character of any individual: for he has some predominant principle; there
> is a certain proportion in which his qualities are mixed; and each affects the
> other. Those qualities check that principle, though at the same time they
> are themselves controlled by it. . . . The force of character is so strong, that
> the most violent passions do not prevail over it; on the contrary, it directs
> them, and gives a particular turn to all their operations. The most pathetic
> expressions, therefore, of all the passions are not true, if they are not accom-
> modated to the character of the person supposed to feel them.[10]

Whatley asserts that Shakespeare avoids the problems of contemporary
tragic writers who do not grasp the importance of "distinguishing peculiari-
ties" and those of "the comic writers [who] have, indeed, frequently caught
them; but then they are apt to fall into an excess the other way, and over-
charge their imitations: they do not suffer the character to show itself, but
are continually pointing it out to observation; and, by thus bidding the spectator take notice of the likeness, tell him all the while it is but a representation" (p. 24). He attributes to Shakespeare the particular genius of creating
unique character, avoiding the extremes of both tragic and comic writers in
the nineteenth century.

Whatley's essay compares two tyrannical usurpers, King Richard III and
Macbeth, in order to show the distinctive principles founding two very different characters. He concludes that "thus, from the beginning of their history to their last moments, are the characters of Macbeth and Richard preserved entire and distinct" (pp. 118–19). Whatley's notion that character
must be "entire and distinct," governed by a "predominant principle," depends upon coherence as the measure of successful character. He also ties
the fate of the theatrical enterprise to the success or failure of character.
Whatley's argument, which refutes criticism of Shakespeare's episodic plot
structure and focuses critical attention on character as the core of drama,
proves to be influential throughout the nineteenth century. Not only is his
own essay reproduced in several editions (the third issued in 1839), but his
ideas are taken up once again in George Steevens's influential scholarly edition of Shakespeare in 1804.

Perhaps most importantly for the performance editions of the period,
Whatley's ideas undoubtedly interested John Philip Kemble. Kemble not

only wrote an essay responding to Whatley's comments on Macbeth in 1786, but also published a much-expanded version of his response in 1817 to argue with Steevens's revival of Whatley's arguments. Kemble did not object to Whatley's assertions about character, but to his assessment of Macbeth's courage. Doubtless biased in part by his own success in the role, Kemble criticized Whatley for doubting Macbeth's valor even though, in the main, he clearly admired Whatley's ideas.

In his 1817 revision, Kemble supports Whatley's view of character explicitly: "Truth of character and passion, the real touchstone and test of dramatic worth, is the unrivalled attribute of Shakspeare's muse."[11] The principle of ruling character is obviously of paramount importance to Kemble's defense of Macbeth: "If we might decide on the ruling character of men from their occasional starts of feeling, this passage would unanswerably prove that, in Mr. Whatley's acceptation of the word, Richard is more timid than Macbeth" (Kemble, *Essay*, p. 147). However, Kemble's argument significantly augments Whatley's idea of coherent and distinct character by insisting that such character must serve a *moral* purpose. Both responses to Whatley open with the claim that "plays are designed, by the joint powers of precept and example, to have a good influence on the lives of men. . . . the cause of morality is promoted only, when, by a catastrophe resulting from principles natural to the agents, who produce it, we are taught to love virtue, and abhor vice."[12] Thus, Kemble bolstered his argument that Macbeth's courage is crucial to the moral lesson of the tyrant's fate by asserting that the fall of a character we merely despise cannot improve our moral sensibilities. Though Kemble extended the significance of character, he did not question the importance of the organizing principle.

Though the characters of *Twelfth Night* are not, generally speaking, part of the debates about the predominant principles governing character, the performances of this period embodied this interest in character clearly. In their linking of theatrical and textual practices, the performance editions also register this reigning principle. As I have already mentioned, the prompt-book alterations of scenic structure that the performance editions adopt rewrite specific characters. At the same time, most introductions and notes to the performance editions make it clear that an interest in character often motivates interest in the play. For example, the editorial introductions and apparatus of the six collected editions I focused on in the previous chapter acknowledge an ongoing interest in Malvolio—certainly the frontispiece illustrations favor scenes with Malvolio, indicating his importance to productions. Francis Gentleman singles out "*Malvolio's* ridiculous self-sufficiency"

(Bell, vol. 4, p. 295) and comments extensively on Malvolio when he first
enters: "A dry assuming importance, quaintly expressed, seems to be the material ingredient of *Malvolio*; who thereby, from future situations, becomes a
very ridiculous object, and indeed shows much originality of character"
(Bell, vol. 4, p. 307). Later performance editions extend this interest to include all three fools that the play represents. As Mrs. Inchbald suggests in
her discussion of Sir Andrew Aguecheek, Feste, and finally Malvolio, Shakespeare "added to his natural fool, and his counterfeit fool—a made fool
[Malvolio]" (Inchbald, p. 4). Oxberry opens his remarks by drawing attention to "that natural fatuity, as shown in Sir Andrew Ague-cheek, [and] con-
ceit, as displayed in Malvolio" (Oxberry, p. i). For Cumberland's edition,
Daniel devotes almost a page to likening Sir Toby to Falstaff, praising Sir
Andrew's follies, and focusing on Malvolio as "an admirable picture of folly
in *another* degree" (Cumberland, p. 6).

The introductions also single out Viola. Oxberry's gives Viola the same
degree of attention that he gives Malvolio and much more vivid praise:
"Viola, more particularly, is a being of the fancy, as bright and impalpable as
the colours of the rainbow; her words are the echos of all that is most sweet
and harmonious in the imagination; to hazard a bold phrase, she is the music of life" (Oxberry, p. i). She is often considered by critics like Inchbald to
be the genuine source of interest in the play, in its serious aspects rather than
in its representation of folly.

The records of benefit performances between 1771 and 1830 offer further
evidence of which roles most interested the nineteenth century.[13] Toward
the end of each season, actors and other theatrical personnel were allowed a
benefit, a performance of the play of their choice, so that they could collect
the evening's profits after expenses.[14] Naturally the actors would choose popular plays, normally ones in which their roles were particularly appreciated.
In the twenty-seven benefit performances of *Twelfth Night* staged at the request of actors between 1741, when the play was first revived, until 1830, sev-
enteen of the total were staged for "fool" roles. Six of these performances
benefited two or more characters, often supporting a pair of actors like
Richard Suett and Robert Palmer, who played Feste and Sir Toby together
for two benefits. Of the benefits for single characters, Andrew Aguecheek
had eight, Suett had one as Feste, Palmer had one as Sir Toby, and Robert
Bensley had one as Malvolio. All in all the pattern of the benefits suggests
both the popularity of Aguecheek's role and the tendency to benefit the
"fool" characters in groups as well as singly.

The remaining ten benefits were produced for the actresses in the play.

These differed from benefits for the fool roles in two important ways. First, each benefit supported only one actress, whereas the "fools" often staged joint productions. Second, whereas the same comic actors, like Suett and Palmer, would often choose a single "fool" role for their benefits in successive seasons, the actresses who chose *Twelfth Night* for their benefits never repeated their roles later. In fact, for all the *Twelfth Night* benefits staged for Viola, it was the actress's first appearance as the character, implying that it was the role itself which was perceived as a draw for the audiences rather than an actress's identification with that role. Anne Barry (1777), Mary Bulkley (1782), and Charlotte Goodall (1789) each chose to play Viola for the first time at their benefits. Unlike the case of Andrew Dodd, who started playing Andrew Aguecheek in 1771 and chose that role for his benefit three times between 1775 and 1795, these actresses relied on the overall popularity of *Twelfth Night* and the interest in seeing a new actress in the role of Viola for their profits. Five different actresses—Isabella Mattocks (1771), Elizabeth Harper (1782), Jane Powell (1793), Anne Biggs (1801), and Clara Ann Dixon (1801)—chose the role of Olivia, with the last two attempting it for the first time. The benefit performances of *Twelfth Night* reinforce the evidence of the introductions: two groups of characters are of particular interest from the late eighteenth century through the nineteenth century, the fools and the female leads.

In analyzing the treatment of character in the nineteenth-century performance editions, I take up Alan Sinfield's recent challenge to examine how playtexts produce "character effects." While vigorously rejecting humanist essentialism, Sinfield explores how features of Renaissance playtexts enable the construction of recognizable individuals.[15] I agree with Sinfield's proposition that Renaissance playtexts—or rather Renaissance performance editions—present sufficient continuity to create the impression of a continuous identity in the characters, at least as long as such coherent identities are ideologically useful. However, I explore how performance editors revised particular characters to promote "character effects" which were acceptable from the late eighteenth century through the nineteenth century.

Character in this period bore a different ideological weight than in the sixteenth and seventeenth centuries. Instead of earlier performance editions' limited invocation of character, the nineteenth-century performance editions recorded new continuities of character, strongly linked to the ways the nineteenth century was beginning to make sense of individual subjectivity. The performance editors revealed a concept of individual identity as they constructed specific characters within the play.[16] In studying how perfor-

mance editors rewrote the fools and the female leads, the two sets of characters which most interested them, I explore the structure and ideological coherence in nineteenth-century "character effects."

### Fashioning the Fool

The treatment of the fools in the performance editions of *Twelfth Night*
recalls Whatley's strategy in contrasting Macbeth and Richard III. As
Mrs. Inchbald contrasts the natural fool, the counterfeit fool, and the made
fool, the performance editors amend Aguecheek, Feste, and Malvolio in order to emphasize the distinctive versions of folly that organize their characters. In the role of the "natural fool," Sir Andrew Aguecheek evidently
needed very little revision. Most of his speeches, in subject and in language,
reflect the "country bumpkin" features associated with the natural clown in
the eighteenth century.[17] His dancing, his natural fatuity, and his gullibility
all allow him to fit readily into an accepted category of fooling without
much adjustment.

Feste and Malvolio, however, pose greater challenges to the performance
editors because they play multiple roles in Olivia's household and in Illyria.
Feste, for example, has all the talents of the court fool, or counterfeit fool,
but he is not connected solely to Olivia's household in the Folio text and
thus operates as a free agent, soliciting payment for his fooling from almost
everyone. The accepted role of court fool, serving a particular distinguished
household, is a character which the performance editors must force upon
him by curtailing his other functions in the Folio text. Malvolio as well,
from his position of authority within Olivia's household, has a mixed role in
the comedy, as he never fully relinquishes his status and respectability as
steward even though he becomes the "made fool" almost from his first interaction with his tormentors. The performance editions concentrate on the
mockery of Malvolio, de-emphasizing his authority and status, traits that he
possesses in the Folio even during his most extreme folly.

The changes to a single scene where all three fools appear demonstrate
how differently performance editors treat Malvolio, Feste, and Aguecheek.
In act 2, scene 3 Malvolio earns the enmity of the group carousing in the
kitchen. The most striking changes are made to Feste's role: all six of the collective performance editions cut the first song which Sir Andrew requests,
transform "Hold thy peace" into a Christmas song, and introduce a drinking song just before Maria urges them to be quiet.

Kemble uses the interpolated drinking song to interrupt Malvolio's appearance. The appropriate musical question "*What is the properest day to*

*drink? / Saturday? Sunday? Monday?"* (p. 26) preoccupies the trio so much that once Malvolio appears to scold them they continue to sing it. Then Malvolio comes down to chastise the carousers. Performance editors, following Kemble's lead, revise his longish Folio speech questioning their good sense and betraying his own self-importance: "My masters, are you mad? Or what are you? Have you no wit, manners, nor honesty, but to gabble like tinkers at this time of night? Do ye make an ale-house of my lady's house, that ye squeak out your coziers' catches without any mitigation or remorse of voice? Is there no respect of place, persons, nor time in you?" (2.3.87–93). Of the six major performance editions, Inchbald cuts only one line: "Do ye make an ale-house of my lady's house, that you squeak out your coziers' catches without any mitigation or remorse of voice?" Kemble and those who follow him cut the speech more drastically and also add musical interruptions, turning Malvolio's diatribe into a dialogue:

> *Malvolio.* My masters, are you mad? or what are you?
> *Sir Andrew.* [sings] *Monday,—*
> *Malvolio.* Have you no wit, manners, nor honesty, but to
>      gabble like tinkers at this time of night?
> *Sir Toby.* [sings] *Saturday—*
> *Malvolio.* Is there no respect of place, persons, nor time, in you?
>
>                                                  (Kemble, p. 26)

Between the cuts to the speech and the interpolated singing, Toby and Aguecheek interrupt Malvolio's complaint from the start. By changing the rhythm of the scene's first interchange between Malvolio and the fools and exaggerating the joke that they are keeping time in their catches, Kemble and those who follow him detract from Malvolio's justifiable and potentially threatening complaint. Consequently, the seriousness of his intrusion, which temporarily stops the revelry in the Folio, transmutes into humor.

Performance editors change Feste's lines in this scene even more substantially; the scene's longest omission (twenty-four lines) includes one of his solo songs and some commentary about him. Without the song and the speeches, which suggest both the range and the degree of Feste's musical skill, these editions limit his role by eliminating his talent for love songs as well as drinking songs and foolery. Most of them also leave off Toby's and Andrew's praise of Feste's "mellifluous voice" and "contagious breath." As the interruptions to Malvolio's largely valid complaint rob him even of his momentary dignity and authority, these changes to Feste's role make his part—and the scene itself—less complex in tone.

In the Folio, the less boisterous song which Feste offers at the beginning
of the scene moderates the merrymaking and emphasizes Sir Andrew's role
as suitor, whereas the catch about "hold thy peace" foreshadows Malvolio's
appearance. The nineteenth-century performance editors shift the balance
of the scene in the direction of misrule over order, revelry over love melancholy. These changes revise and simplify the Folio's representation of Feste's
various talents and eliminate the validity of Malvolio's complaint. Sir Andrew, who becomes the butt of everyone's jokes, maintains his foolish role
more or less intact. Lacking its potentially mournful love songs or serious
complaints, the scene becomes unalloyed comedy, even farce. The treatment
of these three characters is fairly consistent through the play. Sir Andrew's
and Sir Toby's roles receive only minor alterations, but Malvolio and, to an
even greater degree, Feste appear as different figures in the later performance
editions than they are in the Folio.

Feste's part offers a bewildering array of functions and characteristics, from which the performance editors create a household fool whose
principal duty is to Olivia. The major cuts to Feste's role which I have already mentioned seem principally to affect his singing. The omission of
both his first song for Aguecheek and Toby (2.3) and his entire appearance in
act 2, scene 4, where his only real purpose is to sing, is a double alteration to
his role which effectively limits his musical contributions to drunken catches
and the much-maligned epilogue song. In some cases, these cuts could accommodate an actor's lack of singing talent. However, Leigh Hunt's praise
of John Fawcett as Feste in 1820 is particularly based on his singing of the
final song: "We stopped the play out, on purpose to hear him sing that
melancholy-merry song, with its pleasant air." [18] Moreover, the reasons for
curtailing Feste's earlier singing certainly cannot lie in any idea that singing
is inappropriate to the play, especially given that the play's revival in 1820 was
a version transformed into light opera. In reviewing this production, Hunt
observed that *Twelfth Night* though "quite able to stand alone, must also be
allowed to be more fitted [than *The Comedy of Errors*] for the introduction
of songs" (p. 231). While Henry Bishop apparently added memorable music
for Viola and Olivia, Hunt makes no mention of any songs added for Feste.
In fact, a promptbook dated 1820 suggests that this production added six
songs, including a duet for Olivia and Viola and a serenade from Orsino and
his court when they arrive below Olivia's window in a galley, but actually cut
Feste's song in the second act as most other performance editions do. [19]

The omission of Feste's songs may therefore have more to do with the
songs themselves than with the skills of the actors or the nature of the play.
Both are melancholy love songs, in many ways ideally suited to the two un-

requited lovers who request them. Both suggest that Feste is not only aware
of Orsino's and Aguecheek's courtships and their likely degree of success, but
also sensitive to the mood required in singing before a particular suitor.
Feste's song for the carousing Aguecheek anticipates love in "*Present mirth
hath present laughter*" (2.3.49) and emphasizes a *carpe diem* motif in "*Youth's
a stuff will not endure*" (2.3.53). In contrast, his song for Orsino in the very
next scene reflects on the singer-lover's death as "*I am slain by a fair cruel
maid*" (2.4.54). Even though these texts normally keep Viola's later observation that his fooling "craves a kind of wit," that cleverness does not extend to
his singing in these performance editions.

These cuts also limit Feste's flexibility. In the Folio, because of his experiences in both households and his double skills of fooling and singing, Feste
offers illuminating evaluations of the other characters. Nineteenth-century
editions confine him to one household. In the performance editions which
eliminate Feste's visit to Orsino in act 2, he still tells Viola later in the play,
"Foolery, sir, does walk about the orb like the sun, it shines everywhere.
I would be sorry, sir, but the fool should be as oft with your master as with
my mistress" (3.1.39–42). In the Folio, Feste's statement is literally true; in
the performance editions, it is not. Many of Feste's critical observations no
longer exist in the performance editions, possibly because he enacts an aspect of comedy which Whatley most criticizes, by "continually pointing
[distinguishing characteristics] out to observation; and by thus bidding the
spectator take notice of the likeness, tell[ing] him all the while that it is but
a representation" (p. 24). These changes obliterate his similarity to Viola,
who also crosses the boundaries set by Olivia and Orsino. The Folio text
shows Viola, who is challenged by Olivia as a comedian, and Feste, who is
treated often as a messenger, to be figures allied by their roles in the two
households and by their unique status on Illyria's margins.

A closer examination of Malvolio's role reveals that, although not as se-
verely truncated as is Feste's character, his part is edited to emphasize his
comic actions. Not only does he deliver the ring immediately to Viola upon
receiving it from Olivia, but, after Kemble's text, he also duly appears cross-
gartered and dressed in yellow stockings just after Maria calls Toby and
Fabian to witness the event. In the Folio, the two scenes between Sebastian
and Antonio (2.1 and 3.3) intervene on both occasions before Malvolio sets
out to do what he thinks Olivia has asked of him. The performance editions
move these encounters, concentrating attention on Malvolio. In both cases
he is wholly unaware of the true circumstances of his task; he is as ignorant
that he is conveying more than just a ring to Cesario in 2.2 as he is blind to
Olivia's true mood and response to his overtures in 3.4. In the nineteenth-

century editions, the immediacy of his appearances in both sequences keeps the audience's attention focused on his behavior and his comic ignorance.

Paradoxically, these same editions also cut and interrupt his speeches in interesting ways, as in the case of Malvolio's dignified speech scolding the revelers. By adding the song, Kemble disrupts Malvolio's role at the same time that his rearrangements make it more coherent. Leigh Hunt's assessment of that scene's impact in his 1811 review of the play suggests that the effects of mocking Malvolio so thoroughly with interruptions are particularly comic: "The scene of midnight riot, where *Sir Toby, Sir Andrew,* and the *Clown* are in vain interrupted by the entrance and admonitions of *Malvolio,* whose gravity is at once shocked by their incontinence and mortified by their contempt of him, is one of the completest pictures ever drawn of the recklessness of a stupid debauchery; and is sure to convulse the spectators with laughter" (p. 42). By leaving off the less obstreperous song and exacerbating the drunken assault on Malvolio, the nineteenth-century performance editors use Malvolio purely to comic effect.

In fact, they also cut Malvolio's longer speeches throughout the play. When Malvolio in his yellow stockings has presented himself to the bemused Olivia, these editions cut short his meditation on the significance of her response (see fig. 2). Kemble radically cuts the second half of the speech which offers Malvolio's conviction that, without a doubt, he is about to win Olivia. Through these cuts, Kemble's edition eliminates over half of the speech and moves immediately into Malvolio's comic interaction with Toby, Maria, and Aguecheek.[20] By cutting short Malvolio's gleeful self-congratulation and his absolute, if misguided, self-confidence in his interpretation of Olivia, the performance editors reduce the action to interplay between him and the characters who are gulling him.

This impulse to curtail his overweening self-assurance recurs strikingly in the final scene in which he very aggressively asserts his rights to Olivia and repeats his own humiliation. All the collective performance editions except Bell leave off the lines in angle brackets below:

. . . Pray you, peruse that letter.
You must not now deny it is your hand:
Write from it, if you can, in hand, or phrase,
Or say 'tis not your seal, not your invention:
<You can say none of this. Well, grant it then,
And tell me, in the modesty of honour,
Why you have given me such clear lights of favour,
Bade me come smiling and cross-garter'd to you,

BELL (1774)

Oh, ho, do you come near me, now? no worse man than Sir Toby to look to me! this concurs directly with the letter. *Cast thy humble slough,* says she; *be opposite with a kinsman, surly with servants, let thy tongue tang with arguments of state, put thyself into the trick of singularity*; and consequently, sets down the matter how; as a sad face, a reverend carriage, a slow tongue, in the habit of some Sir of note, and so forth. I have lim'd her but it is Jove's doing, and Jove make me thankful! and when she went away, now, *let this fellow be look'd to:* fellow! not Malvolio, nor after my degree, but fellow. Why, every thing adheres together. Well! Jove, not I, is the doer of this, and he is to be thanked.

(vol. 5, p. 338)

OXBERRY (1821)

Oh, ho! do you come near me now? no worse man than Sir Toby to look to me? She sends him on purpose, that I may appear stubborn to him; for she incites me to that in the letter.—I have limed(1) her.—And, when she went away now, *let this fellow be look'd to:*—Fellow!(2) not Malvolio, nor after my degree, but fellow. Why every thing adheres together.—Well, Jove, not I, is the doer of this, and he is to be thanked.

(1) As a bird with bird-lime
(2) *Fellow*, originally signified *companion*. Malvolio takes it in the favorable sense.          (p. 44)

CUMBERLAND (1830)

Oh, ho! do you come near me now? no worse man than Sir Toby to look to me? She sends him on purpose, that I may appear stubborn to him; for she incites me to that in the letter.—I have limed her.—And when she went away now, 'let this fellow be look'd to:'—Fellow! not Malvolio, nor after my degree, but fellow. Why, every thing adheres together.—Well, Jove, not I, is the doer of this, and he is to be thanked.

(p. 46)

**Figure 2.** Malvolio asserting the accuracy of his perceptions.

INCHBALD (1808)

Oh, oh! do you come near me now? no worse man than Sir Toby to look to me! This concurs directly with the letter: she sends him on purpose that I may appear stubborn to him; for she incites me to that in the letter.—Cast thy humble slough, says she; be opposite with a kinsman—surly with servants, let thy tongue tang with arguments of state—put thyself into the trick of singularity;—and; consequently sets down the matter how; as, a sad face, a reverend carriage, a slow tongue, in the habit of some sir of note, and so forth. I have limed her; but it is Jove's doing, and, Jove, make me thankful!

(p. 50)

*Select* KEMBLE (1815) (same as 1811)

Oh, ho! do you come near me now? no worse man than sir Toby to look to me? She sends him on purpose, that I may appear stubborn to him; for she incites me to that in the letter.—I have lim'd her.—And, when she went away now, *Let this fellow be look'd to:*—Fellow! not Malvolio, nor after my degree, but fellow. Why every thing adheres together.—Well, Jove, not I, is the doer of this, and he is to be thanked.

(pp. 46–47)

LACY (1855) (same as Folio)

Oh, ho! do you come near me now? no worse man than Sir Toby to look to me? This concurs with the letter: she sends him on purpose, that I may appear stubborn to him; for she incites me to that in the letter.—"Cast thy humble slough," says she,—"be opposite with a kinsman—surly with servants, let thy tongue tang with arguments of state,—put thyself into the trick of singularity;"—and consequently sets down the matter how; as, a sad face, a reverend carriage, a slow tongue, in the habit of some sir of note and so forth. I have limed her: but it's Jove's doing, and Jove make me thankful.—And, when she went away now, "let this fellow be look'd to:"—Fellow! not Malvolio, nor after my degree, but fellow. Why, every thing adheres together—that no drachm of a scruple, no scruple of a scruple, no obstacle, no incredulous or unsafe circumstance—What can be said? Nothing that can be, can come between me and the full prospect of my hopes.—Well! Jove, not I, is the doer of this, and he is to be thanked.

(p. 42)

To put on yellow stockings, and to frown
Upon Sir Toby, and the lighter people;
And acting this in an obedient hope,
Why have you suffer'd me to be imprison'd,
Kept in a dark house, visited by the priest,
And made the most notorious geck and gull
That e'er invention play'd on? Tell me, why?>
                    (5.1.329–43)

By omitting eleven out of fifteen of his lines in this speech, performance editors gag Malvolio even more effectively than Feste does. Augustine Daly's 1893 edition carries this diminishment of Malvolio to its logical extreme and cuts him entirely from the final scene. By intruding in his serious statements, by focusing attention on his actions through both scenic continuity and stage directions, and by cutting his lengthy speeches of self-justification, the nineteenth-century performance editions present Malvolio purely as a comic scapegoat. Though the Folio allows him to catalog his ills and enlist Olivia's sympathy, these later texts have so thoroughly focused on Malvolio's comic self-importance that they consistently undermine his claims of misuse and cut speeches which might draw sympathy or emphasize his importance to the household.

Both Malvolio's and Feste's parts are cut in their second scene together, the madhouse scene in which Feste poses as Sir Topas to catechize Malvolio in his prison (4.2). The performance editions typically omit about a third of the Folio text in this scene, most importantly the entire sequence where Feste speaks in both his own and Sir Topas's voice. This three-way dialogue between two people functions as Feste's comic tour-de-force and the climax of the Folio scene. Feste's enactment of two roles not only stages a kind of battle for Malvolio's soul but also demonstrates, in eighteen lines, his mastery of comic impersonation.

In effect, the performance editions remove the evidence the Folio offers that Feste, at least, can adopt different types of folly as mere roles. When he plays the court fool as well as the sober priest, Sir Topas, both for fun, his acting denies any organizing principle in his part and even suggests that Malvolio's folly could be a pretense. In this scene and in his adoption of the madman's voice in act 5 (also edited out of the performance editions), Feste threatens to transgress the boundaries of his defining role as court fool: he reveals that the three distinct fools in *Twelfth Night* are merely roles rather than the principles at the heart of "entire and distinct" characters.

However, in cutting the scene by a third in length, performance editors also take out some of the more aggressive teasing which Malvolio experiences. A number of his laments are missing in the performance editions: his insistence on the "hideous darkness" of his prison, his frustration with trying to get Feste's attention, and his repetition of his plight to the Clown: "They have here propertied me: keep me in darkness, send ministers to me, asses, and do all they can to face me out of my wits" (4.2.94–96). The relative shortness of the edited scene undercuts any sympathy Malvolio gains while he is in the power of Sir Toby, Maria, and Feste; Feste promises to bring the pen and paper almost immediately in the performance editions.

By focusing not on his multiple functions in Olivia's household but on his self-delusion, the performance editors readily create Malvolio as a coherent character. Feste's part does not as readily offer some organizing principle which governs his actions; moreover, both his actions and language throughout the Folio insist on the interchangeability of roles, not by altering "essence" but by changing clothes, facial hair, voice, and so forth. Because Feste undoes both his own consistency of character and, by implication, that of other characters in the play, performance editors frequently choose to limit his part as drastically as practically possible.

These substantial changes in Feste's and Malvolio's roles do not occur in isolation. By cutting Feste's role in act 2, scene 4, performance editors revise not only his role but those of other characters as well. By limiting Feste to Olivia's household, they allow Feste's foolery to deflate Olivia's mourning (1.5) but erase his ironic assessment of Orsino's changeability (2.4). Moreover, rearrangements of scenes which make Malvolio's scenes continuous (particularly the 1.5, 2.2, 2.1 reordering) also affect the characters of Olivia and Viola. The editing of the fools inevitably influences the female leads and contributes to the substantial changes in their roles.

### Creating the Perfect Woman and Her Opposite

Nineteenth-century commentaries link Olivia and Viola in unusual ways: praise for Viola and condemnation for Olivia often occupy the same introductions and even the same sentences. Inchbald opens her 1808 introduction to the play by singling out Viola's part as particularly interesting: "the dramatis personae of higher interest are those, with whom Viola is concerned in the serious, more than in the comic occurrences, which befall her; for, with them, she speaks a language that enchants both the ear and the understanding; and produces a happy contrast to the less refined dialogue" (Inchbald, p. 3). In effect, she validates Viola's interactions with characters like Olivia in contrast to Viola's involvement with Feste, Malvolio, and others. However, by the end of her introduction, Inchbald also singles out

Olivia as a character with a "greater reproach to her discretion" since "she actually did fall in love with a domestic" (Inchbald, p. 4).

The editing of their roles is similarly linked because both characters potentially enact nineteenth-century ideologies of gender. Viola displays a thoroughly admirable devotion and submissiveness—by nineteenth-century standards—and Olivia's self-imposed restriction within her home, selfless commitment to mourning, and rejection of suitors accord well with the evolving image of the Lady in the House. The alterations to both roles indicate an ongoing concern with consistency of character, specifically with acceptable female character. Performance editors remove those aspects of Viola's part that deviate from the submissive modesty considered to be the hallmark of her character: they limit her sarcastic wit, the impropriety of her male disguise, and her occasional identification with the wordplay of Feste. They also cut Olivia's part in order to weed out the contradictions which her character expresses, especially the contradiction between her ability to rule her own household and her inability to rule her feelings. For both Viola and Olivia, the internal consistency which these performance editions seek derives from nineteenth-century ideologies of gender which position gentlewomen as passive rather than passionate, submissive rather than aggressive, and modest rather than self-assertive. The alterations in these editions demonstrate a struggle to conform both Olivia and Viola to nineteenth-century perceptions of woman's nature.

However, because of the nineteenth-century assumption that extremes of passion did not touch true gentlewomen, the contradiction between Olivia's status as a woman of means and her vulnerability to passion represented an intolerable conflict which the performance editors tried to efface. When that effort foundered because of Olivia's violent passion, performance editors emphasized the ideal in Viola in contrast to Olivia and her shortcomings. The opposition between the two women proved essential because even the most extreme cutting could not excise Olivia's bold courtship of Cesario. Viola, on the other hand, seems to express proper maidenly modesty and even merits inclusion as one of Shakespeare's model heroines in John Ruskin's "Of Queens' Gardens." [21]

As a result, by the end of the nineteenth century, the insistence on the contrast between Viola and Olivia became even more extreme. In William Winter's introduction to Daly's 1893 performance edition, he posits Olivia principally as a foil to Viola's perfections: "*Viola* is as gay as she is gentle, and as guileless and simple as she is generous and sincere. The poet has emphasized his meaning, furthermore, by the expedient of contrast of the two women. *Olivia*—self-absorbed, ostentatious in her mourning, acquisitive and voracious in her love, self-willed in her conduct, conventional in her character, physically very beautiful but spiritually insignificant—while she is precisely the sort of woman for whom men go wild, serves but to throw the immeasurable superiority of Viola into stronger relief." [22] Whether Olivia in the Folio text actually contrasts with the superior Viola, the performance editors of the nineteenth-century performance editions certainly tried to produce this effect.

In the Folio *Twelfth Night*, mutual challenge and competition for control characterize the first encounter between the two characters. As Viola has refused to leave the gate, she also persists in her somewhat insulting questions about who is the lady of the house. She challenges Olivia by accusing her of usurping herself, by turning the conversation always back to the text she has memorized, and finally by daring Olivia to speak with her alone about matters "as secret as maidenhead." Nineteenth-century performance editors modified all of these tactics. In the Kemble text and its successors, Viola only asks once which is the lady of the house, and Olivia seems unaware that she is being mocked by yet another comedian. Because all these texts limit Viola's references to her own part, her persistence is not as obvious as it is in the Folio. In the performance editions, she no longer frames her promise to deliver "divinity" to Olivia in private conference as a challenge to maidenhead, a cut that smacks of bowdlerization but also removes the implied intimacy of Viola's appeal to Olivia.

If Viola's aggression in the scene is muted by these cuts, so is Olivia's recognition of the situation and vigorous response to her visitor. For example, these texts cut Olivia's repeated demands that the messenger come to the point, removing as well Viola's insistence on her speech of praise:

> *Viola.* . . . But this is from my commission. I will on with my speech in
> your praise, and then show you the heart of my message.
> *Olivia.* Come to what is important in't: I forgive you the praise.
> *Viola.* Alas, I took great pains to study it, and 'tis poetical.
> *Olivia.* It is the more like to be feigned; I pray you keep it in.
>
> (1.5.190–98)

All six collective editions also cut later lines indicating Olivia's authority, including Maria's suggestion that Cesario "hoist sail" and Olivia's direct challenge to the messenger: "Sure you have some hideous matter to deliver, when the courtesy of it is so fearful. Speak your office" (1.5.208–10). Through her impatience with Orsino's text and his rude messenger, Olivia demonstrates her insight into the situation she faces, yet many of her reactions and commands are cut in the performance editions from Inchbald

(1808) to Cumberland (1830), leaving an Olivia who is far less witty and far less capable of judging the conversation or taking control over it.

The nineteenth-century performance editors remove both Olivia's display of her authority and Viola's persistent flouting of that authority. As a result, they transform Viola from sarcastic to modest and demure while changing Olivia from her equal in a match of wits to confused acquiescence. Kemble's edition paves the way for Olivia's bemused dullness by interpolating the following lines as Olivia puts on her veil for the messenger's arrival: "What means his message to me? / I have denied his access o'er and o'er: / Then what means this?" (Kemble, p. 18). In this speech, which both Oxberry and Lacy pick up, Kemble emphasizes her curiosity about the Duke's persistence rather than about his messenger. Although in the Folio text Olivia knows exactly what to expect of Orsino from the moment when Viola arrives, Kemble takes pains to underscore her lack of understanding.

Once the two women depart from Orsino's script with Viola's request to see Olivia's face, the nineteenth-century performance editions again depart from Shakespeare's script, cutting this exchange:

> *Olivia.* Is't not well done?
> *Viola.* Excellently done, if God did all.
> *Olivia.* 'Tis in grain, sir, 'twill endure wind and weather.
>
> (1.5.238–41)

By removing this bit of conversation, performance editors effectively blunt the edge of their private encounter at the crucial moment when Olivia has removed her veil. These texts move directly from Olivia's comment that "such a one I was this present" (1.5.237–38) to Viola's spontaneous speech in Olivia's praise.[23] Consequently both characters are rendered less assertive and, to modern eyes, less interesting.

Though Viola's lines remain mostly intact for the rest of the scene, the performance editors continue to revise Olivia's lines, as if more restraint would excuse her sudden love for Cesario. The Folio *Twelfth Night* consistently draws attention to Olivia's unusual combination of power and vulnerability—showing her face to Cesario in private conference is itself a gesture that suggests both her accountability only to herself and her developing weakness for the messenger. Since performance editors could not cut the unveiling or the private conversation, they eliminated speeches that recall Olivia's position of power and wealth in her household. For example, the four collected performance editions from Inchbald to Cumberland omit Olivia's catalog of her beauty: "I will give out divers schedules of my beauty.

It shall be inventoried, and every particle and utensil labelled to my will. As, item, two lips indifferent red; item, two grey eyes, with lids to them; item, one neck, one chin, and so forth" (1.5.247–52). In the Folio, Olivia's defense against Cesario's insistence that she leave the world a copy of her beauty (i.e., a child) is to turn the leaving of her beauty into a legal matter, items to be appended to her will. The performance editors remove this pointed reminder of Olivia's status as a woman of substantial means, rendering her both a more modest woman and one less willing to use and bestow her own resources.

They also cut several lines that demonstrate Olivia's own awareness of the contradictions in her behavior. Performance editions from Inchbald (1808) through Lacy (1855) leave off her commentary on Orsino after she insists that she cannot love him: "Yet I suppose him virtuous, know him noble, / Of great estate, of fresh and stainless youth; / In voices well divulg'd, free, learn'd, and valiant, / And in dimension, and the shape of nature, / A gracious person. But yet I cannot love him" (1.5.262–66). In this curious speech, Olivia recognizes the paradox of her inability to love Orsino despite his evident virtues. The removal of this speech takes away Olivia's self-awareness in order to downplay the inescapable contradictions expressed in her character.

As act 1, scene 5 shows, certain aspects of both Viola and Olivia troubled the nineteenth-century performance editors. In Viola's case, editors diminished the aggressiveness and persistence of her surrogate wooing of Olivia as well as her self-consciousness about the role she is playing. These alterations are part of an idealization of Viola which leads the scene to focus on her eloquent speeches at the end rather than her complex wit throughout. At the same time, performance editors undercut Olivia's authority over her household and over the conversation, leaving a character wholly ruled by fickle emotions from the moment Cesario first appears. These strategies focus attention on Viola's sentimental wooing at the expense of Olivia's wit and her own.

The performance editors' treatment of Olivia's role for the balance of the play shows the same goal: they rendered her character more consistent, often by eliminating the aspects of her role which affirm her power in favor of those which suggest her vulnerability. As early as the eighteenth century, John Potter, in the *Theatrical Review* (1771), demonstrated both the distaste Olivia's character inspired and the concurrent desire to excuse or even modify her behavior: "If any one of the [characters] can be said to be reprehensible, it is *Olivia*, whose sudden love for *Viola* in man's attire, and pr cipitate [*sic*] marriage with *Sebastian*, thro' mistake of dress, is not altogether consistent with a woman of her exalted situation; and yet, we frequently meet with instances of this sort, in real life, which derive their origin from chaste love, and have their foundation in the principles of honour and virtue."[24] As Potter's comments about her "exalted position" imply, because of Olivia's status as lady, her fully acceptable self-confinement in the domestic sphere, and even her coldness to the Duke's suit, she should represent the feminine ideal developing in the early nineteenth century. Unfortunately, the boldness she shows in pursuing Cesario and her insistence on a secret marriage contradict the feminine ideals suggested by her status and domestic seclusion.

This contradiction is so disturbing that performance editors even removed references to Olivia's contradictory behavior, as when they cut Sebastian's description. Overtaken by Olivia's desire for Cesario, Sebastian is almost ready to believe that he is mad, "Or else the lady's mad; yet if 'twere so, / She could not sway her house, command her followers, / Take and give back affairs and their dispatch, / With such a smooth, discreet, and stable bearing / As I perceive she does. There's something in't / That is deceivable" (4.3.16–21). Performance editors undercut a seeming contradiction in her character, her apparent madness in contrast to her rule over her household, in order to downplay the conflict between her "exalted situation," as Potter terms it, and her wooing of Cesario/Sebastian.

Inevitably, the speech of Olivia's which causes performance editors of this period the most trouble is her declaration of love to Cesario (see cover art). There are three distinct versions of this speech in the performance editions (see fig. 3). The cuts in *Bell's Shakspeare* remove only the first four lines of the speech that Olivia apparently speaks in an aside to herself, thus limiting her declaration to an open address to Cesario. Though the rest keep the first two lines about Cesario's beauty, they omit the two lines which set up Olivia's compulsion to reveal herself and the oddly negative cast to that compulsion, in which she likens her love to "murderous guilt." In the Folio text, the paradoxical appeal of Cesario's scorn and the unusual comparison of her love to murderous guilt suggest that Olivia's reactions to her feelings are mixed and complex. In the nineteenth-century performance editions, however, Olivia appeals to Cesario without acknowledging or reflecting upon the unusual nature of her declaration. When all nineteenth-century performance editions after Bell's cut the final four lines, they remove Olivia's attempts to explain her declaration and justify its open demand for Cesario's love. In the performance editions, her speech ends with the confession that neither "wit nor reason" can hide her love, even though the Folio shows her *trying,*

BELL (1774)
*Cesario*, by the roses of the spring,
By maid-hood, honour, truth and ev'rything,
I love thee so, that maugre all thy pride,
Nor wit nor reason can my passion hide.
Do not extort thy reasons from this clause,
For that I woo, thou therefore hath no cause;
But reason thus with reason fetter,
Love sought is good; but given unsought better.
(pp. 331–32)

KEMBLE (1815) (same as OXBERRY [1821]
and CUMBERLAND [1830])
O, what a deal of scorn looks beautiful
In the contempt and anger of his lip!
Cesario, by the roses of the spring,
By maidhood, honour, truth and everything,
I love thee so, that, maugre all thy pride,
Nor wit, nor reason, can my passion hide.
(p. 41)

**Figure 3.** Olivia's declaration to Viola
(3.1.147–58).

INCHBALD (1808)
Cesario, by the roses of the spring,
By maidhood, honour, truth and everything,
I love thee so, that, maugre all thy pride,
Nor wit nor reason can my passion hide.
(p. 43)

Folio (1623)
O what a deal of scorn, lookes beautifull?
In the contempt and anger of his lip,
A murderous guilt shewes not it selfe more
soone,
Then love that would seeme hid; Loves night, is
noone.
Cesario, by the Roses of the Spring,
By maid-hood, honor, truth and everything,
I love thee so, that maugre all thy pride,
Nor wit, nor reason, can my passion hide.
Do not extort thy reasons from this clause,
For that I woo, thou therefore hath no cause;
But reason thus, with reason fetter,
Love sought, is good, but given unsought, is
better.                                        (pp. 265–66)

nonetheless, to reason her way through her actions. As they cut the Folio's lengthy declaration, performance editors shifted its focus radically—toward her direct appeal to Cesario and away from her self-conscious efforts to describe and excuse the nature of her passionate claim. Through this editing, Olivia loses self-awareness but also avoids indicting herself and revealing her own recognition that there is something "guilty" about her actions.

Thus the performance editing diminishes the sense that Olivia's status is at odds with her behavior, a contradiction which the Folio text emphasizes. However, performance editors also limited Olivia's references to Viola as part of the problem (they cut "A fiend like thee might bear my soul to hell" [3.4.219]) and any identification of her character with Viola's. Without the frame of her attempts to reason about her feelings, Olivia does indeed seem bold and haughty, most unlike Viola. With her self-conscious speeches as they appear in the Folio, her analysis of her love comes far closer to the ways in which Viola talks about her love for Orsino.

Even through the last scene of the play, performance editions continue to undermine her authority over her wealth and household as well as any suggestions that she and Viola are alike. From Inchbald to Lacy, her exhortations to Cesario to overcome his fear and her audience with Malvolio are cut short. Most striking, all these editions remove her offer to Orsino that they celebrate their marriages at her house, "at [her] proper cost" (5.1.318) and leave off her line to Viola, "A sister! you are she" (5.1.325). Thus, all omit the suggestion that she still controls her wealth and insure that she and Viola are not identified as sisters even momentarily. This subtle editing effectively shifts the authority and benefits of kinship to Orsino, now the kinsman who outranks her.[25] All these changes eliminate the paradoxes in Olivia in favor of a more coherent, and much less powerful, character.

The adjustments to Viola's role—and attention to her character—are considerably greater, as suggested by the rearrangements. Along with the fools, Viola is the character who merits the most attention in the prefaces. By the end of the nineteenth-century, William Winter outdoes Inchbald's praise of Viola, by fulsomely valuing her above Rosalind: "the tender loveliness, the poetic beauty, the ardent, unselfish emotion, the exquisite glee and radiant grace crystallize around her. *Viola* is Shakespeare's ideal of the patient idolatry and devoted, silent self-sacrifice of perfect love. . . . She loves and she is simply herself; and she will submit, without a murmur, to any sorrow that may await her. 'She never told her love.' *Rosalind* is a woman. *Viola* is a poem. *Rosalind* is very human. *Viola* is human, too, but she is also celestial" (p. 5). In the same introduction that so devastatingly critiques Olivia, Viola's character bears the weight of all maidenly virtue. However, she needs some amendment to do so.

The changes in Viola's character fall into two broad categories: cuts or additions designed to promote consistency and rearrangements of scenes affecting the dilemmas that she faces. When her first appearance opens the play, performance editions offer a practical staging move as well as a symbolic gesture indicating her centrality in the nineteenth century. In the case of the second rearrangement (1.5, 2.2, 2.1), Viola's actions, like Malvolio's, flow continuously; with her soliloquy about the ring is the culmination of her interview with Olivia and its immediate result. These shifts in order both revise the presentation of Viola herself and establish her primacy among the passionate lovers in Illyria.

Her character changes so dramatically with the reordering of the play's scenes that the cuts and additions to her role might appear to be more local and consequently less important changes. Certainly, some editing to her part resembles the more "functional" cuts evident in other characters. For example, performance editors cut apparent duplicate speeches or added com-

ments like Kemble's interpolated speech in the opening scene which allows
Viola to explain her intentions quite explicitly, because she asks to be a "page
unto him [Orsino] / Of gentle breeding, and my name, Cesario: / That
trunk, the reliques of my sea-drowned brother, / Will furnish man's apparel
to my need" (Kemble, p. 7). However, even small changes revise Viola's participation in the Duke's household in significant ways. The pre-Kemble texts
cut all of Viola's interchange with her fellow servant Valentine. This cut limits Viola's interaction with the other servants and emphasizes her relationship with Orsino, thus foreshadowing the extensive omissions at the beginning of act 2, scene 4. All six collective performance editions also trim
Orsino's responses to Viola's comment that there may be a woman who loves
him as he loves Olivia, removing his damning assessment of women's love.
As a result, the scene concentrates on Viola's idealized love without any
pointed reminders from Orsino of either women's frailty or their loss of
beauty. This editing emphasizes the speech in *Twelfth Night* that nineteenth-
century commentators designated the most beautiful, Viola's description of
"Patience on a monument."[26] These lines express the central declaration of
Viola's consistent character, the palpable evidence of her superior silence and
modesty in opposition to Olivia's frank and improper declarations of love.

The only problem is that Viola's crossdressing itself contradicts the apparent perfection of her character in nineteenth-century terms. As a result,
throughout the performance editions, the most extensive editing to Viola's
part concerns her disguise. The single most significant omission occurs
when Malvolio overtakes Viola with the ring (2.2). All six collective performance editions excise the following crucial lines from Viola's soliloquy:
"Disguise, I see thou art a wickedness, / Wherein the pregnant enemy does
much. / How easy is it for the proper false / In women's waxen hearts to set
their forms! / Alas, our frailty is the cause, not we, / For such as we are made
of, such we be. / How will this fadge? My master loves her dearly, / And I,
poor monster, fond as much on him, / And she, mistaken, seems to dote on
me" (2.2.26–34). Needless to say, there is no compelling theatrical or scenic
reason to abbreviate Viola's speech. In fact even though eighteenth- and
nineteenth-century critics urged that a character fulfill a moral purpose, performance editors consistently removed Viola's moral objections to her disguise. This cut underscores the problematic status of cross-gender disguise
in both performances and performance editions.

In its denigration of her inappropriate appearance, her soliloquy draws
attention to her crossdressing, an aspect of the role that the nineteenth-
century performance editors were as eager to conceal as to exploit. The lure

of so-called breeches parts on the eighteenth- and nineteenth-century stage was quite different from the sixteenth-century's supposedly unhealthy interest in young boys playing female parts. With an actress in the role of Viola, her adoption of male clothing became a rare opportunity to see female legs exposed. This motive for the revival of crossdressing comedies was distinctly at odds with the praise for Viola's character and sensibility, as Leigh Hunt acknowledged: "the disguise of women in male attire, though it continues, and is likely to continue, welcome in the spectators from causes unconnected with dramatic decorum, always strikes one as a gross violation of probability, especially if represented as accompanied with delicacy of mind" (p. 42).[27]

Hunt's own reviews offer evidence of the "causes unconnected with dramatic decorum": he devotes a full paragraph in extravagant praise of Maria Tree's legs when she played Viola. He closes his commentary by saying that "it is impossible not to be struck . . . with a leg like this. It is fit for a statue; still fitter for where it is" (p. 228). Despite his distaste for the unseemly interest in breeches roles, he himself spends more time discussing Miss Tree's limbs than her acting. Elizabeth Howe, analyzing the situation facing the first English actresses from the Restoration through the eighteenth century, and Michael Baker, examining the conditions endured by Victorian actresses, argue persuasively that the crossdressed roles adopted throughout this period exploited the sexual display of the actress's body for financial gain.[28] By the late nineteenth century, Baker notes that "serious actresses might even shun Shakespeare where the plot demanded male disguise" (p. 101).

In the Folio soliloquy, Viola's vocal self-consciousness about her male disguise inevitably draws attention to the sexual appeal in the role at odds with the fine idealized sensibility so valued in the nineteenth century. Her "wicked disguise" conflicts with her delicacy of mind. As in the case of Olivia's commentary about her passion, Viola's lines underscore aspects of her character which the nineteenth century would just as soon ignore. The performance editors' attention to this speech is especially significant since the excised section links her disguise (and its implication that she is an actress playing a part) to female sexual vulnerability. Viola's avowal of frailty here runs all too close to the nineteenth-century perception that actresses were sexually tainted by their willingness to adopt and display themselves publicly in male disguise.[29] The transvestite actress, with her strong economic draw and her erotic appeal to both sexes, challenged emerging gender hierarchies of public versus private and exceeded the heterosexual oppositions of male desire and female submission. Performance editors secure Viola's ideal femininity through careful editing of those lines which draw attention to her as an actress playing a part or which associate her disguise with female frailty.

However, the most important reason for the cuts in Viola's soliloquy may be that her acknowledgment of female frailty draws her too close to Olivia's justification for her weakness: "ourselves we do not owe. / What is decreed, must be: and be this so" (1.5.314–15). Anxieties about the similarities in these two characters pervade both performance editions and criticism. In the late eighteenth century, Mrs. Elizabeth Griffith, author of *The Morality of Shakespeare's Play Illustrated*, indicts Olivia in the following scathing terms: "In the last speech of this Act, Olivia speaks in the usual manner of all infatuated persons, who are apt to make the Fates answerable for those follies or vices which they have not sense or virtue enough to extricate themselves from, by their own exertions."[30] However, Griffith also attributes to Olivia (albeit inverted) two of Viola's lines omitted from this very soliloquy as further evidence of Olivia's weakness: "She [Olivia] repeats the same idle apology for herself, again, in the second Scene of the next Act: For such as we are made, if such we be, / Alas! Our frailty is the cause, not we" (p. 121). As this error suggests, Olivia's "frailty" could easily become Viola's as well.

The performance editors' investment in Viola's feminine identity, like their work on Olivia, extends through the final scene. In the eighteenth and nineteenth centuries, performance editors almost entirely eliminate the obstacles that Viola herself raises to the revelation of her identity. For example, from Bell in 1774 to Augustine Daly in 1893, all the performance editions remove this section of Viola's and Sebastian's mutual recognition:

> *Viola.* My father had a mole upon his brow.
> *Seb.* And so had mine.
> *Viola.* And died that day when Viola from her birth
>         Had number'd thirteen years.
> *Seb.* O, that record is lively in my soul!
>         He finished indeed his mortal act
>         That day that made my sister thirteen years.
>                                   (5.1. 240–46)

For the nineteenth-century performance editors, the sooner Viola accepts her proper role the better.

The successive treatments of Viola's ultimate acknowledgment that she is Sebastian's sister underscore this urgency to establish her identity (see fig. 4).

Folio (1623)
If nothing lets to make us happie both,
But this my masculine usurp'd attyre:
Do not embrace me, till each circumstance,
Of place, time, fortune, do co-here and jumpe
That I am *Viola*, which to confirme,
Ile bring you to a Captaine in this Towne,
Where lye my maiden weeds: by whose gentle helpe,
I was preserv'd to serve this Noble Count:
And all the occurrence of my fortune since
Hath beene betweene this Lady and this Lord.
(p. 274)

**Figure 4.** Viola's acknowledgment of her identity (5.1.247–56).

BELL (1774) (same as INCHBALD [1808])
If nothing lets to make us happy both,
But this my masculine usurp'd attire;
Do not embrace me, till each circumstance,
Of place, time, fortune, do cohere and jump
That I am *Viola*:                          (p. 325)

KEMBLE (1815) (same as OXBERRY [1821],
CUMBERLAND [1830], and LACY [1855])
If nothing lets to make us happy both,
But this my masculine usurp'd attire,
Away with doubt:—each other circumstance
Of place, time, fortune, doth cohere, and jump,
That I am Viola,—your sister Viola. [they
embrace]                                    (p. 69)

Until Inchbald, performance editors simply cut the last five and a half lines of Viola's speech in the Folio, leaving intact her injunction that Sebastian not embrace her. Kemble, however, also revised the first part of the speech and completely reversed the Folio text, by interpolating "Away with doubt" and reiterating Cesario's identity: "I am Viola—your sister, Viola" (p. 69). He even offered a stage direction requiring the embrace which the Folio apparently denies. This cutting of Viola's recognition scene obviously tightens the action and weeds out repetition—Viola does mention the captain and her garments later. However, these changes also underscore distinctly different treatments of Viola in the nineteenth-century and Folio performance editions. In the Folio, Viola's social identity as Sebastian's sibling and sexual identity as female are separate but related concerns, drawn out during the construction of her new identity in Illyria. In the nineteenth-century texts, she acknowledges her identity immediately and equally swiftly surrenders that identity to become Orsino's wife. Some of the differences between these two sets of texts reflect changes in acting conventions. The Folio *Twelfth Night* stages the gradual revelation of Viola as a reconstruction of the boy-actress in the role of a woman rather than a youth. Since actresses played Viola on the nineteenth-century stage, performances did not need to re-establish her feminine identity so carefully. In fact, Viola's gender was so obvious that Sebastian's provisional acknowledgment "Were you a woman, as the rest goes even" (5.1.237) accelerates a recognition scene which no longer requires such elaborate proof of kinship since the evidence of gender is so clear. Performance editors insisted on an embrace that ratifies the end of Viola's cross-dressed disguise.

Despite these efforts to downplay the transgressions in Viola's crossdressing and eliminate her aggression, the contrast between Olivia and Viola, secured by editing both roles, always threatens to collapse into likeness. If Olivia's sudden passion for Cesario is out of place given her mourning and status, then so is Viola's inquiry about Orsino's bachelorhood just after her brother has drowned. If Olivia's willful wooing of Cesario reveals an uncontrolled sexual boldness, so the display of Viola's legs in male attire signals her sexual appeal. The performance editors underscored the differences between the two women successfully to a degree, but the effects of Viola's disguise on the nineteenth-century stage established in her character just as contradictory a blend of nobility and sexual boldness as in Olivia.

### Variations in Revision

By offering these summaries of the changes made in late-eighteenth- and nineteenth-century performance editions, I run the risk of obscuring the evolution in this series of performance editions. The variations in the individual texts show an ever-shifting boundary between what is inside and what is outside the text, a boundary which each performance editor renegotiated. Bell's edition of *Twelfth Night* is unique in this array because it does not rearrange the text but does include many of the cuts. In fact, many of the cuts that affect characters originated in the late eighteenth century rather than the nineteenth century and reflected eighteenth-century concerns about the transgressive actress as well as emerging interests in character and moral purpose. By using more cutting, later performance editors pursued further similar goals, recasting characters in more focused and consistent roles—by nineteenth-century standards, of course.

With the Inchbald edition, introducing added speeches and altering the order of scenes became part of the performance editor's strategy, but John Philip Kemble actually introduced the widespread changes which characterize the later performance editions.[31] Kemble's influence, registered in three published versions of his promptbook *Twelfth Night* texts, continued long after the end of his tenure at Drury Lane. His rearrangements and additions persisted throughout the nineteenth century in the Oxberry, Cumberland, and French editions as well as numerous promptbooks. Even Lacy's edition, which restored some of the Folio text, nonetheless kept the rearrangements.

Indeed, by the end of the nineteenth century, rearrangements are increasingly part of performance editing as deliberate combinations of rearrangement and cutting appear. Charles Calvert's 1873 *Twelfth Night* edited both Orsino's opening scene (1.1) and his first appearance with Viola (1.4) in order to splice the two scenes together as one late in act 1.[32] Henry Irving's 1884 text uses the same combination, while the *Memorial Theatre* text (1882) freely shifts other sections of scenes around to create combined scenes. Certainly, the increasingly elaborate sets created in the late nineteenth century contributed to these combined scenes. Equally, this growing willingness to cut and paste scenes and sections of scenes together may be the logical extreme of the pursuit of unity of action and character which Kemble introduced in his early performance editions.

Throughout the nineteenth century, both cuts and rearrangements were acceptable methods of performance editing; rearrangements actually increased even as some of the text was reinstated. These strategies produced a variety of texts, most of which twentieth-century scholars would judge irrelevant to *Twelfth Night*'s textual history. Because these texts are so obviously different from the Folio, scholars take those differences as hierarchical: the Folio is a "good" text, and the performance editions are flawed rather than merely different. Thus omissions from the Shakespearean text are always reductions, losses rather than changes, even though Shakespearean texts are almost always cut in performance.[33] By switching the scenes around, performance editors so clearly flout the seventeenth-century text that their editing practically constitutes a violation. And, to current academic sensibilities, additions to Shakespeare's text are so presumptuous that any version of clarity created by such amendment is automatically suspect. Our inflated valuation of the "authentic" Shakespearean text too often blinds us to what changes, especially extreme ones, reveal about the historical reworking of texts.

Nineteenth-century cuts and rearrangements to the Folio *Twelfth Night* reveal the shifting attitudes toward major character roles—at least those considered most important to nineteenth-century critics and editors. The contrast between the Folio and later performance editions exposes features of both. The distinctive functions of both Feste and Malvolio and the contradictions and discontinuities in Viola's *and* Olivia's behavior in the early text stand out in the context of nineteenth-century characterizations of folly and editing to produce Viola's perfection and reduce Olivia's willfulness. As they revised seventeenth-century characters, nineteenth-century performance editors also eliminated these characters' perspectives on each other: Orsino's unwitting evaluation of Viola's love, Olivia's understanding of Cesario's scorn, Feste's judgments and misjudgments that pervade the Folio

*Twelfth Night.* Nineteenth-century opinions about Viola's virtue, Olivia's inconsistencies, and Feste's value replaced the Folio's complex network of evaluations of character and behavior. With these changes, performance editions reveal starkly how historically grounded values reproduce varying Shakespearean texts.

# Textual Perversity in Illyria

For nineteenth-century audiences, as we have seen, poignant moments of seductive interaction between Viola and Olivia provoked fears about sexual transgression. As a result, the femininity of Viola and Olivia became a serious concern for critics and performance editors alike, ultimately masking the erotic aggression in both characters. Nineteenth-century critics of *Twelfth Night* also approached its homoerotic aspects only in the most roundabout ways. However, as in the case of feminine identity, performance editions reflected with great sensitivity the shifting perceptions of sexual roles and the implications of those historical changes for Shakespeare's plays. While scholarly editors during this period wrestled with and rewrote the homoeroticism within the sonnets, the performance editors worked radical changes in the text *Twelfth Night* that register cultural anxieties about the play's homoeroticism.[1]

The most striking of these are the changes to Antonio and Sebastian, especially in the context of the pervasive rearrangements of their scenes. Just as the shifting scenes between Viola and Olivia set up new character constructions, so too the shifting of Antonio's scenes with Sebastian in the nineteenth century reworked that relationship. In the second case, instead of an implicit modesty being made explicit, the performance editors achieved the opposite effect: the openly declared love of Antonio for Sebastian was effectively silenced and denied.

In some cases, rearrangements that created unified actions for Viola or Olivia also repositioned Antonio's scenes with Sebastian. For example, the switch which allows Viola's scene with Malvolio (2.2) to follow Olivia's action of sending the ring (1.5) also dislocates Sebastian's scene with Antonio (2.1). This displacement becomes even more significant when we discover that Sebastian's second scene with Antonio (3.3) was moved almost as frequently as the opening scenes; in five performance editions from 1794 to 1855, it shifted to follow the gulling of Malvolio (2.5). Through 1915, that scene appeared in five different places in the play in production (after 2.5, 2.3, 3.1, 1.5, and 2.4) and in three different places in published editions (after 2.5, 2.3, and 3.1).[2]

Like the other two major rearrangements, the displacement of 3.3 was often justified in terms of nineteenth-century staging conditions. According to the *Memorial Theatre* edition (1882), this rearrangement avoids "a great delay in change of scenery . . . nearly the whole of Act III. and the whole of Act IV. being played in Olivia's garden" (*Memorial Theatre*, p. vi). However, in contrast to their other rearrangements, performance editors seemed to be unable to find any specific new place for this scene. Throughout the nineteenth century, they continued to move the two scenes between Antonio and Sebastian restlessly around the play. The only sequential demands on either scene are that the first must occur before anyone else in Illyria sees Sebastian and the second must occur before Antonio asks Viola for his purse. Within these *termini ad quem*, both scenes show up in several places in the performance editions yet are never cut entirely from the play. As a result, these texts reveal a curious fact about the structure of the Folio *Twelfth Night*: the crucial plot surrounding the twin's appearance, which is so tightly interconnected to the main action in *The Comedy of Errors*, is essential yet not anchored in place in this comedy. Exploiting this, performance editors attempted to isolate the relationship between Antonio and Sebastian with its implications of explicit homoerotic desire.[3]

Nineteenth-century concepts of the ideal woman and of folly produced revisions in scenic order, but those changes did more than just unify the actions of those characters who most interested the performance editors— they also rewrote Antonio and Sebastian. Subtle revisions of implicit homoerotic connections between Orsino and Cesario and between Olivia and Viola in these later editions echo and reinforce their amendments to Antonio's desire. This performance editing suggests a growing uneasiness about the same-sex relationships in the play, particularly in the case of Antonio, but also for other characters.

### Displacing Antonio

Antonio enacts the most direct homoerotic desire in *Twelfth Night*. His passion differs in important ways from the others represented in the play. For one thing Antonio is the only character whose homoerotic desire does not arise from the gender deception of Viola. Unlike Olivia, who pursues the image of Sebastian, or Viola, who can only woo Orsino in disguise, Antonio pursues Sebastian himself. Antonio is also the only character who is not "restored" to heterosexual union by the substitution of one twin for the other. Antonio's position is unusual: his close tie to Sebastian is *not* presented in relationship to a woman, as Orsino's affection for Cesario self-evidently is during the courtship of Olivia. Only at the end of the comedy, when Orsino realizes that he and Cesario are rivals for Olivia, can he openly express his love: "Come, boy, with me; my thoughts are ripe in mischief: / I'll sacrifice the lamb that I do love" (5.1.127–28). Antonio's love, however, requires no woman for its expression. His feelings are not homosocial bonding as Eve Sedgwick defines that concept, but rather, as Joseph Pequigney suggests, a direct, open passion.[4]

In fact, Antonio's rejection of a female third in his relationship with Sebastian is most striking in the final scene. Critics make much of the lengthy mutual identification of brother and sister, but mostly ignore the response of the other character who knows about the twins. Aside from the siblings themselves, only Antonio knows that there are an identical sister and brother, yet he cannot even begin to imagine who Viola might be. In fact, Antonio introduces the term "twin" into the play: "How have you made division of yourself? / An apple cleft in two is not more twin / Than these two creatures. Which is Sebastian?" (5.1.220–22). Not only is Antonio the one character in the play who does not "swerve," as Stephen Greenblatt puts it, in either gender or beloved, but his final words in the play indicate that he continues to desire only Sebastian.[5] Antonio's feelings admit no female third party, no substitution. This very directness in Antonio's love provoked the most serious alterations in the nineteenth-century performance editions. Ironically, in his case, the nineteenth-century performance editors modified a character who already has a single organizing force within an integrated personality: all of Antonio's actions and speeches arise from and relate to his love for Sebastian, at least in the Folio text.

Beyond the widespread rearrangements which I have already discussed, the nineteenth-century performance editors worked hard to distinguish Antonio's pursuit of Sebastian from the other romantic entanglements of the plot. They used multiple strategies: diminishing the parallels which the

Folio sets up between his love and that of the others, removing the romantic language though not necessarily the sexual innuendo in his speeches, and, finally, revising both rescues of Sebastian. The restless shifting around of his scenes with Sebastian is only one sign of the impulse to displace or replace Antonio's love; the more convincing indicators are the cuts which remove his constant references to his love and reshape the emphasis of his speeches to undermine his unwavering attention to Sebastian. Through significant editing, Antonio loses fully a third of his lines in his first scene with Sebastian and almost twenty percent from his part throughout the play.[6]

In the first scene between the two men (2.1), many performance editions cut all or most of his only speech alone onstage. In the Folio, after Sebastian has exited, Antonio gives the following impassioned, if brief, soliloquy: "The gentleness of all the gods go with thee! / I have many enemies in Orsino's court, / Else would I very shortly see thee there: / But come what may, I do adore thee so, / That danger shall seem sport, and I will go" (2.1.43–47). Inchbald's text cuts all five lines, while the other five collected performance editions cut the last four, as do eight individual performance editions up to 1883. Kemble not only eliminates Antonio's speech but also interpolates a "Fare thee well" (p. 24) from Sebastian, giving *him* the final words in the scene and insuring that Antonio has *no* lines alone onstage. In the effort to limit Antonio's avowed passion for Sebastian, these texts omit both Antonio's abrupt reversal of intention and his declaration of love. This could be interpreted as promoting consistency of character—removing the contradictory purposes in Antonio's four-line speech—but also conveniently leaves out his adoration.

In actuality, both the danger Antonio faces and his intended actions affect the plot. Cutting Antonio's soliloquy removes the important information that he will pursue his friend into Illyria despite the dangers. Surely the omission of his stated intention to follow Sebastian makes his reappearance in act 3 (or wherever it might occur) more surprising and thus more striking. Like so many of the other changes made in Antonio's role, omitting his brief soliloquy ultimately compounds the problem of his motivation. The attempt to limit or control his love actually underscores how essential that love is to the plot.

These cuts and additions to Antonio's soliloquy also curtail the parallel endings of the three-scene sequence in the Folio: Viola's wooing of Olivia (1.5), Antonio's pursuit of Sebastian (2.1), and Malvolio's insistence that Viola receive the ring (2.2). Each of these scenes ends with a soliloquy: Olivia's acknowledgment of her love, Antonio's declaration of love, and Viola's longer, more fully developed meditation on her love and Olivia's. In the

Folio, all these soliloquies occur within ninety lines, building from Olivia's interrupted meditation on the youth's perfections to Antonio's five-line declaration to Viola's twenty-four-line soliloquy addressing the situation as she sees it. All three of these characters reveal their own implication in homoerotic relationships within these speeches. Olivia unwittingly exposes her love for another woman, Antonio quite consciously undertakes to act on his love for a man, and Viola contemplates a tangle of desires that appear to be homoerotic—her love for Orsino and Olivia's love for her. When the performance editors move Antonio's scene with Sebastian after Viola's soliloquy and cut Antonio's decision to pursue his love, they effectively undo the parallels which the Folio *Twelfth Night* develops. Although Viola's soliloquy continues to be the last word on gender confusions and same-sex desire, Antonio's love is displaced from consideration.

The cuts to the second scene between Antonio and Sebastian shorten their interchange more radically. One conspicuous omission, originating in Kemble's edition, occurs when Antonio explains his reappearance (3.3—see fig. 5). Because his vow to follow Sebastian does not occur in the earlier scene, Antonio's explanation should be all the more crucial. Kemble (1808) first cut the three lines which express Antonio's love and jealousy. He then interpolated "I fear'd besides, what might befall your travel" in the place of the three lines he excised and transformed "fear" to "doubt" in the next to last line. Though Kemble left in the telling phrase, "desire, / More sharp than filed steel" (3.3.4–5), he downplayed considerably the extremes of emotion, both love and fear, in his revision.[7] Kemble balanced the fear and love in Antonio's speech, providing a combined motive for his reappearance. In the Folio, Antonio's syntax equates his desire with the love which would have drawn him "to a longer voyage" (3.3.7), but those lines disappear, as does the suggestion that his anxiety about Sebastian's safety is tied to his love. "Jealousy what might befall [his] travel" (3.3.8) clearly links his love to his anxieties about the dangers Sebastian might encounter. The Kemble editions not only offer Antonio's second appearance as a surprise, but also subtly shift the emphasis of the speech explaining his pursuit of Sebastian.

In addition, the collective performance editions after Inchbald's cut the seven lines in which Antonio justifies (to the extent that he does) his inability to walk freely in Illyria:

*Sebastian.* Belike you slew great number of his people.
*Antonio.* Th'offence is not of such a bloody nature,
                Albeit the quality of the time and quarrel
                Might well have given us bloody argument.

It might have since been answer'd in repaying
What we took from them, which for traffic's sake
Most of our city did. Only myself stood out,
For which, if I be lapsed in this place,
I shall pay dear.

(3.3.29–37)

By removing Sebastian and Antonio's discussion about the bloody or not-so-bloody nature of Antonio's quarrel with Orsino, performance editors undermine the risk he faces for his friend. Equally importantly, this cut drops a quarter of his lines in the scene.

As a result, the nineteenth-century performance editors omit both Sebastian's questions about the bloody exploits of his friend and Antonio's own equivocations about the nature of the argument. Moreover, the removal of Antonio's refusal to pay Orsino also eliminates the Folio's interesting juxtaposition of Antonio's apparent parsimony in dealing with Orsino and his notable generosity in giving Sebastian his purse. That inconsistency may be one reason that the nineteenth-century performance editors dropped Antonio's explanation. However, this editing also undoes the parallel the Folio establishes between his unexplained refusal to repay Orsino (3.3) and Sebastian/Cesario's apparently inexplicable refusal to return Antonio's money to him in the next scene (3.4), an issue to which I will return later.[8]

Even when Antonio addresses Viola instead of Sebastian, the nineteenth-

---

Folio (1623)
I could not stay behinde you; my desire
(More sharpe than filed steele) did spurre me
forth,
But not all love to see you (though so much
As might have drawne one to a longer voyage)
But jealousie, what might befall your rravell,
Being skillesse in these parts: which to a
stranger,
Unguided, and unfriended, often prove
Rough, and unhospitable. My willing love,
The rather by these arguments of feare
Set forth in your pursuite.          (p. 266)

KEMBLE (1815)
I could not stay behind you; my desire,
More sharp than filed steel, did spur me forth;
I fear'd besides, what might befall your travel,
Being skilless in these parts; which to a
stranger,
Unguided, and unfriended, often prove
Rough and unhospitable: My willing love,
The rather by these arguments of doubt,
Set forth in your pursuit.          (p. 37)

**Figure 5.** Antonio's explanation for following Sebastian (3.3.4–13).

century performance editions limit his declarations. When the officers capture him as he defends Cesario (3.4), Kemble cuts only two half-lines below
(omissions in the performance editions are indicated in angle brackets), but
nonetheless utterly changes the tone of his first speech: "I must obey. [*To Viola*]—This comes with seeking you; / But there's no remedy, <I shall answer
it. / What will you do,> now my necessity / Makes me to ask you for my
purse<?> It grieves me / Much more for what I cannot do for you, / Than
what befalls myself" (3.4.340–45). In Kemble's text, and those which follow
his, the phrase "there's no remedy" anticipates his request for money rather
than his stoic determination to face the consequences of pursuing Sebastian.
Of course, since Kemble has removed Antonio's earlier explanation that his
answering to charges depends upon repayment, he has already undercut the
logic which justifies Antonio's request for his purse. In the Folio text, where
these lines follow directly Antonio's explanation in the next scene that the argument "might have since been answer'd in repaying / What we took from
them" (3.3.33–34), the urgency of Antonio's financial dilemma and the sense
of his claim that "I shall answer it" are both clear. Moreover, given how important Antonio's ability to pay has suddenly become, his obvious concern
for what will befall Sebastian without the purse is all the more striking in the
Folio text. Kemble's editing shifts emphasis away from strong concern for
Sebastian with the transformation of Antonio's worried question about what
his friend will do without money into a simple statement: "Now my necessity / Makes me to ask you for my purse."

The performance editions' tendency to efface the love which Antonio
expresses becomes even clearer late in this same scene. Kemble, and those
texts which follow his, combine Antonio's two speeches challenging Viola
to acknowledge her debt to him, but in the process they remove Antonio's
important characterization of his action in saving Sebastian: "I snatch'd
[him] one half out of the jaws of death, / <Reliev'd him with such sanctity of
love;> / And to his image, which methought did promise / Most venerable
worth, did I devotion" (3.4.369–72). His devotion remains, but his love is
lost in these texts. This pattern of cutting Antonio's declarations of love,
though not necessarily his most suggestive lines, persists in his final appearance. Unlike Malvolio, Antonio is allowed to give his long speech, lament-
ing and blaming Cesario's indifference, yet, once again, the lines where he
describes his heroic action in saving Sebastian are omitted: "That most in-
grateful boy there by your side, / From the rude sea's enrag'd and foamy
mouth / Did I redeem. A wrack past hope he was. / His life I gave him, <and
did thereto add / My love, without retention or restraint, / All his in dedica-
tion>. For his sake / Did I expose myself (pure for his love) / Into the dan-

ger of this adverse town" (5.1.75–82). Beginning with Kemble's text, even "pure for his love" is left out of Antonio's speech. Removing these particular lines obliterates an interesting echo in the Folio text as Antonio adopts the language of love "without retention or restraint," which we have heard throughout the play in Orsino's claims to love Olivia.

Consistently, the performance editions erase parallels which link Antonio and the other lovers in the Folio text. He no longer announces his love in the contexts of Olivia's and Viola's declarations; he no longer echoes Orsino's language of love. More specifically, his references to his own love for Sebastian are often removed, even if the cuts undermine the logic of the plot. After all, without his vow to follow Sebastian for love, Antonio's second appearance in Illyria is a complete surprise.

Perhaps most strikingly, these texts sever his rescues of Sebastian from the love which he explicitly associates with those heroic deeds. Though the Antonio in the Folio text never mentions saving Sebastian's life without also announcing his love, the nineteenth-century performance editions keep only the rescue. This insistence on Antonio's heroism responds, in part, to a historical shift in the characterization of male-male love. As Randolph Trumbach notes, in the Renaissance, sodomy was almost always associated with the rake, as an aspect of his excessive sexuality. However, by the nineteenth century, erotic desire between men came to be associated with effeminacy.[9] Thus the attention drawn to his manly deeds completed the elimination of Antonio's effeminate love.

A significant addition to Orsino's lines in the final scene also recasts Antonio's second rescue of his friend, when he mistakes Viola for Sebastian and saves her during the duel. Orsino's pardon of Antonio, which is published in eight editions between 1791 and 1855, intervenes in the middle of Orsino's final speech and highlights the problems posed by the relationship between Antonio and Sebastian (see fig. 6). The pardon occurs in two versions, the first originating in the individual Lowndes (1791) text and persisting until Kemble revises it in 1810. The Lowndes version signals the departure of the officers and the inclusion of Antonio as Sebastian's friend. Kemble's version shifts the exit of the officers and recasts more emphatically the forgiveness Orsino offers: "Henceforth, be forgotten / All cause of anger" (p. 72). In both versions, this speech resolves the theatrical problem of Antonio's presence onstage at the end, alone and under guard, by overtly acknowledging a character who is frequently suppressed elsewhere in the play.

Orsino's last-minute change of heart reinterprets Antonio's defense of his beloved Sebastian as the more acceptable defense of a maiden. Female distress calling forth male protection is a dominant theme in Victorian drama,

Folio (1623)

He hath not told us of the Captaine yet,
When that is knowne, and golden time convents
A solemn Combination shall be made
Of our deere soules. Meane time, sweet sister,
We will not part from hence.
<interpolated pardon>
            *Cesario* come
(For so you shall be while you are a man:)
But when in other habites you are seene,
*Orsino's* Mistris, and his fancies Queene.
                                    (p. 275)

**Figure 6.** Antonio's pardon (interpolated at 5.1.384).

LOWNDES (1791)
Antonio, thou hast well deserv'd our thanks,
Thy kind protection of Cesario's person,
(Altho' you knew not then for whom you fought)
Merits our favour: officers, release him!
                [Exeunt. Officers
Henceforth be free—thou hast a noble spirit,
And as Sebastian's friend be ever near him.
                                    (p. 58)

KEMBLE (1810)
. . . Go, officers;
We do discharge you of your prisoner.
                [exeunt officers]
Antonio, thou hast well deserv'd our thanks:
Thy kind protection of Cesario's person,
(Although you knew'st not then for whom thou fought'st,)
Merits our favour: Henceforth, be forgotten
All cause of anger: Thou hast a noble spirit,
And as Sebastian's friend be ever near him.
                                    (p. 72)

a theme which Joseph Donohue argues "emphasizes the strong connection in nineteenth-century cultural attitudes . . . between maiden innocence and the likelihood that its possessor is in difficulty, and further suggests a prime value placed on the importance of the rescue. The rescuer is, of course, male." [10] By placing Antonio in that familiar position of rescuer, the pardon interpolates him within the conventional Victorian gender distinction between manly rescuer and distressed maiden. While the Folio text supplies appropriate sexual substitutes for Olivia's longing for Viola and Orsino's interest in his page, the nineteenth-century performance editions also offer Antonio's recuperation into the heterosexual ending once his "desire, / More sharp than filed steel" (3.3.4–5) is reframed in his rescue of Cesario. The severe editing of Antonio's part reflects nineteenth-century editorial anxieties created by homoeroticism throughout the play; his incorporation into the ending thus resolves the "problem" of his love once and for all.

However, the very placement of this belated acknowledgment of a character whose words and presence are cut so frequently can actually recall, rather than banish, homoeroticism. After all, Orsino pardons Antonio in the same speech in which he asserts that Viola shall remain Cesario until she is properly dressed to be his fancy's queen. The sudden reunion of Antonio and Sebastian again potentially reinforces the ambiguity of Orsino's insistence that Viola remain a boy. Consequently, a speech which seems designed to point out Antonio's error and draw him into heterosexual comic union occurs at a point that actually could revive the homoerotic passions operating in the play. Moreover, "be ever near him" is an implicit stage direction which should send Antonio to Sebastian's side as Cesario stands next to Orsino (at least one marked promptbook, Kemble's, records this stage direction explicitly).[11] It is worth noting that neither of the two performance editions with a diagram of the closing tableau places Antonio and Sebastian together. Both Lacy and Oxberry include Antonio's pardon, though their final positions show that Orsino's suggestion remains unacted upon. Oxberry shows him at the opposite end of the stage, whereas Lacy puts him on the other side of Olivia from Sebastian.

Both these performance editions even register their uneasiness about Antonio typographically. Oxberry transforms him into a woman in the final tableau by designating him as "Antonia [*sic*]" (p. 71). More radically, Lacy's text leaves off an entire line from the pardon so that its closing benediction reads:

> Thy kind protection of Cesario's person,
> Although you knew'st not then, for whom thou fought'st,
> Merits our favour: Henceforth, be forgotten
> And, as Sebastian's friend, be ever near him.          (p. 66)

This typographical error functions as the unconscious of the text, revealing through accident the contradiction at the heart of Antonio's treatment in the pardon and in the promptbooks.[12] Like Lacy's pardon, the promptbooks and the performance editions try simultaneously to forget the love Antonio bears Sebastian and to reunite them within the comic union the other characters achieve.

The paradoxical effects of Orsino's pardon underscore the difficulties which bedevil much of the performance editing of Antonio's role. Attempts to limit his love or transform it into heroic, but selfless generosity collide with the importance of his extreme interest in Sebastian, the love which motivates all of his actions in the comedy. While the scenic rearrangements reveal how even the Folio text isolates Antonio's interactions with Sebastian, the other alterations, like the pardon, recall how necessary his love is to the progress of the plot.

This suggestive treatment of Antonio in the nineteenth century is strongly linked to changing perceptions of homosexuality. As Alan Bray argues, there was a major shift in perspective concerning homosexuality from the Renaissance to the late Restoration.[13] Given the public status of sodomy in the Renaissance as outside the natural order and in fact an undoing of that order, Bray conjectures that the man involved in such activity could either go against the Renaissance perspective, invoking the Greeks perhaps, or simply avoid the issue completely.[14] He suggests that the person "could keep at two opposite poles the social pressures bearing down on him and his own discordant sexual behavior, and avoid recognizing it for what it was" (p. 67). At the same time that erotic relationships between men were almost unimaginably disruptive, intimate friendships between men were absolutely necessary to Renaissance social and political realities in the English court.[15] Bray's argument has interesting implications for the ways in which the Folio *Twelfth Night* isolates yet requires the desire of Antonio.[16] However, the paradoxes necessary to the representation of Antonio's homoerotic love in the Renaissance became an intolerable contradiction by the nineteenth century, both because of the insistence on coherence in character and because of growing awareness and persecution of homosexuality.

In the early eighteenth century, homosexuality was distinguished from the more generalized notion of debauchery; a homosexual "culture" grew up around the molly houses and the intermittent persecution both the houses and their participants experienced. The growing awareness of what we now call homosexuality as a characteristic of a specific group of people was a new development, though there is still considerable debate about exactly when the shift occurs. Looking at the evidence of trials and executions under the statutes against homosexuality from 1740 through the mid-1800s, Louis Crompton explores in detail the virulent punishment of homosexuality in the late eighteenth century and early nineteenth century, noting that England was unusual in its prosecution of homosexuals. In a period of judicial reform in Europe, punishment of homosexuality actually increased in England so that "by 1806 the number of executions had risen to an average of two a year and remained there for three decades, though executions for every other capital offense decreased dramatically."[17] According to Crompton, though the numbers may represent only a minority of those involved in homosexual acts at the time, the threat of prosecution was constant. Even if the offender did not receive the death penalty—and evidence of completed homosexual encounter was necessary—lesser crimes like solicitation could land him in the pillory, where mob wrath against the individual might easily result in serious harm or death. The violence of both the punishment and public response to homosexuality led Byron's friends to expurgate his letters and disguise the subjects of his poems, if he had not already done so himself.

Avoiding even the imputation of love between men was absolutely crucial in the early nineteenth century.

This recognition of the "homosexual" may have affected the late-eighteenth-century and early-nineteenth-century responses to Antonio. Certainly, the impulse to cut and shift his scenes shows a desire to limit his role, arising perhaps from a new perception of what that role might be. Antonio's love for Sebastian cannot fall into the acceptable nineteenth-century cult of romantic friendship between boys (infatuations between boys at public schools were widely acknowledged and accepted according to Crompton's account). Nineteenth-century critics and performance editors alike preferred to see and promote: "Antonio, the sea-captain, [as] a delightful specimen of that frank, open, and prodigal nature so common in the nautical character—at all events, in the English sailor."[18] However, this assertion of his nautical role in conjunction with his love for Sebastian is a loaded compliment since, as Crompton points out, naval courts were just as vigorous in their punishment of love between men, hanging twenty sailors between 1800 and 1830 (p. 18). As a result, references to Antonio's love for Sebastian had to be removed from the text. Although we are now very aware of the charged sexual language that signals Antonio's passion, the nineteenth-century editors were most sensitive to an "inappropriate" romantic love addressed to Sebastian.

### Hetero/Homoeroticism in Sebastian and Orsino

Sebastian and Orsino are the two men most closely associated with Antonio's much edited love, and both their parts are affected. Sebastian's connection is clear: he is the object of Antonio's demonstrative affections. Although Antonio has no female third party to his love for Sebastian, *Sebastian* invokes a woman from the very beginning, well before his betrothal to Olivia supersedes his bond with Antonio. In their first scene together, Sebastian explains his deception, which has merely been of name, not gender, in terms of his sister. In admitting Antonio's claim on him, he introduces Viola into the conversation, "[my father] left behind him myself and a sister, both born in an hour: if the heavens had been pleased, would we had so ended! But you, sir, altered that, for some hour before you took me from the breach of the sea was my sister drowned" (2.1.18–22). Sebastian's tears for his sister become his tears at parting with Antonio. He frames his connection with Antonio and, more importantly, the revelation of his name by invoking his sister, but Antonio does not see his relationship to Sebastian in terms of a woman and indeed pays scant attention to Sebastian's strong ties to Viola.

In fact, the performance editing of Antonio's role reveals that the only third party who figures in his pursuit of Sebastian is Orsino. When the performance texts cut elements from Antonio's part which emphasize his love for Sebastian, they also remove allusions to his relationship with Orsino, like Antonio's acknowledgment of the "many enemies in Orsino's court" (2.1.44). In effect, the performance edition cuts downplay any personal quarrel between Orsino and Antonio and emphasize Antonio's suggestion that he is in danger in Illyria only because he did not pay: "Only myself stood out" (3.3.35). However, that shift in emphasis only underscores another curious aspect of the Folio scene. Immediately after affirming that he would not pay back Orsino, Antonio hands over his purse to Sebastian, who has not asked for money and, in fact, questions the gift. The conjunction of an unknown mercantile problem with Orsino and the sudden, yet crucial, gift of money to Sebastian establishes Antonio's position in Illyria, poised between his love for Sebastian and his enmity with Orsino. Added to this is the violence with which Antonio responds when Sebastian apparently refuses to pay back the money as Antonio himself has refused to repay Orsino. Orsino's persistent importance to Antonio's situation—also reflected in his interpolated pardon—positions him, rather than a woman, as the mediating third party in Antonio's love for Sebastian.

The final scene reinforces this view of Antonio's association with the Duke. He finally faces Orsino, whose response is, oddly enough, praise for him, "With which such scathful grapple did he make / With the most noble bottom of our fleet, / That very envy and the tongue of loss / Cried fame and honour on him" (5.1.54–57). By portraying Antonio as an honorable fighter from a woefully inadequate ship, Orsino, like Antonio, presents the dispute as being about goods. In fact, this initial greeting is frankly admiring. It is the first officer who brings up the bloody consequences of Antonio's sea fight, "this is he that did the Tiger board, / When your young nephew Titus lost his leg" (5.1.60–61). Antonio is not directly blamed for the young man's injury, yet Orsino's subsequent response reiterates the very terms in which Antonio has portrayed his danger: "What foolish boldness brought thee to their mercies, / Whom thou in terms so bloody and so dear / Hast made thine enemies?" (5.1.68–70). The abrupt change in Orsino's tone and Antonio's immediate challenge to the Duke's claim on Cesario reveal that the issue is not goods at all—the connection which joins them is the young man. Orsino's and Antonio's initial argument originated over the body of a (castrated) young man; in the final scene, their quarrel resurfaces, this time explicitly as rivalry over another youth who lacks something of a man.

Nineteenth-century commentators ignored both Sebastian and Orsino almost as thoroughly as they avoided Antonio; however, performance editing linked both to Antonio's homoerotic passion in the play. Sebastian is Antonio's beloved, and Orsino, in his love for Sebastian's twin, functions as Antonio's rival and enemy. As a result of these interconnections, both roles experience revealing alterations in the nineteenth-century performance texts, but the different treatment of the two is equally significant.

The connection between Sebastian and Antonio is essential to the structure of the play, although many productions and performance editions seem to wish it were not. Both the cuts and the rearrangements of scenes have a very different impact on Sebastian's role than on Antonio's. The movement of Sebastian's scenes underscores how scripted his role becomes once he encounters the people of Illyria. After his second meeting with Antonio (3.3), like Antipholus of Syracuse in *The Comedy of Errors*, Sebastian constantly finds himself inscribed as suitor, rival, husband; in short, he finds himself in a series of heterosexual roles which he accepts. Before the Illyrians encounter him and begin to control his actions, Sebastian has no fixed place, but Antonio *never* has a place. Moreover, compared to Antonio's role, Sebastian's suffers surprisingly few cuts. Even in their first scene together where Sebastian confesses his gratuitous imposture, the performance editions only cut two lines out of one of his speeches: "She is drowned already, sir, with salt water, though I seem to drown her remembrance again with more" (2.1.29–31). Some performance editions, like Kemble's, treat this speech as an internal stage direction, omitting the lines and giving instead the stage direction—"[He weeps.]."

The performance editors also undercut the extravagancy of Sebastian's emotions in their later scene together, by excising his excessive thanks and his apology for having only that to offer in return for Antonio's kindness: "And thanks, and ever thanks; and oft good turns / Are shuffled off with such uncurrent pay: / But were my worth, as is my conscience, firm, / You should find better dealing. What's to do?" (3.3.15–18). Unlike Viola, who has rewarded her sea captain for the mere suggestion that Sebastian might have survived, Sebastian appears unable to repay Antonio for his rescue. Without Sebastian's desire to offer more valuable gratitude, Antonio's gift of his purse is all the more remarkable because it is wholly unprovoked generosity.

Even in the final scene of the play, where Sebastian's role experiences most of its editing, the lines he loses are more strongly associated with others than with his own character. For example, the truncation of Viola's dialogue of self-identification affects Sebastian's lines as well, since his lines in response are also cut. More interestingly, one major cut to his role in the scene, the removal of his evaluation of Olivia's position, works together with other editing to the scene which seeks to obscure any possible sexual connection between the two women. The priest's assertion before Viola that she and Olivia have kissed and Olivia's acknowledgment of "a most extracting frenzy of my own" (5.1.279) both vanish, and so does Sebastian's emphasis on Olivia's passion for another woman: "So comes it, lady, you have been mistook. / <But nature to her bias drew in that. / You would have been contracted to a maid; / Nor are you therein, by my life, deceiv'd: / You are betroth'd both to a maid and man>" (5.1.257–61). The near-universal omission of these lines is significant. This statement most overtly directs attention to the homoeroticism of Olivia's love for Viola and apparently asserts her ongoing error as she is still betrothed to both maid and man (Greenblatt, p. 71). They are also the lines which offer Sebastian's version of the "master-mistress" of the sonnets, a formulation which Orsino invokes even more directly. Here Sebastian apparently identifies himself in both sexual roles, a blending of "maid" and "man" which the performance editors always cut. Otherwise, his declarations of friendship remain intact, perhaps because they are not as vivid or as homoerotically charged as those of Antonio. After all, Sebastian only mentions love once in the entire play, when he speaks to Antonio about "your love." His necessary alliance with Olivia insures his heterosexual place in Illyria's circuit of desire even though he first appears as the object of Antonio's love.

Orsino, by contrast, suffers severe cutting. The changes to his role reflect not only nineteenth-century efforts to achieve coherent character, but also anxieties associated with his likeness to Antonio in being attracted to the beautiful boy Cesario. Like Sebastian, Orsino's homoerotic involvement is counterbalanced by his predominantly heterosexual yearning for Olivia. However, in Orsino's case, his dual attraction—to Cesario and to Olivia—is not sequential but simultaneous. Whereas Sebastian moves from Antonio's protective and devoted love to Olivia's, Orsino's admiration for Cesario coexists with his devotion to the Lady Olivia. Even though his declaration that Cesario is "the lamb that I do love" comes only with Olivia's ultimate rejection, his attraction to Cesario is recorded in a variety of ways throughout the Folio text. In fact, his utter shift of allegiance from Olivia to Viola makes sense only if he has been attracted to both all along, but that represents an intolerable contradiction in his nature. Orsino is most problematic in the nineteenth century precisely because of his reversal at the end of the play. While Antonio's direct love for Sebastian prompts the revision of his organizing principle from devoted love to heroic generosity and Sebastian's betrothal to Olivia apparently makes it unnecessary to edit his early association with Antonio, Orsino's inconsistency, in love and in language, results in a tangle of editing that arises from multiple causes.

His social position in the play exacerbates the difficulties posed by his inconsistent character. Orsino is the ranking gentleman in the comedy, the suitor of Olivia, and, most importantly from the nineteenth-century perspective, the man for whom Viola exhibits her exemplary devotion. Considerable anxiety attended his role simply because of his association with Viola. Mrs. M. L. Elliott, who wrote *Shakspeare's Garden of Girls* in 1885, expressed just such reservations about Orsino: "It is earnestly to be hoped that Viola won as good a husband as she deserved. Orsino is no hero. There is something effeminate in his love-sickness. . . . All we can do is to believe that Viola's depth of passionate devotion found a worthy object in the man of her choice."[19] If he is not noble and worthy, if his character's coherence rests on his preoccupation with love, then he is no fit object for *her* love. In fact, Orsino was taken to be the principal flaw in the comedy by some nineteenth-century critics, including Arthur Symons: "But the great defect of Twelfth Night as an acting comedy lies, no doubt, in the fact that the love interest never takes very much hold on our sympathies. Viola is a charming young woman and makes a very pretty boy; but who can possibly sympathize with her in her ardent pursuit of such a lover as Orsino, a man whose elaborate sentimentality reminds one of those delicacies which cloy rather than delight the palate, and whose plastic readiness to transfer his affections makes one suspect they were, after all, scarcely worth such trouble to win?"[20] The difficulties performance editors faced only grew because his sentimentality and effeminacy could be associated with homoeroticism in the nineteenth century (Trumbach, pp. 134–35). Though many alterations were aimed at creating a greater consistency in his speeches, their editing also reveals an impulse to moderate both the extravagance of his declared love for Olivia and his implicit interest in Cesario. Their maneuverings register an increasing willingness simply to limit his role, cutting proportionately more of his part than anyone else's.[21] The extravagance of his love is most thoroughly cut, starting with his opening speech, which loses twelve lines.

In the first scene Orsino and Cesario have together (1.3), the performance editions cut the scene to mute Orsino's favoring of his new page. Not only does Valentine's admiration (or envy) of how close Cesario has become to Orsino disappear (totally or in part), so does some of Orsino's telling description of how well the youth will suit the task of courting Olivia. In their first discussion, Orsino catalogs the reasons why Viola is the ideal emissary to Olivia, but the performance editions leave off his most revealing com-

ment: "And all is semblative a woman's part" (1.4.34). Though relatively little
is cut from the scene, all the lines omitted point to Orsino's growing interest
in his page and the transparency of Viola's disguise.

Some individual editions (and occasional promptbooks) from the late
nineteenth century not only move Orsino's opening scene (1.1) but also
combine it with his first scene with Cesario (1.4), condensing the Folio text's
gradual but thorough exploration of Orsino's shifting attentions. This
change, first published in Charles Calvert's 1873 edition and later more
widely in Henry Irving's 1884 individual performance edition, is the logical
extension of Kemble's earlier attempts to unify scenic action and to render
Orsino less changeable and hence less blameworthy. Calvert's text basically
appends the second scene to the first, making Orsino's request for Cesario
bridge the gap. His scene opens with a song which does not appear any-
where in *Twelfth Night* and which focuses quite deliberately on service to the
beloved: "Being your slave, what should I do but tend / Upon the hours and
times of your desire" (Calvert, p. 10). This broad hint about Viola's love for
Orsino precedes and prepares for her declaration at the end of the scene. Irving's individual edition opens this composite scene not with song but with
the conversation between Viola and Valentine which gives way to Orsino's
first speech from the opening. By combining the scenes, these two late performance editions eliminate the dynamics of Orsino's household and his
courtship before Cesario's arrival; in fact, he never appears onstage without
her. As a result these alterations focus attention more on Viola's unrequited
love than on Orsino's futile courtship. Even though these editorial changes
restore some of Orsino's role, they also disguise his extravagance and changeability by creating a coherent action: learning of Olivia's rejection leads immediately to his decision to send another emissary, Cesario.

The second scene between Viola and Orsino (2.4) demonstrates how the
multiple impulses in editing Orsino's part, working together, result in dras-
tic reductions in his lines. His role, like Feste's, is curtailed in the extensive
cutting of the dialogues where Orsino calls for a song and then discusses the
nature of love with Viola (2.4). Not only do these editions leave off Feste's
revealing comment that Orsino should have his "doublet of changeable
taffeta, for [his] mind is a very opal" (2.4.74–75), but the rest of the cuts also
eliminate the proof Orsino himself offers that Feste's assessment is correct.
The nineteenth-century performance editors consistently omit Orsino's
spectacular reversal in the middle of the scene where he abruptly contradicts
his own claim that "such as I am, all true lovers are, / Unstaid and skittish in
all motions else, / Save in the constant image of the creature / That is
belov'd" (2.4.17–20). Orsino's advice to Cesario to choose a woman younger

than himself, though a sentiment nineteenth-century commentators frequently approved, is removed along with his revealing reasoning: "For boy, however we do praise ourselves, / Our fancies are more giddy and unfirm, / More longing, wavering, sooner lost and worn / Than women's are" (2.4.32–35). These same editions also excise his further explanation why men's affection "cannot hold the bent" (2.4.37).

Cuts to Orsino's role intensify the focus on Viola's eloquent speech about her imaginary sister. However, they also render *Orsino's* character more consistent in a scene that the Folio text uses to exactly the opposite effect. Orsino's assertion of men's shifting fancies is important not just because it reflects all too clearly on his own behavior but also because it offers the unflattering implication that Viola is but a flower which, "once display'd, doth fall that very hour" (2.4.39). By eliminating nearly half of this scene, performance editions also noticeably and significantly limit the intimacy of Orsino's and Cesario's mutual confidences. As Viola and Orsino listen to music together, discuss Cesario's love, and exchange opinions about women's love, the scene demonstrates a striking closeness between the two in the Folio text. The nineteenth-century performance editors remove both Orsino's inconsistent evaluation of male and female love and the ample evidence the scene offers of how thoroughly Orsino has opened to Viola "the book even of [his] secret soul" (1.4.14). Consequently, his interest in whom Cesario might love is less pointed, and the emphasis on Viola's oft-quoted speech about her sister's love is greater.

Similar cuts occur to Orsino's part in the final scene, removing many lines that signal his intimacy with Cesario. For example, these editions omit Orsino's reply that Antonio's claims are madness by insisting, "Three months this youth hath tended upon me" (5.1.97). The removal of these lines also limits the implicit, potentially disturbing parallel to Antonio's assertion that "for three months before / No int'rim, not a minute's vacancy, / Both day and night did we keep company" (5.1.92–94). To downplay further the impropriety of Viola's stay in Orsino's house, these same editors leave off his evaluation of her service: "Your master quits you; and for your service done him, / <So much against the mettle of your sex, / So far beneath your soft and tender breeding, / And since you call'd me master for so long,> / Here is my hand; you shall from this time be / Your master's mistress" (5.1.320–25). The performance editors carefully cut lines that recall how long Viola served the Duke and the intimacy of her connection with him. These same editions also curtail his response to Olivia's rejection: "Why should I not, had I the heart to do it, / Like to th'Egyptian thief at point of death, / Kill what I love?—<a savage jealousy / That sometime

savours nobly.> But hear me this: / <Since you to non-regardance cast my faith, / And that I partly know the instrument / That screws me from my true place in your favour,> / Live you the marble-breasted tyrant still" (5.1.115–22). While removing the echo of Antonio's jealousy, nineteenth-century performance editors undertake to limit Orsino's assertions of "his true place" in Olivia's favor as well as his reference to Viola as a mere instrument. Cutting these lines leaves the balance of the speech more focused on the lamb he loves than on his response to Olivia. In the final scene, as throughout *Twelfth Night*, the performance editions are uneasily poised between limiting Orsino's intimacy with Viola and explaining his abrupt decision to marry her rather than Olivia at the end of the play.

The contradictions in Orsino's character arise in the Folio from the ambiguity in his attraction to Cesario. Because his inconsistency became potentially homoerotic effeminacy in the nineteenth century, his character prompted many performance editing strategies. Even though actresses playing Viola in the nineteenth-century doubtless diminished the overtness of Orsino's homoeroticism, the performance editors still faced the problem of an intimacy between the two characters which is necessary given their ultimate marriage but which is also improper, whether she is a young woman or a young man.

### Olivia and Viola: Love between Women

An actress playing Viola mitigates Orsino's attraction to Cesario, but at the same time aggravates the homoeroticism in Olivia's love for the youth. If Viola/Cesario's femininity is apparent enough to justify Orsino's sudden proposal to his page, then surely it is also apparent in Olivia's relationship with him/her. The appearance of one woman desiring another is further underscored by the impropriety of Viola's masculine dress and its association with the dangers of certain close relationships between women. My intention here is not to review the performance editing already explored in chapter 3. Instead, I suggest that the homoeroticism implicit in Olivia's love was potentially visible and contributes to the ways that nineteenth-century performance editors and critics tried to distinguish these two women from each other.[22] The strategies used to "improve" Olivia's character and to deflect attention from Viola's disguise also worked to redeem Olivia from her "misplaced" desire and to downplay the sexual provocativeness of Viola's male attire and witty demeanor, especially when she arouses Olivia's desires.

One signal that such desire was accessible to nineteenth-century audiences of *Twelfth Night* appears in the poem "Viola and Olivia," by John Lucas Tupper: "Olivia / Loveth, her eye abused by a thin wall / Of custom, but her spirit's eyes were clear."[23] These verses and the accompanying etching of the same name by Walter Deverell were published at the start of the April 1850 edition of the Pre-Raphaelite journal the *Germ*. Together they demonstrate that the nineteenth-century audience could perceive mutual love between Olivia and Viola. Citing the poem and its accompanying etching as a clue to the overwhelming popularity of Olivia's unveiling among illustrators, Barbara Melchiori is interested "to find such an early treatment by a Shakespearean illustrator and by a poet of the theme of lesbianism."[24] However, the poem is not lesbian in the twentieth-century understanding of the term, but demonstrates that Olivia's love for Viola could have been readily interpreted as "romantic friendship," an intense loving friendship between women that in the nineteenth century carried few erotic connotations.[25]

In fact, the last stanza imagines a reciprocity in Viola's feelings for Olivia and a marriage of their souls which the play itself never approaches:

> . . . We have oft been curious to know
> The after-fortunes of those lovers dear;
> Having a steady faith some deed must show
> That they were married souls—unmarried here—
> Having inward faith that love, called so
> In verity, is of the spirit, clear
> Of earth and dress and sex—it may be near
>     What Viola returned Olivia?
>         (Tupper, p. 145)

This imagined extension of the relationship acknowledges Olivia's passion and even adds Viola's love, both apparently spiritual and ennobling.

This poem imagines an idyllic spiritual marriage between Viola and Olivia, but most nineteenth-century criticism and performance editing emphasized their differences and incompatibility. The relationship between Olivia and Viola clearly elicited complex responses which Lillian Faderman's arguments about romantic friendship can help to clarify. She argues that passionate loves between women were accepted, even admired, in part because sexual love between women seemed impossible. According to her survey of these relationships, such passionate friendships only drew criticism when the women defied patriarchal controls by crossdressing or by adopting and maintaining masculine behaviors. Viola and Olivia, of course, do both; Viola dresses as a boy, and Olivia boldly woos Cesario, thus usurping the male role in courtship. Olivia's passion is further complicated by the fact that she is not pursuing an idealized friendship with another woman, but a

marriage with a boy—her love anticipates consummation in ways Faderman
suggests were unthinkable for female friends of the late eighteenth and early
nineteenth centuries. The "masculine" behavior of both Olivia and Viola
compromises the acceptable love imagined in the poem and produces anxieties centered around those aspects of their characters. The excessive concern expressed by the critics about both Viola's crossdressing and Olivia's
amorous pursuit of her masks a larger anxiety about the potential homoeroticism of their relationship. The treatment of Viola and particularly
Olivia supports recent revisions of Faderman's work like that of Lisa Moore,
who argues that the vigorous criticism of crossdressers and "masculine
women" as inappropriate figures for passionate friendship indicates an ongoing anxiety about such close relationships between women.[26]

Certainly, the impulse to idealize Viola responded to the disturbing crossdressing in the role and her strong sexual appeal in male dress. As I suggested
in the previous chapter, there is a sexual attraction to the breeches parts, acknowledged by critics like Leigh Hunt in their reviews. Even when the theatrical critic does not attack the impropriety of the actress's costume, the
review must still take up the issue of crossdressing. In *Oxberry's Dramatic Biography*, the author of Miss Maria Tree's "souvenir" quotes a review clearly
interested in emphasizing her modesty in breeches parts like Viola's: "Nothing, perhaps, can be a stronger proof of native modesty, than the manner in
which [Miss Tree] played in male attire: the sternest objector to feminine (or
rather in most cases *un*feminine) stage-personations of man, would have
made an exception in her favour. She was so gentle, so unaffectedly timid, so
unconscious of wrong—her mind seemed so absorbed in the passion which
suggested and warranted the disguise, that no sense of impropriety could
find its way into the thoughts of the spectator, any more than to her own."[27]
Notably, the impropriety which would not occur to any spectator must
nonetheless be warded off by Miss Tree's "native modesty." More strikingly,
there seems to be nothing paradoxical about following this description of
Miss Tree's modesty with an analysis of her "feminine" physical appeal in
these roles: "To our taste, indeed, we confess she never looked *so* feminine, as
when habited in the costume of the other sex. . . . her figure was beautifully
formed; and her 'masculine usurped attire,' which was always the most taste-
ful and becoming imaginable, displayed it to peculiar advantage" ("Memoir," pp. 205–6). The juxtaposition here of assertions that nothing improper
will occur to the viewer watching Miss Tree as Viola and the frank admiration expressed for her figure "displayed . . . to peculiar advantage" in male attire illustrates the principal paradox expressed in performance editing associ-

ated with Viola's crossdressing: the character's remarkable virtue must coexist with the actress's inevitably revealing male costume.

In fact, the transparent femininity of Viola in disguise is crucial, if William Winter's response to Viola Allen's performance is to be believed. Apparently, Allen tried to present Viola's disguise as successful, possibly encouraged by several current stories of women who successfully masqueraded as men. Winter is horrified at the attempt to portray the disguise as a realistic transformation:

> The delicate, almost spiritual, yet absolutely feminine *Viola*, lovelorn for the lord whom she serves, was not only to be so perfectly disguised in male apparel as to be esteemed, by all her interlocutors, a young man; she was to appear so to her auditors. The abnegation of sex was to be literal, as in the instances occasionally reported in contemporaneous life, wherein a woman, for a long time, passes for a man. . . . Miss Allen's notion about *Viola* seems to have rested on the fact that such deception is *possible*. . . . The woman of fact who succeeds in passing herself off as a man is abnormal, unfeminine, and the success of her imposition depends upon her being so. Shakespeare's *Viola* is not a woman of that kind.[28]

Viola's male attire must necessarily reveal that she is in fact a woman, or she runs the risk of appearing "abnormal, unfeminine." Yet that revelation of her femaleness relies on appearance as much as demeanor, on the actress's form revealed in breeches as much as on Viola's "feminine" behavior.

Another signal of Viola's appeal in breeches is less direct but more pervasive in the nineteenth century. Rarely is Viola's disguise mentioned in literary criticism without an accompanying defensiveness about the *character's* modest virtue. In her influential 1833 book, *Characteristics of Women, Moral, Political and Historical*, Anna Jameson comments first on how "the exquisite refinement of Viola triumphs over her masculine attire."[29] She then draws attention to the results of Viola's disguise as she appeals to both the Duke and Olivia: "In her character of a youthful page, she attracts the favor of Olivia, and excites the jealousy of her lord. The situation is critical and delicate; but how exquisitely is the character of Viola fitted to her part, carrying her through the ordeal with all the inward and spiritual grace of modesty!" (Jameson, p. 247). Viola overcomes the inherent impropriety of these complications through her exemplary modesty. The attraction she exercises over Olivia becomes a "delicate" situation which she can handle because of her virtue.

In 1895, Louis Lewes is similarly struck by Viola's "charming appearance, even in male clothes, her amiable, prudent, and yet attractive demeanour, [which] work with magic power upon the Duke."[30] He focuses on her response to discovering that Olivia loves her, singling out that moment as the greatest test to her character: "Viola, who had left no ring, understands the important and delicate nature of the situation, but her character helps her to overcome *its doubtful side* without causing her womanly modesty to suffer" (p. 229; my emphasis). The "doubtful side" of her relationship with Olivia, that is, its apparent homoerotic love, challenges her modesty; in fact, that doubtful side *requires* the assertion of Viola's modesty. Mrs. Elliott (1885) makes still more clear how Olivia's desires are connected to Viola's modesty: "[Olivia] says mournfully 'I would you were as I would have you be.' This is intolerable to Viola. . . . Moreover, it is an offense against her modesty" (p. 212). Olivia's love not only violates her own modesty, but Viola's as well, particularly in the way it draws attention to the homoerotic appeal of her masculine dress. Mrs. Elliott, who does not openly acknowledge the obstacle Viola's crossdressing poses to her total representation of female virtue, nonetheless reveals her concern with strikingly extreme declarations of Viola's virtue: "Her inviolate modesty, her unswerving devotion, her unselfish endurance, her dauntless fearlessness, all commend themselves to our strongest personal sympathies. . . . In Viola we have the very personification of modesty" (p. 215).

Other critics, like Stephen Meany in 1859, argue that this modesty is explicitly revealed in Viola's own response to her crossdressing: "it is hard to say whether Viola's sleepless disquiet, or Rosalind's perfect composure, under the contradiction between her dress and her sex, be more expressive of maiden modesty."[31] Meany, like Jameson, discovers Viola's modesty most vividly expressed in her self-consciousness about the role she is playing. However, such self-consciousness in performance could easily have the opposite effect, drawing attention to her state of dress rather than to her modest uneasiness.

Attributing Viola's discomfort about her disguise *only* to modesty and virtue is itself an interesting strategy. After all, in the Folio text, she shows no concern either in planning to adopt male disguise or in presenting herself before Orsino. Given that other modest Shakespearean crossdressers, including Jessica in *Merchant of Venice* and Julia in *Two Gentlemen of Verona*, express their misgivings immediately upon adopting their new clothes, Viola's initial complacence is noteworthy.[32] In fact, only when she appears before Olivia as surrogate lover for Orsino does she begin to express her self-consciousness about her apparel. Her discomfort reaches its peak when she realizes that Olivia loves her, a disquiet signaled by the solitary meditation on her disguise and the frailty of women. The critics often quote these same lines as evidence of her inherently modest self-consciousness about her inappropriately revealing clothes, but the performance editions just as often cut them to avoid emphasizing the actress's necessarily immodest apparel.

Despite her uneasiness when she discovers that her disguise has seduced Olivia, Viola continues that same disguise without apparent distress before Orsino. In speaking to him, she can even readily discuss her love for a woman "Of your complexion. . . . About your years, my lord" (2.4.26, 28). Whereas she draws attention to her disguise through nervous hints about not being "not that I play" (1.5.185) with Olivia, she exposes her true womanhood to Orsino through careful, controlled indirection, in the much-beloved story of the sister who is herself. The nineteenth-century interest in the "Patience on the monument" speech accords with their view of Viola's modest character, but reveals an interesting contradiction to the twentieth-century reader. A careful assessment of Viola's suggestion that "she never told her love" (2.4.111), which the nineteenth century takes at face value, proves that Viola does reveal her love—and just as vehemently as Olivia does.

The scene in which Viola makes the claim includes three indirect revelations of her love: her assertions that the person she loves resembles Orsino in complexion and years and the story of her imagined sister. In act 5 her declarations are still more vigorous, as she tells Orsino that "I most jocund, apt, and willingly, / To do you rest, a thousand deaths would die" (5.1.130–31). This speech, which nineteenth-century critics typically construe as evidence of her self-sacrificing love, is followed immediately by a still more blatant declaration: "After him I love / More than I love these eyes, more than my life, / <More, by all mores, than e'er I shall love wife.> / If I do feign, you witnesses above / Punish my life, for tainting of my love" (5.1.132–36). Far from eliminating Viola's declaration of love, which is every bit as passionate as Olivia's have been, the performance editors only remove the bracketed line. These texts defuse any suggestion of Viola's possible love for a wife, omitting even a remote reference which would position Viola as a "female husband," one common term for women who love other women in the nineteenth century.[33]

The performance editions hide Viola's possible relationship to Olivia, while keeping her declaration of love for Orsino. The difference between the two characters is not, then, that Viola is silent while Olivia declares her love; the difference is that Viola always states her love in the context of self-denial.

Submissiveness, not silence, characterizes her love, while Olivia's more disturbing passion is represented as an urge to dominate, even as she asks Sebastian to "be rul'd by me!" (4.1.63).

Moreover, Viola's frequent visits to Olivia, at Orsino's behest, consistently foreground Olivia's love for a girl and necessitate an explanation of Viola's continued willingness to court her. Most nineteenth-century critics address this continued courtship by extolling in Viola an absolutely selfless devotion. Mrs. Elliott is particularly vivid in her explanation of Viola's continued addresses to Olivia: "Viola's love . . . leads her to forget everything, but *his* future happiness; should Olivia consent, *her* whole future would be a blank. . . . But this thought never once stops her. In season and out of season she devotes herself, body and soul, to her master's interests" (p. 212). William Winter praises Viola's "true love, which desires not its own happiness first, but the happiness of its object, and which feels, without conscious knowledge, that itself is the perfection of human attainment and that it may be better to lose than to win. Shakespeare has incarnated that lovely spirit in a person of equal loveliness, and has inspired it with the exuberant glee that is only possible to perfect innocence" (p. 38). This insistence on Viola's "perfect innocence" in conjunction with the selfless courtship she pursues in wooing Olivia attributes to Viola yet another virtue, produced by the need to explain aspects of her behavior which are otherwise understandable only in terms of her involvement with Olivia as well as with Orsino.

The performance editions themselves do not address the issue of Viola's continuing attendance on Olivia except by muting their interchanges and Olivia's declarations. However, both Charles Kean's promptbook for 1850–59 and J. B. Buckstone's 1867 promptbook attempt to limit Viola's courtship of Olivia by cutting entirely their penultimate meeting in 3.4. By omitting Olivia's acknowledgment of her "headstrong potent fault" and Viola's reappearance after she has claimed that "never more / Will I my master's tears to you deplore" (3.1.163–64), these performances cut back the courtship even more drastically than in the performance editions.

Even though Olivia's dress does not suggest the sexual immodesty that Viola's does, her infatuation with Cesario and open wooing of him ultimately create much greater and less easily dismissed uneasiness than Viola's behavior. Like Viola, Olivia transgresses gender boundaries, and perhaps her violation of gender hierarchy is more disturbing because she more readily appears, at first, to fit the discourses of domesticity and privacy which define womanliness in the nineteenth century. Some critics, like William Winter, explicitly vilify Olivia; others defend her, but in peculiarly revealing terms. Jameson offers Olivia only backhanded compliments: "The distance of

rank which separates the countess from the youthful page—the real sex of
Viola—the dignified elegance of Olivia's deportment, except where passion
gets the better of her pride—her consistent coldness towards the duke—the
description of that 'smooth, discreet, and stable bearing' with which she
rules her household [also cut in performance editions]—her generous care
for her steward Malvolio, in the midst of her own distress,—all these circumstances raise Olivia in our fancy, and render her caprice for the page a
source of amusement and interest, not a subject of reproach" (pp. 250–51).
The vindication offered for Olivia's behavior suggests more severe criticism
of the character, as well as more various extenuating factors which are
brought to bear in saving her passion from "reproach."

   For several critics, only the genius of Shakespeare could have preserved
Olivia's virtue at all. After contrasting the plot of *Twelfth Night* with its
possible sources, Charles Knight concludes that "the love of Olivia, wilful
as it is, is not in the slightest degree repulsive. With the old stories before
him, nothing but the refined delicacy of Shakspere's conception of the female character could have redeemed Olivia from approaching to the anti-
feminine."[34] Whereas Viola's character is transparently feminine, even in or
especially in male disguise, Olivia's character seems constantly in danger of
becoming anti-feminine, as Charles Cowden Clarke suggests: "No one but
Shakespeare, with his reverence for what is due to *real* refinement in the female character, could have redeemed Olivia from the charge of violating the
principles of delicacy inherent in women; for, instead of being the retiring
and attracting, she is the seeking party. The love of Olivia, however, wilful as
it is, is in no one instance masculine in character or repulsive in manner"
(pp. 196–97). But her love *would* be masculine and repulsive in manner
were it not for Shakespeare's skill. Whereas critics find Viola an inherently
refined character, only *Shakespeare's* refinement rescues Olivia's reputation.

   In an essay published several years later, Henry Hudson also wonders
about Olivia: "it were well worth the while to know, if we could, how someone so perverse in certain spots can manage notwithstanding to be so agree-
able as a whole."[35] The terms which both Hudson and Clarke use to describe Olivia are significant. She is "perverse," a term whose rich history and
associations with sexual difference Jonathan Dollimore traces in *Sexual Dissidence*.[36] When the nineteenth-century critics concentrate on the potential
repulsiveness of her masculine pursuit and the danger that she might become antifeminine, they displace and hide what is perverse about Olivia's
desires. They find her aggressiveness in courtship, rather than her attraction
to the page, the nearly "repulsive" aspect of her behavior, although the two
are clearly connected.

The defenses of Olivia cannot rely on general claims of modesty and virtue which attend Viola's actions. Not only does Olivia openly declare her love, but she also initiates her own courtship, whereas Viola is "only" acting on Orsino's behalf. More to the point, whereas Viola's disguise runs the risk of being improper and implicates her character in the controversies about transvestite actresses and female husbands, Olivia's behavior clearly runs the risk of being repulsive and masculine. She crosses the boundary between an acceptable, spiritual passion for another woman and a dangerous usurpation of male prerogative, in courtship if not in sexual desire.

Both the reluctance to allow Olivia her passion and the near-idealization of Viola herself function in part as responses to the love which she inspires in Olivia. The overwhelming insistence that Viola's femininity shows through her disguise—thus revealing the true heterosexuality of her love for Orsino and Orsino's attraction to her—renders Olivia's love for Viola more disturbingly homoerotic. Viola's male attire has a sexual appeal which responses to performances demonstrate; the effect of that appeal on Olivia provokes various editorial strategies. However, no matter which cuts are used, Olivia still pursues Cesario, an action which critics from Inchbald on deplore. The distress created by a lady taking the masculine role in courtship and falling in love with a woman is palpable in the language of these essays as they endeavor so mightily to assure their readers that Olivia is *not* repulsive.

In addition to the other considerations like staging, the nineteenth-century performance editors responded to gender and eroticism, particularly to the transgression of clear sexual roles in characters like Antonio. Critics complained of Orsino's effeminacy even as they saw Olivia on the edge of being unfeminine or even masculine. The extravagant praises of Viola suggest that her virtues derive from an exquisite femininity which is, at least partially, constructed through performance editing and critical rhetoric to defend her character from the implications of its own disguise. So both nineteenth-century literary critics and performance editors treated Olivia and Orsino as occupying troubling sexual roles while they redeemed the heterosexually appropriate gender role in the image of Viola's perfect womanliness. Ironically, in the Folio text Viola's perfect femininity is constructed only as a role to be played by a boy.

# The Video Editions

A t the beginning of the twentieth century, performance editions undergo serious changes. In 1884, Henry Irving publishes his *Twelfth Night*, and Augustine Daly has his performance edition privately published in 1893. Two performance editions of *Twelfth Night* appear before 1915: Henry Beerbohm Tree's souvenir edition of *Twelfth Night* in 1901 and Harley Granville-Barker's *Twelfth Night: An Acting Edition*, published and sold in the lobby during his famous 1912 production.[1] Early in the twentieth century, individual performance editions of other plays, like *Othello* "as arranged for the stage by J. Forbes-Robertson and presented at the Lyric Theatre on Monday, December 15, 1902," and *The Tempest* "as arranged for the stage by Herbert Beerbohm Tree" (1904), are also published.[2] Intermittently throughout the twentieth century, recognizable performance editions appear in conjunction with stage productions, but the practice is far less influential or consistent than it was in the nineteenth century.[3] Instead editions are published that seem to offer performance editing but actually conflate performance and scholarly materials. The bibliographic materials and photographic images come from theatrical practitioners, but the text has become canonically fixed.

For example, even though late-nineteenth-century and early-twentieth-century performance editors like Henry Irving and Harley Granville-Barker continued to produce individual performance editions using promptbook changes, they offered the full Folio text in their collected editions. The

*Henry Irving Shakespeare* (1888) offers no performance revisions at all, nor does Granville-Barker's misleadingly named *The Player's Shakespeare.*[4] Although Granville-Barker's introduction to those volumes acknowledges that productions alter Shakespeare's texts, he tells the reader that "we must retrain both our tongue to Shakespeare and our ears. . . . It is to this end among others that the Folio text has been chosen for these books" (p. 58). Moreover, both Irving and Granville-Barker offer introductions to their individual performance editions which are subsequently adopted or adapted as scholarly projects. William Winter writes the introductions to Irving's performance editions, which, in extended form, become his two-volume *Shakespeare on Stage*, and Granville-Barker himself writes prefaces to his performance editions, some of which then appear in *The Player's Shakespeare.*[5]

Similarly, the Folio series editions in the 1960s and 1970s link their texts to the theatre by offering introductions from recent directors and illustrations by stage designers. For example, Peter Hall introduces *Twelfth Night*, and Lila di Nobili contributes illustrations.[6] But the texts themselves come from the New Temple Shakespeare, edited by M. R. Ridley. For those texts, the series editors "decided to provide their own simple 'editorial apparatus' avoiding foot-notes as tending to distract the eye, while adding a Glossary."[7] Despite echoes of Bell's introduction, these texts are so far removed from representing performance that the speech headings are printed in a different color, "not for reasons of aesthetics, but so that the reader's eye could more easily ignore them, if he or she wished to concentrate on the poetry alone" (Ede, p. 10). When the apparatus is linked to performance but the text is obviously not, these twentieth-century texts depart from the nineteenth-century performance tradition.

However, a logical extension of the nineteenth-century performance edition does begin to appear with the development of filmed performances: screenplay texts. These range from the very early "motion picture edition" of George Cukor's *Romeo and Juliet*, published in 1936 with commentary by both actors and director, to Kenneth Branagh's screenplay text, published almost at the same time that his film of *Much Ado About Nothing* came out on videotape. The performance edition of *Romeo and Juliet* offers both the playtext and the "scenario version" in which all the verse is written as prose so that the actors are able "to unite, to fuse together, the beauty of the verse with the realism and intimacy demanded by the screen."[8] Branagh's performance edition of *Much Ado* offers a single text in prose and appears under a title worthy of any nineteenth-century performance edition: *Much Ado about Nothing, by William Shakespeare, Screenplay, Introduction and Notes on the Making of the Movie by Kenneth Branagh*. This edition includes filming directions about shot angle and composition as well as the text and a general introduction that explains Branagh's revisions to the play and affirms that "nothing 'difficult' was changed. No words were altered for easier understanding. The adaptation was at the service of our attempt to find an essence in the piece, to find the spirit of the play itself."[9] Once again a performance edition presents its historically specific material presentation as "the play itself."

Screenplay texts appear for only two *Twelfth Night* video editions, the BBC *Twelfth Night* and the *Animated Twelfth Night*. In both cases, the publication in print and on tape was practically simultaneous. The BBC *Twelfth Night* was published in 1979, and the video edition had its debut on BBC television in 1980. The *Animated Twelfth Night* and its companion text appeared in bookstores simultaneously in 1993. For both, pedagogy may be the motivation. Certainly the *Animated Twelfth Night* text, with its own study guide, announces its educational goal. In both these screenplays, the editors include texts that exceed the production. The BBC *Twelfth Night* text incorporates the Folio text, and "cuts are marked by vertical lines and by a note in the margins."[10] The margins are also the location of character movements that the editors deem important enough to mention. The Animated Tales produce a wholly different version in the text from the cartoon; the text is longer, including a more extensive final scene which does include characters beyond the two sets of lovers featured in the final encounter of the Animated Tale.

Screenplays may seem to be the direct descendants of the nineteenth-century performance editions, but, unlike the earlier editions which are published while the plays are performed onstage, the screenplays are published at the same time that the "performances" are themselves mechanically reproduced. In effect, two related "performance editions" appear simultaneously: a film version which combines multiple media—language, music, sound, spectacle, moving images—and a print version which represents those several facets in text, stage directions, still photographs, and the descriptions of camera and character movements. Together, they register the changes that new possibilities for mechanical reproduction have introduced into performance editing. With the ability to reproduce performance in several media, the twentieth century ushers in multiple new types of performance editions.

The shift of performance editing into different media may actually start with Orson Welles's *Mercury Shakespeare* texts (1934). Welles's texts, "Edited for reading and Arranged for staging," first appeared as *Everybody's Shakespeare*. Welles's *Twelfth Night*, less rearranged but more curtailed than

Kemble's popular nineteenth-century edition, prominently announces its connections to other forms of reproducing Shakespeare: "Stage business set in this manner (behind vertical lines) is in addition to that recorded phonographically on Mercury Text Records. On these records the cast acts the entire play and Orson Welles, as a narrator, adds the descriptive matter enclosed in parentheses."[11] The text includes two kinds of stage directions, those in parentheses, which Welles reads on the record, and those marked by a vertical bar, which are much more extensive and inflected with the emotional tenor of the characters. Thus the text anticipates two readings, one with a sound recording which does not need extensive narration and one without which requires elaborate explanations of every move. Punctuated with periodic indications of which record should be played to accompany the written text, the *Mercury Shakespeare* is also profusely illustrated with line drawings in the margins and at the head of scenes. The drawings most frequently offer sketched postures for the actors, but also include set designs (the only illustrations accompanying Antonio's first meeting with Sebastian) and occasionally more elaborate drawings of specific actors. Both Ada Rehan and Julia Marlowe appear as Viola, for example. These drawings complement the extensive stage directions. Together text, image, and sound promise to recreate performance more thoroughly than any earlier performance edition.

Various publications linked to performance appear throughout the twentieth century. Scholarly texts are reprinted with introductions and illustrations from the theatre. Sound recordings from the *Mercury Shakespeare* and Caedman series in the 1960s provide alternative performance editions to texts.[12] Screenplays are published to complement film productions. These multiple reproductions revise the relationship between the reproducibility first associated with texts and the uniqueness attributed to performance. Such illustrated texts, sound recordings, and screenplays are important in their own right and shift performance editing into new forms. However, the twentieth-century innovation that most radically advances performance editing is reproduction on film. Consequently, in this chapter, I concentrate on the video editions.

From the silent Shakespearean films of the early 1900s to contemporary video editions which are marketed to academics daily, Shakespeare's plays now reach their audiences in a distinctive new form. The precursors of the bricolage of image, sound, movement, and artifact which John Collick discovers in film are the earlier performance editions where *Bell's Shakspeare, A Select British Theatre*, and others link Shakespeare's words, engraved images, and stage materials.[13] Performance editions offered not a transitory event, but a marketable material object. Until fairly recently that object was, of necessity, a printed text; now videotape has made film equally available, equally reproducible.

As the printing press transformed writing, so film technology has transformed performance. Now Shakespearean films and videos have important affinities with earlier performance editions. The texts published as performed by Wm. Oxberry, Comedian, as produced by John Philip Kemble, and as appearing in *Bell's Shakspeare* have certain clear similarities to our current video editions: Olivier's *Hamlet*, Polanski's *Macbeth*, and the BBC Shakespeare Plays.[14] Beyond the obvious fact that Shakespeare shares top billing with contemporary actors, directors, and producers, all of these are published editions which ground their authority in particular performances rather than in a reconstructed Shakespearean "original." They are reproducible artifacts which represent performance; they are sequentially (and nonsequentially) "readable," available to interpretation and reinterpretation through close reading now possible using computer and video technology.[15] Most importantly, they are culturally and historically specific enactments of Shakespeare's plays; like their nineteenth-century counterparts, they are related to canonical Shakespeare texts but rarely reproduce the entire Folio or quarto texts.

Nonetheless, these video editions also differ significantly from printed texts—in the technology they employ, in their insistence on the visual and aural aspects of the play over the written text, and in the aspects of performance which they reproduce. Consequently, video editions both are and are not performance editions. If we examine the published scripts that sometimes accompany the video editions, then film/video looks more like performance in contrast to these texts. However, if we look at the reproducible features of the video edition, its positioning of versions of Shakespeare's plays identified with performers, series, and directors, this new form of performance edition clearly moves us toward multimedia reproducibility that will truly revolutionize all editorial traditions.

Since theatre and film share terminology as well as tactics of representation, careful distinctions are crucial. Similarly, the textual editing analyzed in the last two chapters and the film editing in *Twelfth Night*'s video editions are not the same procedures. The differences are sometimes extreme. For example, "cuts" in theatrical performance or in the performance editions are omissions of sections of the working script, but a "cut" in film is an "instantaneous change" from one shot and the next.[16] The literal cutting and splicing of film is obviously very different from script changes that leave out material on stage or on film, even though a film cut can mark such changes.

Similarly textual editing, the construction and annotation of a text for publication, differs from film editing, which, according to David Bordwell and Kristin Thompson, "may be thought of as the co-ordination of one shot with the next" (p. 151). Of the many techniques that come into play in relating one set of images recorded by the camera to the next set, many have no obvious analogs in the nineteenth-century performance editions: the fade-out, the dissolve, manipulations of sound like the voiceover, and, of course, the cut.

Even more general terms shared by theatre and film are slightly different for the two forms. "Mise-en-scène," literally "put in the scene," is a theatrical term referring to the sets, props, and scenic backgrounds which together produce the physical context for theatrical action. In terms of performance editing, mise-en-scène often supplies details not mentioned in the play but nonetheless significant to a particular production's representation.[17] Such features are, by and large, represented sparsely in the nineteenth-century performance editions. Although mise-en-scène in film does include these theatrical elements, in the video edition the term also includes film direction, "the director's control over what appears in the film frame" (Bordwell and Thompson, p. 75). The camera's directed gaze on specific details can create the context of character and action and establish elements of setting and action as signifiers within the cinematic structuring of the audience's view.

### Multiple Films of *Twelfth Night*

The video editions of *Twelfth Night* include (in chronological order): the Vitagraph 1910 silent film of *Twelfth Night*, the Lenfilm Russian production (1955), the 1970 John Dexter/Joan Plowright *Twelfth Night*, the 1972 soft-core production, the 1980 BBC *Twelfth Night*, the 1990 Renaissance Theatre Company (RTC) production, and the *Animated Twelfth Night*.[18] These productions address a range of imagined audiences and fit several different "genres" of film. Despite widely differing degrees of cinematic sophistication and variant film conventions, these seven video editions all represent and manipulate *Twelfth Night* in ways which resemble the nineteenth-century performance editing.

Of necessity, a film of *Twelfth Night* only ten minutes long must eliminate most of the verbal text and curtail considerably the action of the play; nonetheless, the editing choices in the 1910 Vitagraph silent film of *Twelfth Night* underscore the connections between Victorian stage productions and early films.[19] Aside from a brief sequence of Viola and Sebastian, dressed in similar clothes and embracing, the film narrative opens as many performance editions do: Viola appears on the seashore, with her brother's trunk. Then Sebastian is rescued from the sea in an invented scene which offers the only allusion to Antonio in this particular film text. This presentation of the two shipwrecks at the beginning of the film echoes Daly's treatment of the twins and recurs in later video editions.

With 1.3 removed entirely, the opening sequence of the Vitagraph *Twelfth Night* is followed immediately by a scene in Orsino's house, combining 1.1 and 1.4. This conflated scene, which resembles both Charles Calvert's and Henry Irving's composite texts of 1.1 and 1.4, becomes the only private encounter between Orsino and Cesario, as the film text cuts Cesario's second scene with Orsino (2.4) even more completely than the performance editions do, removing it entirely. The Vitagraph *Twelfth Night* presents Olivia's sending of the ring and Viola's receipt of it continuously then plunges immediately into the gulling of Malvolio (2.5).

The substantial changes in the second half involve not only the near-complete omission of Sebastian (and the complete absence of Antonio), but also the curtailment of Malvolio's part by leaving out entirely his imprisonment and several of the scenes leading up to his gulling. Feste's role is effectively reduced to two brief scenes, his immediate dismissal in 1.5 and a short scene of motley tumbling at the end, where he is also quickly dismissed. Although the omission of Sebastian until the very end and the absence of Antonio may be obvious choices for such an abbreviated production, these changes are also logical extensions of the uneasiness with those two characters which the earlier performance editions register. Similarly, the cuts to Malvolio's and Feste's roles are more radical versions of previous efforts to present Malvolio as the comic scapegoat and to limit Feste's mobility and commentary. Obviously, the Vitagraph *Twelfth Night* offers an extreme case, both in the extent of its cutting and in its necessary reliance on the visual rather than the verbal text, yet its treatment of *Twelfth Night* foreshadows the persistence of nineteenth-century performance editing in film and television editions.

The Lenfilm *Twelfth Night* (1955) is a Russian feature film, produced soon after Joseph Stalin's death. Some of the alterations to the Folio text result from the translation of the comedy into Russian, complete with Russian folksongs to replace Feste's repertoire. Moreover, additional changes occur because Yakov Borukhovich Friedland (Y. Frid), the director of the film, also uses a technique that influences his treatment of the text—"combinatory filming," which allows Katya Luchko to play both Viola and Sebastian for the production, sometimes showing up in the same scene.

Friedland employs familiar textual changes. Like the Vitagraph production, the Lenfilm *Twelfth Night* uses an extended version of Viola's first scene, intercut with other materials, and presents the rescue of Sebastian immediately after Viola appears. Both the first scene between Antonio and Sebastian and the second are shifted in the film and experience cuts. Since Antonio strolls off with Sebastian in the first scene, he does not declare his adoration in soliloquy. Their second scene also experiences important textual cuts removing Antonio's jealousy and love. The rearrangements of the opening and the treatment of Antonio and Sebastian's scenes together resemble the movements and cutting in the early performance editions, even though Soviet film directors would clearly neither know nor follow English theatrical practices.

John Dexter's production of *Twelfth Night* (1970), starring Joan Plowright as both Viola and Sebastian, has obvious affinities with the Russian video edition: one actress in both twin roles, substantial reworking of the opening, and interesting movements and shifts in the scenes between Antonio and Sebastian. However, Dexter's *Twelfth Night* is a television version, complete with fadeouts at appropriate moments for commercial breaks. While the Lenfilm production takes full advantage of the big screen, exploiting wide-angle and long shots as well as numerous outdoor scenes shot on location, Dexter's production is designed for television and thus yields tightness of focus, insistence on closeups, and obvious use of indoor studio sets.

Its major textual changes are clustered in the opening and around Antonio's and Sebastian's scenes. Dexter reworks Viola's first scene so that it contains Orsino's opening scene in the Folio. His treatment of the opening prefigures the radical changes he makes later in the text, most notably combining Sebastian's first and second appearances and relocating the resulting scene much later in the play, after 2.4. Both his cuts and his rearrangements echo changes made in the nineteenth-century performance editions.

A close contemporary of Dexter's production, Ron Wertheim's *Twelfth Night* (1972) offers the greatest departure from the Folio text. Imbued with the seventies spirit of free love and guided by a *Playboy*-like soft-core mandate, Wertheim's adaptation transforms Orsino into an aging rock star in search of a "sincere relationship" with Olivia, the starlet widow of an aged movie mogul. Though most of the characters keep their Shakespearean names, Malvoglio [*sic*] has become a priggish accountant, while Antonio has changed race and gender, becoming a statuesque black woman named Antonia. Feste, whom Wertheim himself plays, functions as a combination gardener/chauffeur for the reclusive Olivia. Inevitably, each scene is intercut with soft-core "erotica," as when Orsino's opening song(!) serves as the background to assorted pseudo-orgy images.

Given such extreme alterations to the Folio situations, it is hardly surprising to find scenic reordering as well. Yet Wertheim's production opens with Orsino and then shows Viola's arrival, keeping at least the initial scenes in order. The second sequence, which presents Viola's surrogate courtship of Olivia and the first appearance of Sebastian, is completely reworked. Sebastian's meeting with "Antonia" on the beach is moved earlier in the play, preceding Orsino's request that Cesario go to see Olivia. More radically still, the entire ring episode is eliminated: Olivia doesn't send a ring; Malvolio doesn't carry it; and Viola doesn't receive it. Given the omission of large sections of plot and near-complete rewriting of the play's language, this production of *Twelfth Night* is perhaps more an adaptation than a video edition. Nonetheless, its treatment of gender and homoeroticism underscores the significant effects of doubling the roles of Viola and Sebastian, played in Wertheim's film by Nikki Gentile. As a result, this production complements similar doubling in the Lenfilm and Dexter productions.

The BBC *Twelfth Night* (1980) is a British television production, like the Dexter/Plowright version. Part of the BBC televised canon of Shakespeare's plays, it marks a distinct kind of video edition designed for an academic audience. Both the BBC Shakespeare plays and the RTC production are perpetually advertised in *Films for the Humanities* and offered to university, college, and high school libraries as educational aids. Though these video editions are as widely available as nineteenth-century performance editions, they are clearly aimed at the academic videotape market rather than the playgoer or filmgoer. The 1980 BBC and 1990 RTC versions walk a fine line between the demand for the Folio *Twelfth Night* and the possibilities of performance editing.

Since Cedric Messina's avowed purpose as the series producer for the BBC Shakespeare Plays is to offer the canonical Shakespeare, presumably his production should present a straight Folio text of *Twelfth Night*. We would definitely expect the scenic order to follow the Folio, but the BBC uses the now-familiar rearrangement of 1.5, 2.2, and 2.1. Moreover, the filming of that sequence contrasts the three soliloquies that appear at the end of those scenes in order to establish Viola's role as a mediator of desire. Nonetheless, the BBC's textual cuts are minimal, although its film cutting and shot manipulation rework the comedy's homoerotic dimensions.

Paul Kafno's 1990 Renaissance Theatre Company video edition of *Twelfth Night*, also designed for television, is a filmed version of a stage production.

This edition inverts the first two scenes, using Viola's introduction of the performance to set a tone of melancholy. Kafno also rearranges 1.5, 2.1, and 2.2. Even though it uses the same nineteenth-century inversion of 2.1 and 2.2 that the BBC production does, the RTC video edition produces a wholly different reading of the relationship between Antonio and Sebastian. Like the BBC version, the RTC *Twelfth Night* keeps the Folio text largely intact, relying on film editing and set choices to reinforce its rearrangements of scenic order.

Finally, the most recent video edition is the *Animated Twelfth Night* (1993), produced jointly by Soyuzmultfilm animation studios in Russia and a Welsh television production company. Pitched to younger viewers and possibly envisioned in response to the newly required Shakespeare examinations faced by British fourteen-year-olds, the *Animated Twelfth Night* resembles the Vitagraph edition in its extreme reduction of the Folio text. Of the six Shakespearean plays produced in the first Animated Tales series, the production of *Twelfth Night* makes the largest number of rearrangements in scenic order.

The *Animated Twelfth Night* runs only thirty minutes and rearranges the play in very familiar ways. The play as a whole is curtailed, of course, but two areas in particular receive striking treatment, Antonio's scenes with Sebastian and the final two scenes (4.3 and 5.1). The production combines both of the private conversations between Antonio and Sebastian and displaces that composite scene well past their first appearance in the Folio text to very late in the play, after Viola has been to court Olivia on Orsino's behalf twice. More interesting still, the animated version disperses Viola's soliloquy from act 2, scene 2, so that only a small part of it serves as Viola's response to Malvolio while the rest is intercut with Sebastian and Antonio's scene together, as Viola walks back and forth behind them in the most complexly filmed sequence of the animated production. Not only does this strategy delay Viola's full acknowledgment of her problem and implicitly excuse her continued attentions to Olivia, but it also strongly emphasizes Sebastian's appearance as the solution to her problems rather than yet another version of homoerotic desire.

The directors chose puppets over the cartooning used for *Macbeth*, *A Midsummer Night's Dream*, *Romeo and Juliet*, and *Hamlet* and were, as a result, able to "layer" these scenes: Viola's meditation on the ring (2.2) and a combined scene between Antonio and Sebastian (2.1 and 3.3) occur simultaneously in the background and foreground. Puppetry, with its complex and time-consuming stop-action photography, also influences the radical cuts at the end of the production. This tale cuts both Malvolio's scene in the madhouse (4.2) and his return in act 5. In fact, the final scene is radically pared down to just the confrontation when Viola and Orsino meet Olivia and Sebastian dancing in her courtyard. This limits the number of puppets and separate manipulations required. The "natural perspective" of the identical twins may also be one reason for the choice of puppets, but it seems as if *Twelfth Night* requires that even an animated performance present bodies, in their similarities and their differences, in order to present the play's interactions.

Despite the widely ranging film techniques and audiences of these productions, all seven use rearrangements and some of the cuts that originate in the nineteenth-century performance editions. There are several possible explanations for the persistence of the nineteenth-century revisions. For example, the Folio registers a radically different theatrical structure from the proscenium stage, whose invisible fourth wall film adopts. The alterations in stage structure and production of spectacle influence performance editing in the nineteenth century in ways that could equally apply to the twentieth-century video editions. Moreover, significant differences in ideas about sexuality over the last three centuries affect both sequences of action and articulations of gender. Equally, the influence of two hundred years of theatrical production may have effectively rewritten the performance possibilities of *Twelfth Night*. Although there is no sign that film directors research and then reinscribe nineteenth-century performance choices, their rewriting of the playtext quite possibly grows from ongoing assumptions about how theatre and film work and how *Twelfth Night* "should" work.

### Filming Viola First

Even though the demands of stage scenery do not require that the seashore scene come first on film, many video editions continue the common nineteenth-century reversal of the first two scenes. Although this inversion continues to establish Viola's centrality in production, the three video editions that make the switch—the Lenfilm, Dexter, and Kafno productions—encode Viola's importance in varying ways. These range from visual motifs of character to manipulations of point of view to the establishment of tone and mood. Because their representation of performance is more complete than that of the nineteenth-century editions, the video editions that open with Viola's scene underscore the very different effects her introduction can produce.

When the Lenfilm Russian production presents Viola's and Sebastian's initial scenes together, it contrasts the twins by presenting crucial characteristics of each. After an initial elaborate storm sequence, Frid reveals Illyria first through Viola's approach to the city. In a long tracking shot, the camera moves with them as they enter the city; Viola, with the sea captain to her right, walks forward through one arch into the light and then through a second arch into darkness. Her emergence from the arch forms a framing shot that establishes her association with movement and boundaries.

Viola's initial entrance represents her liminal status, initiating a visual pattern which persists throughout the film. Repeatedly, Viola is displayed crossing thresholds, usually through Olivia's various doorways. In act 1, scene 5 she kicks the closed portal to Olivia's castle before gaining entrance and later appears dwarfed by a doorway three times her height when she enters Olivia's great hall. In fact, she never meets with Olivia without some archway or arched trellis in the frame. In act 5 Olivia's coy, yet encouraging glances, Orsino's resulting murderous rage, and the various accusations of Aguecheek and Toby all occur in the context of Viola's movements through the doors, arched hallways, and front portal of Olivia's castle.

The Lenfilm opening offers a series of scenic details which lead to the revelation of Sebastian. After the camera cuts from the long shot of Viola, it offers a much closer image of a woman who dances and swirls her red skirt before moving into the background to the center of a circle of dancing men. The camera then shifts slightly and focuses on two men sitting at a table, playing dice. A serving woman carrying drinks crosses in front, drawing the camera back with her to screen right. With this image begins the voiceover of Sebastian, "My father . . . left behind him myself and a sister" (2.1.18). However, no sooner does the camera present Antonio and Sebastian than a man behind them, apparently drunk and attempting to grab one of the serving women, inadvertently jostles Sebastian. Antonio rises and pulls the man off while Sebastian half-rises and tosses his drink in the fellow's face. Antonio pulls the offender around to face him and hits him.

This display of figures in the marketplace anticipates the series of situations which Sebastian will face. The woman surrounded by men/suitors prefigures Olivia, who first appears to Sebastian in a deep maroon dress surrounded by her kinsmen and followers. Similarly, the drunk who bumps into him and ends up fighting with him foreshadows Toby's and Aguecheek's various assaults as well as Antonio's role as protector. While the Lenfilm production defines Viola's liminal status in the framing shots of the arches, the relative paucity of information about Sebastian is augmented and reinforced by foreshadowing of his later activities.

In addition to exploiting the visual introduction of the twins, this opening situates *Twelfth Night* within the context of the Soviet cultural thaw after the death of Stalin.[20] The vivid storm, followed by a peaceful, beautiful

Illyria, where the only problem appears to be love, provides an image of escape from the suffering and familial disintegration in Russia under Stalin's rule. In fact, the director himself emphasizes this goal in his comments on the film just after its release: "The inexhaustible and life-giving optimism of *Twelfth Night* attracted us."[21] Viola's crossing of thresholds and Sebastian's involvement in the minor and easily resolved strife of carnival-like celebration not only fit the comedy's concerns but also resonate with the cultural situation of Russia two years after Stalin's death.

John Dexter's 1970 *Twelfth Night* also places Viola's scene first, but Dexter interpolates act 1, scene 1 (rather than 2.1) into Viola's scene. The crosscutting to Orsino's scene offers both an introduction to Orsino and Olivia and a bridge between Viola's learning of the situation in Illyria and her decision upon a course of action. By actively reworking Viola's opening scene to introduce the other principal characters, Dexter makes visually explicit the effects of putting Viola's speeches first. He deliberately uses the intimacy of television production to set out all the comedy's situations as quickly as possible, thus engaging his audience's attention before the first commercial break.

Specifically, he presents images of Orsino and Olivia at appropriate moments in Viola's discussion with the sea captain by employing dissolves, in which one image blurs out of focus and the return to focus presents a different image (Bordwell and Thompson, p. 152). As Viola says, "Orsino? I have heard my father name him," her image dissolves, replaced by a closeup of Orsino. The conversation continues in a voice off—Viola's voice is heard saying, "He was a bachelor then" (1.2.28–29), but she is out of the frame.[22] When the sea captain comments on Orsino's suit, which is "fresh in murmur," the image of Orsino's face dissolves into a long shot revealing that he and his musicians are serenading underneath a window. As the camera pulls back, Olivia becomes partially visible in the window. At "the fair Olivia," Dexter replaces the long shot of Orsino and his court with the image of Olivia framed by her window. She appears in focus at Viola's question, "What's she?" (1.2.35). When the sea captain's voiceover reaches the mention of her father's death, Olivia's image is supplanted by a long shot of Orsino and his company. At "for whose dear love," her face reappears (1.2.39). These dissolves follow quickly one after another, interweaving Orsino's courtship and Olivia's rejection as the sea captain describes them. Viola's lament "O that I serv'd that lady" (1.2.42) draws the camera back to her face after the final dissolve of the sequence.

Dexter uses Viola's voice from within the narrative of the film, but dislocates the voice from the speaker in order to present other characters. His empowerment of the voice here is another signal of her initial importance. Kaja Silverman contends that classic cinema uses dislocated male voices as extradiegetic, outside the frame, and therefore identified with agency and control over the images presented. Female voices, she suggests, are thoroughly confined with the narrative world created by the film so that the dislocated female voice (that of the hypnotized female patient reciting her history to the analyst, for example) signals lack of control.[23] Dexter's strategies ultimately bear out this analysis, even though this production initially positions Viola's voice outside the narrative of Orsino's courtship and thus able to invoke it and speak over it. When the sea captain's voice offers the history and explanation of the situation, Viola's authority diminishes. Because of the dissolve and the voiceover, Viola's perspective introduces the play's situation, but her verbal control over the situation is distinctly limited.

The Renaissance Theater Company production (1990) also reverses the first two scenes, opening with Viola's appearance at the end of credits which run against the backdrop of the sounds and sights of the storm. The RTC production uses the turbulent sky and music to establish the context for Viola's ragged appearance and her vivid worry about her brother. Unlike the Plowright and Lenfilm Violas, who are both clean and dry, the RTC heroine has clearly just escaped from the storm. Her clothes are tattered and damp, all but torn from her back; she is thoroughly wet and breathing heavily. Kafno establishes an intimacy with her situation through closeups which reveal the visible anguish of her tears for Sebastian and the aural evidence of her voice, which nearly breaks several times. Her obviously justified distress establishes a tone of melancholy which spills over into Orsino's first scene.

Opening with the psychological intensity of Viola's misery could make Orsino's amorous difficulties look trivial, but film techniques link the two scenes and make Orsino's unhappiness seem serious and justifiable. The similarity in lighting emphasizes the connection; a bluish cast to the setting in Orsino's scene offers a somewhat lighter version of the lighting employed for Viola's opening. The persistence of inclement weather also reinforces Orsino's lament as an extension of Viola's. In addition, the pace of his scene is noticeably slower than hers, as if he has been worn down by his unhappiness. The result is two well-balanced scenes that are close to the same length. In effect, the RTC production uses the inversion of the first two scenes to distinguish its tone and approach from the British television productions which precede it. The emphasis on melancholy humor contrasts with the high spirits in both the Dexter/Plowright and BBC productions.

In the Lenfilm, Dexter/Plowright, and RTC productions, Viola's appearance in the opening scene echoes the strategies of the nineteenth-century performance editions. However, through the reproduction of sound, image, and movement as well as the characters' lines, the video editions surpass the nineteenth-century performance editions by revealing surprising contrasts in the effects different productions achieve with the same reordering of scenes. As these video editions show, Viola's centrality, which the revision necessarily creates, can introduce a production's major images, accelerate the plot information for television, and even set the whole tone for the play. Film editing itself introduces new ways of exploring familiar textual changes.

### Rearrangements in the Video Canon

The "canonical" film texts, the RTC and BBC versions of *Twelfth Night*, are constrained by their proposed academic audiences to keeping the text more or less intact. Nonetheless, both these video editions also use rearrangements of the Folio scene order. In the process of reordering the sequence of scenes from Viola's first meeting with Olivia (1.5) through her receipt of Olivia's ring (2.2), these films establish distinctive slants on Viola's courtship, Sebastian's appearance with Antonio, and Olivia's revelation of her passion. Because these video editions keep most of the text, their approaches to the relationship between Antonio and Sebastian rely more heavily on film editing than textual editing to represent (or disguise) the homoeroticism which has become increasingly obvious to twentieth-century readers and audiences.

Of the three points of substantial rearrangements in the early performance editions, the only change that the BBC adopts is the second rearrangement (1.5, 2.2, 2.1). Apparently, John Wilders, the literary advisor, was generally uncomfortable with such changes in sequence, "but conceded to some of the rationales, as in this case, where the irony of twinness is not lost, merely inverted." [24] Wilders's discomfort or perhaps the canonical assertions of the series producer required that the introduction to the accompanying published text explain the choice. As John Gorrie explains, "It's important that you get the geography: that the outside [of Olivia's country house] relates to the inside, that you see people in television terms—you can't do this on stage—that you can see them when they leave the room going out through the garden or from the garden you can see them through the windows of the house. The whole thing has a geography, a location, which I hope the viewer will get to know, feel a part of and thereby become more involved." [25] This intimacy with the country house ties *Twelfth Night* to other popular BBC productions like *Upstairs, Downstairs* and places the play firmly within the BBC's larger commitment to English culture and manners. [26]

Gorrie's desire to locate his audience within Olivia's house and estate motivates the rearrangement of the ring sequence. The BBC *Twelfth Night* text also quotes script editor Alan Shawcross, whose explanation of the transposition will sound familiar: "We made the transposition because we wanted to give a continuous movement and keep unity of time and place, which we could do because of the composite set—we can see Malvolio leave Olivia and overtake Viola. It's a good example of the way that the television studio affects the order of scenes. On stage Shakespeare needed the Antonio/Sebastian scene as a break simply to provide a space of time for Malvolio to leave Olivia and find Viola" (p. 21). Both the casual dismissal of Antonio and Sebastian as "simply" a necessary break and the clearly erroneous assertion that the stage *requires* such a break founder on the tradition of performance editing which leads up to the film text. This particular claim for the unique effects of the television studio ignores the fact that performance editions since 1810 have taken the very same transposition onstage. Nor is the appeal to the unity of time and place at all new. Not only does the BBC text use the *Memorial Theatre* edition's strategy of setting off omitted material typographically and mentioning transpositions, but the logic offered in its introduction also echoes the earlier performance edition in claiming the unique demands of material production as the motive for all changes.

However, just because a certain effect is possible onstage or in the television studio does not make it *necessary* that such an effect take place—the medium opens up opportunities but does not force decisions about the forms the comedy will take. The individual directors or producers may attribute their choices to their production conditions, but their decisions—to use the elaborate scenery of the Victorian stage or the composite set of the sound stage—have other motives as well. Gorrie's interest in space here also invokes an essential film "difference": the capacity to oppose interior, enclosed spaces with exterior spaces. But this preoccupation with geography, and particularly with *Olivia's* house, goes beyond seeing "people in television terms," especially when we view this concern in light of the Victorian performance editions' efforts to transform Olivia into their ideal Lady in the House. The perceived importance of involving the viewer with the ins and outs of Olivia's house—sufficient to override Folio scenic order—results in a video edition that echoes the earlier performance editions and comparably controls and limits access to Olivia. In the BBC's self-promotion, the claims for the unique abilities of film take the place of any clear explanation of why such exhaustive invocations of Olivia's defined space are so crucial or why the interactions between Antonio and Sebastian can be so easily dismissed as merely requirements of the stage.

Even though the BBC producers characterize Antonio's first scene with Sebastian (2.1) as merely a break in the action for staging purposes, their displacement of the scene and treatment of the three soliloquies at the end of 1.5, 2.1, and 2.2 demonstrate that the esthetic reasons offered obscure the serious ideological effects of the change—the establishment of Viola's centrality and her role as the heterosexual mediator of desire. The BBC does not cut these soliloquies the way earlier performance editions do, but the shift in the scenes places Viola's solitary meditation between Olivia's realization that she desires Cesario and Antonio's possibly amorous pursuit of Sebastian and emphasizes Viola's pivotal position.

Moreover, the filming of those scenes uses shot angle and character movement to contrast the closing soliloquies of the three characters. Olivia sits and delivers her soliloquy up to the camera, and Viola speaks hers as she stoops to pick up the ring in a high-angle shot and then rises to face the camera. Antonio is the only one who never sits or stoops during his soliloquy and also the only one who looks directly at the camera. Both Olivia and Viola consistently look off camera left or right. Antonio, by contrast, looks almost directly at the camera from the moment when he says, "The gentleness of all the gods go with thee!" (2.1.43). Whereas Olivia and Viola are evidently speaking to themselves, Antonio appears to put the viewer in the place of Sebastian, specifically speaking to us. Like Olivia, Antonio remains essentially in one place as the camera closes in on him from a medium shot to a closeup. We seem to draw closer to him as he decides to pursue Sebastian despite the dangers he will face.

In effect, the filming of these three crucial soliloquies reinforces the rearrangement of the scenes by displaying Viola's as the mediating soliloquy. Visually, she moves between sitting, like Olivia, and standing, like Antonio, and between the high-angle shots and level shots which register Olivia's and Antonio's respective responses to their desires. Torn between her love for Orsino and Olivia's unwitting homoerotic attraction to herself, Viola shortcuts Olivia's desire at the same time that she foreshadows and undoes the passion which Antonio feels for the man he wishes to serve. She becomes the heterosexual norm which denies Olivia's desire and mitigates Antonio's love.

Paul Kafno's RTC production of *Twelfth Night* also takes the second scenic rearrangement, staging Viola's wooing scene, Sebastian's arrival, and Viola's receipt of the ring in the familiar reworked sequence (1.5, 2.2, 2.1). Here the reversal of these scenes cannot arise from any concerns about continuity of action because the sequence acts as the "cliffhanger" at the end of the first part. In fact, Sebastian's entrance with Antonio seems designed to be an utter contrast to the previous two scenes. Olivia and Viola appear full face and in bright daylight, but Sebastian emerges slowly from the fog on a darkened set, followed by Antonio. Olivia and Malvolio take a scornful tone in their respective interactions, but Sebastian is merely emotional and Antonio warmly solicitous. Olivia and Malvolio thrust the ring away in rejection; Antonio hands Sebastian his duffel with a smile. These contrasts in setting, tone, and action distinguish the scene introducing Antonio and Sebastian from the earlier scenes. Although Kafno keeps the entire text, he uses casting, body language, and film strategies to set off Antonio's affection from the erotic dilemmas of the two women.

The RTC production also casts one actor, Tim Barker, as both Viola's bearded sea captain and Sebastian's cleanshaven one. This doubling distracts from any erotic element in Antonio's attentions by reinforcing the comparison of the two sea captains. Moreover, not only is Barker substantially older than Sebastian, but Kafno also establishes a physical distance between the two men for the first part of the scene which is reinforced when Sebastian sits down to explain his situation while Antonio remains standing, arms akimbo. As Sebastian reveals his name and his sister's death, Kafno intercuts reaction shots of Antonio on the lines "my father was that Sebastian of Messaline" and "for some hour before you took me from the breach of the sea" (2.1.16–17, 21–22). He chooses to establish Antonio as a fatherly protector, an identification which carries through in act 3: even though Antonio is claiming to love Sebastian, he spends the entire scene walking back and forth checking for danger. Whatever he says, his actions emphasize that his concern for Sebastian's safety has brought him into Illyria.

Even Antonio's soliloquy in act 2 displays his interest in danger. His comments contrast with those of the women in a variety of ways. Both Olivia and Viola consistently face the camera while discussing their passion and their indecisiveness—Viola even addresses the camera directly! Antonio, however, at first bids Sebastian farewell and even turns away to leave, revealing fully for the first time the large birthmark covering his cheek. This detail concentrates audience attention on his appearance rather than his words when he changes his mind and turns back on "I do adore thee so" (2.1.46). Ultimately, the emphasis of the soliloquy falls on the notion that "danger shall seem sport" (2.1.47). Antonio's action, in this staging, is decisive and based on adventure as much as on affection for Sebastian. Through strategies like these, Kafno manages to keep all of Antonio's lines while focusing attention more on the protectiveness and adventurousness of Antonio than on his vows of love.

In contrast, the BBC production appears remarkably receptive to the homoeroticism of Antonio's love. For example, in its initial scene, the camera cuts away from a closeup of Sebastian's face in the middle of his speech about his sister at the point where he claims that Viola was "a lady, sir, though it was said she much resembled me, was yet of many accounted beautiful" (2.1.24–25). Gorrie gives a reaction shot of Antonio at the word "beautiful," showing him smiling fondly, even amorously, at Sebastian and then cutting back to Sebastian for the rest of his speech. In their second scene together (3.3), Sebastian enters in front of Antonio and begins to undress. It is not immediately apparent that he is taking off his jacket and loosening his shirt in order to wash in the fountain, so there is a moment of near-sexual intimacy. Moreover, the filming of Antonio's soliloquy at the end of 2.1 reflects the fact that his declaration is much more straightforward than either Viola's or Olivia's; even though he is deciding to place himself in danger, he does not express any of the self-doubt that the women do. He loves Sebastian and will go after him. To this extent, the BBC production seems to accept the homoerotic love he expresses.

However, the filming at the end of his soliloquy complicates Antonio's direct, apparently homoerotic desire. At the moment of his declaration of love, Antonio's attention is inexplicably split. He looks straight at the camera while acknowledging his love, but looks to his left at the end of the speech as if looking after the man he is planning to follow. So whom is Antonio addressing so intimately? Sebastian as he has walked offstage? Then who is to Antonio's left and why look there? This split in perspective persists in Antonio's exit—he promises to follow Sebastian, but he exits to the rear of the set, obviously in a different direction from the one we have seen Sebastian take earlier in the scene. Even if we argue that the glance to the left which breaks our implication in Antonio's gaze establishes the direction of his exit to the rear of the set, the question remains: why does Antonio exit in a different direction from the man he has decided to follow? The filming of Antonio's exit transforms his sexual orientation into a vividly spatial disorientation in the BBC video edition. Through the ambiguity which arises in Antonio's divided glance and different exit the production undoes the directness of his passion and the audience's identification, however temporary, with the object of that passion as Antonio looks at us while acknowledging his love.

*Twelfth Night*'s depiction of same-sex love still influences video editions, although in different ways than it affected nineteenth-century performance editions. Consistently, the filming of his scenes manipulates the weight of

Antonio's avowals of love for Sebastian. The efforts which these film texts make to address the play's homoeroticism arise in part from the twentieth-century's greater awareness of homosexuality but also reflect, as the nineteenth-century texts do, how rearrangements of the scenes in act 2 especially affect Antonio and the representation of homoerotic love.

## One Face, One Voice, One Habit, and One Person

For the other video editions of *Twelfth Night*, the constraints of a potential academic audience do not operate to keep the text intact. The radical cuts and rearrangements in these film texts respond more obviously to homoeroticism in the play. An important factor complicating that response is the double casting of a single actress to play both Viola and Sebastian, in effect inverting the Renaissance convention of using boys to portray both twins. Such a shift in casting affects the video editions and produces variations just as striking as the changes which result when women begin to play the female characters and the figure of the actress first influences the editing of Viola and Olivia. Although Kate Terry did play both twins in 1865 (no performance edition is available), only film and the editing possible with the camera make such doubling practical and even common—three of these video editions use the strategy.

Perhaps not surprisingly, the presence of the female body in both roles leads to revised erotic relationships between the male characters. For Orsino to be drawn to the woman beneath Cesario's disguise is acceptable, even desirable; however, for Antonio to be in love with Sebastian, played by the actress, is to risk breaking the "illusion" of Sebastian's masculinity. The verisimilitude of Olivia's mistaking Sebastian for Cesario is achieved at the expense of careful construction and maintenance of gender distinctions between the twins. Moreover, the double casting shifts attention substantially toward the lesbian homoeroticism in the play while suppressing the male homoeroticism which dominates the Renaissance text.

In the Lenfilm production, the details of the opening scene establish gender distinctions in addition to character differences between the twins, played by Katya Luchko. Film brings different techniques to bear in the production of Sebastian's masculinity while using the nineteenth-century strategy of cutting his lines to eliminate effeminacy. By placing Viola's scene first, the Lenfilm *Twelfth Night* reinforces the twins' basic differences. For both roles, the relationship with the sea captain is a deciding factor, evoking and reinforcing Viola's femininity as well as Sebastian's masculinity. Viola's dependence on the paternal information and help of her savior contrasts with the pugnacious camaraderie of Sebastian and Antonio as they immediately

join a barroom brawl. In contrast to the Folio text, Antonio's comforting of
Sebastian is unsentimental and interrupted; the physical encounter of the
fight replaces most of Sebastian's references to his sister and his tears.

Also, though Sebastian leaves to "bear his evils alone," Antonio immediately follows him and offers to be his servant. The Lenfilm movement of Antonio's scene effectively undoes the series of soliloquies by Olivia, Antonio,
and Viola; in fact, the film omits Antonio's declaration of love entirely.
Moreover this film initially gives no hint that Antonio faces any unusual
danger in Illyria and shows the two men going off together in amiable fel-
lowship, not Antonio pursuing Sebastian despite persistent rejection. This
simplification of their relationship and Antonio's situation edits his love as
much as any earlier performance edition.

The second encounter between Antonio and Sebastian (3.3) is similarly
abbreviated and displaced, appearing right after the trick on Malvolio (2.5).
All Antonio's references to desire, love, and jealousy are conspicuously absent as the sequence concentrates totally on the dangers of Illyria. Antonio
and Sebastian are physically separated by the hazard; Sebastian stands
openly on the road into town while Antonio is hiding under a rock overhang
near the arch Sebastian is about to enter. When they agree to meet again,
Antonio slaps his friend genially on the back before heading off. Brief,
unemotional, and obviously functional, this scene immediately precedes
Viola's interrupted duel. The limitations set on Antonio's affection are
clearly linked to editing which "improves" Sebastian's masculinity. Luchko's
male persona benefits from his association with an Antonio who acts and
looks like a pirate with a kerchief tied around his head and swashbuck-
ling gestures.

All the sentiment is removed from their association, even during Antonio's intervention on Viola's behalf (3.4). In fact, his long and largely successful assault on the local constabulary so dominates the scene that his
claims on Viola's friendship are comparatively insignificant. Antonio also
appears as a swashbuckler in his final scene, in which he essentially has no
role in the recognition of the twins—even his speech claiming Viola's loyalty
is cut. Instead of initiating the reunion, he actually takes advantage of the
confusion which follows Viola's cry of "Sebastian" to sneak away from his
guards and ride off on a horse. The treatment of Antonio in the Lenfilm
production suppresses the male homoeroticism, largely by omission, possibly reflecting Soviet attitudes under Stalin, when homosexuality was alter-
nately denounced as a criminal act or designated a medical condition to be
"cured" by marriage.[27]

However, the film text takes a different approach to the potential homoeroticism between Olivia and Cesario/Sebastian, starting with Viola's un-willing and unwittingly effective courtship of Olivia. The visual display of Viola's vulnerability begins before the scene opens, when she kicks at the massive door to Olivia's castle, and continues during her entrance into the cavernous great hall. Not only does the room dwarf Viola, but all the women she meets are so deeply veiled that the film audience, as well as she, has con-siderable difficulty discerning which is the lady of the house. Viola's ques-tions and her boldness appear greatly diminished in these circumstances; this production establishes and justifies her extreme discomfort.

Olivia, on the other hand, becomes the iconographic woman in cinema. When she agrees to unveil, the camera offers just the sort of lingering, soft-focus shot in which the woman is presented as an object of the controlling male gaze. The film even registers the temporary suspension of narrative which Laura Mulvey notes accompanies these shots in classic American cin-ema.[28] Olivia's coy expression, the soft-focus, and the surprising length of the shot combine with her question "Is't not well done?" (1.5.237) to invite the male gaze and stop the forward action. Even though the gaze she solicits here is actually female, as Viola's bewildered expression reminds us, the clas-sic film convention which the Russian film text adopts here initiates a process of idealizing Olivia and encoding her desire as heterosexual while ironically "masculinizing" Viola within the scene's exchanges of gazes.

Later images carry through and redefine the static, soft-focus displays of Olivia which mark her and, later, Sebastian as idealized, objectified figures. For example, after Viola rides off, the scene shifts to night and the camera again offers a lingering shot of Olivia, this time focusing on her head and shoulders while she weeps and prays almost inaudibly before going to bed. This close echo of the earlier soft-focus shot establishes virtuous grief as the action-stopper. However, once again it is the deceiving female gaze rather than the male one which the camera records. Maria observes Olivia's beau-tifully liquid prayers and takes advantage of her mistress's inattention to steal her seal for the trick on Malvolio. Though the camera work suggests static contemplation of Olivia's beauty again, the narrative action continues, enabled by the female gaze which observes Olivia's inactivity but, far from stopping to contemplate her beauty, takes her stillness for an opportunity to act.

Olivia's soft-focus image promotes her idealization and even potentially neutralizes her earlier flirtatiousness, since her tears and obliviousness sig-nal overwhelming grief for her brother. Just as importantly, this sequence re-veals that she is not only outside the action but also practically unaware of it. While idealizing Olivia, in accord with the Soviet tendency to present

Shakespearean women as purely virtuous, the Lenfilm production also establishes oblivious innocence as the necessary condition for the comedic action. Olivia's ignorance of both the deceitful female gaze and the later male gaze of Malvolio with its impulse to control and possess her is amply established in these shots. They operate in part as Mulvey suggests—objectifying her and suspending the narrative—but, more importantly, they offer her inactivity as iconographic female virtue.

These images of Olivia are significant because the Lenfilm production uses and transforms this strategy once again in displaying her with Sebastian. The video edition interpolates a largely silent scene between the two after Olivia interrupts Sir Toby's assault and Sebastian agrees to go with her. Once they enter her house, Olivia starts up the stairs and turns back to look at Sebastian. Initially it appears that another soft-focus, worshipful shot of Olivia is about to occur, but instead the image changes, through a series of fadeouts, to show Olivia and Sebastian drawing closer and closer to each other on the stairs. There are three transitions in this sequence: Olivia looking down at Sebastian from the distance of a few steps/fade-out /Olivia and Sebastian looking at each other, but now closer, about a step apart/fade-out/ Olivia and Sebastian now close enough to touch with his arm near hers on the banister. In this last shot, Olivia and Sebastian appear in a tighter closeup and are near enough to kiss, though they do not. This sequence, which is as silent as the image of Olivia's unveiling in act 1, uses its close, soft-focus scrutiny to signal that the two are falling in love.

This creation of Olivia and Sebastian as a couple establishes them as an object of our gaze and consequently, within the logic of the film, signals both deception and inactivity in their love. To put it another way, this sequence shows Olivia and Sebastian drawing closer and closer to each other without either of them actually moving; it displays their love while foreclosing any physical enactment, even when stepping nearer to each other. Incorporating Sebastian into the static images which have established Olivia's function in the film is almost an acknowledgment that he, like Olivia, is static and oblivious. Their mutual absorption also plays up their differences: Sebastian's black hair to Olivia's blonde, his dark clothes to her red dress, his lower position on the steps to her ascendancy. At the end of this set of images, the Lenfilm film text grafts what little it preserves of their mutual vows (4.3). The production cuts Sebastian's soliloquy worrying about his missing friend and the lady's potential madness and rule of her house, including only Olivia's request that he follow her to the chantry. In place of that scene exploring Sebastian's thoughts about the situation and Olivia's proposal, the Lenfilm offers the visual representation of their mutual affection and another invented scene, the exchange of rings in the church. Their entrance into the church is framed by Malvolio, who watches from his prison as Olivia weds Sebastian; their kiss at the altar is a brief long shot, filmed with far less intimacy than the earlier sequence of increasing closeups.

By manipulating the filming and the context of the scenes which establish Olivia's relationship with Sebastian, this film offers a very complex representation of the love between the two characters, both played by women. In the first invented sequence, the soft-focus shots ally Sebastian with Olivia in a film strategy that the production resolutely associates with both inactivity and lack of awareness. The film text takes advantage of fade-outs to move the two women together without either of them appearing to move. The second sequence, their union at the altar, is framed by Malvolio's jealous gaze, which both establishes a distanced perspective on the events in the church and directs attention to the class boundaries which Olivia is transgressing. With Malvolio watching, Sebastian's status as a servant is emphasized rather than his "real" gender.

Like the Lenfilm production, the Dexter/Plowright *Twelfth Night* in effect eliminates all homoeroticism in the relationship between Antonio and Sebastian. In the first two acts, it appears as if the first meeting between Antonio and Sebastian (2.1) has been cut entirely. The complications and apparent insolubility of the gender confusion build to the end of Cesario's second scene with Orsino (2.4), when a camera dissolve replaces Viola's face with Sebastian's after she completes the story of her hypothetical sister. Viola's final comment, "I am all the daughters of my father's house / And all the brothers too: and yet I know not" (2.4.121–22), dissolves into Sebastian's aggressive direct address to the camera: "my name is Sebastian" (2.1.15–16). By juxtaposing the two scenes and allowing one role to supplant the other, Dexter uses Sebastian's entrance to answer Viola's lament, in the same manner that the frequent reversal of 2.1 and 2.2 in the nineteenth-century editions presents Sebastian as the answer to Viola's problems.

The audacity of demanding a comparison between Joan Plowright as Viola and as Sebastian is matched by the daring extremes of the cutting and staging of a single scene combining the introduction of Antonio and Sebastian (2.1) and their second meeting in the town (3.3). In the Dexter production Antonio and Sebastian meet once late in act 2. Resembling almost every earlier performance edition, this composite scene cuts all of Antonio's brief soliloquy, in which he promises to pursue Sebastian. Moreover, the Dexter/Plowright production also cuts most of Antonio's other potentially erotic lines from the two scenes. He does not plead, "If you will not murder me for my love, let me be your servant" (2.1.34–35); nor does he mention his jealousy, his willing love, or his "desire more sharp than filed steel" (3.3.5). Antonio also spends relatively little time discussing the dangers he faces on Sebastian's behalf and gives his purse almost as an afterthought. The greatest intimacy between the two is their sharing of a jug. Antonio throws the jug to Sebastian as he apologizes for Sebastian's "bad entertainment" (2.1.32), Sebastian pushes it back while apologizing for Antonio's pains, and finally Antonio pitches it forcefully into the sea while saying that he has "many enemies in Orsino's court" (2.1.44). The overall effect is that of vigorous male bonding with no hint of sexual attraction.

The complete absence of any erotic or emotional connection between these two drinking buddies seems necessary for the crossdressing fiction. Plowright, as Sebastian, cannot allow even the suggestion of her true gender, including any obvious attractiveness to Antonio. However, the striking lack of any initial attraction detracts from the power of the later lines where Antonio claims Sebastian has betrayed his love. Though Dexter allows Antonio's passionate accusations of Viola, Antonio becomes noticeably silent when Sebastian once again appears with him in the last act. Antonio does not even participate in the recognition scene, since Sebastian sees his sister almost immediately.

Antonio's principal role in the final scene, beyond his accusation of Viola's witchcraft before Sebastian enters, is to participate in the camera trickery creating the twins. It is Antonio's arm over Sebastian's shoulder which establishes him as Sebastian in a series of shots in the final scene. The camera then gives an over-the-shoulder shot of Viola to show both twins in the frame. The necessary intimacy of Antonio's gesture complicates the distance between the two characters which this production achieves by cutting his speeches. When his gesture must be repeated to maintain the fiction, the several apparent embraces of the final scene strain the nonerotic camaraderie which the rest of the production works so hard to attain. In fact, although somewhat undermined in the final scene, Antonio's macho behavior is a major contributor to Sebastian's "masculinity."

Interestingly, Plowright also establishes Sebastian's maleness by manipulating her voice. Consequently, Cesario's voiceover leads into Sebastian's claim of his identity in a voice of much lower pitch. Since the two figures look strikingly alike and the dissolve provokes comparison, the change in voice proves to be one determining factor of Sebastian's male identity. The appearance of Sebastian and the dominance of "his" voice actually silence the brief voiceovers which Viola has been allowed. The greatest contrast between the two in terms of voice occurs in their soliloquies and demonstrates still further the constraints on Viola's voice. Viola's soliloquy (2.2) takes place in a busy courtyard whose noises are blanked out as the film text presents her speech mostly as an interior monologue. She gives the first two lines aloud but otherwise only breaks into speech once to say, "She loves me sure" (2.2.21). Speaking this line aloud underscores Viola's vulnerability when her very thoughts can be overheard. A number of people turn to look at her, and she covers her mouth self-consciously. The embodied voiceover which represents thought brings the potentially powerful position of the voiceover into a position of complete diegetic interiority, wholly within the narrative rather than outside it with access to the apparatus which creates and masters it. As Kaja Silverman suggests, classic film "equates diegetic interiority with discursive impotence and lack of control, thereby rendering that situation culturally unacceptable for the 'normal' male subject" (p. 54).

Certainly, in the Dexter/Plowright production, the soliloquy of the "normal" male Sebastian is not presented as interior monologue or available for anyone to overhear. "He" speaks his lines about Olivia and her household aloud and alone in her garden. His only internal monologue is brief, occurring when he first meets Olivia. He is not surprised into embarrassing speech and only speaks openly thereafter. Sebastian's maleness is secured by his consistently embodied voice, which gains authority rather than losing it. Conversely, Viola's femininity is established through her increasing constraint within the film narrative. Moreover, all the erotic potential of Cesario's role is concentrated quite thoroughly in her relationship with Orsino. She attends Orsino's bedside as he awakens, turning her back discreetly when he undresses and is robed by his attendants. She embraces him as she puts his belt around him and puts his shoes on him by sitting between his legs with her back to him while he fondles her hair. By contrast, her lack of physical intimacy with Olivia is noticeable, even though she kisses Olivia's hand on one occasion.

The Dexter/Plowright production handles both Olivia's unveiling and her passion very differently from the Lenfilm video edition. For the first part of their interview, Olivia is veiled but nonetheless visible through the sheer fabric. When Cesario sits and requests to see her face, Olivia starts to draw back the veil, but a careful film cut shifts perspective from showing Olivia's partially hidden face to an over-the-shoulder shot of Viola's face once Olivia is unveiled. Consequently, Olivia's question "Is't not well done?" (1.5.237) does not invite the film audience to gaze at her admiringly as it does in the Lenfilm production. Instead the camera focuses on Viola, who looks briefly, rises, and walks away from Olivia before turning to challenge the lady's beauty: "Excellently done, if God did all" (1.5.238–39). The closeup in this sequence features Viola's face as she challenges Olivia; only then does the camera show Olivia, who defends her beauty as being "in grain." The concentration on Viola, rather than Olivia, in this series of shots carries through in the rest of the scene, which consistently downplays Olivia's desirability and desires in order to focus on Viola's dilemma. During the willow cabin speech, which instigates Olivia's passion in this production, the camera focuses only on Viola and shows Olivia's reaction ("you might do much") in the background over Viola's shoulder. In general, Viola's face dominates the frame much more than Olivia's. The two characters so frequently face or look in opposite directions when they speak to each other that their very spatial orientation suggests that their interests do not connect. This strategy of concentrating attention on Viola persists in their other scenes together. Most strikingly, when Olivia declares her love, she falls to her knees behind Cesario, who is facing the camera and dominating the frame even during Olivia's most passionate declaration. This diminishment of Olivia's passion through perspective continues when Sebastian appears. After she interrupts the duel and asks him to follow, all her statements are presented in a long shot over *Sebastian's* shoulder.

The Lenfilm and Dexter productions control the homoerotic connection between Viola and Olivia even more carefully than they do the relationship between Antonio and Sebastian. Moreover, as in earlier performance editions, Antonio's part is vulnerable to textual editing in ways that Olivia's and Viola's are not, since the play's plot and situations depend far more on Olivia's passionate love for Cesario/Viola than they do on Antonio's love for Sebastian. Consequently, film editing, rather than textual changes, is more dominant in limiting the homoeroticism between Viola and Olivia, especially when that homoeroticism is reinforced by casting the same woman as both Viola and Sebastian.

Ron Wertheim's adaptation of the play uses the same twinning of Viola and Sebastian which characterizes the other two film texts, but this production blatantly represents the homoerotic relationship between Viola and Olivia. Despite the liberties in characterization and setting, this video edition retains significant sections of act 1, scene 5 from the Folio text, at least in the opening dialogue within Olivia's household. Moreover, Wertheim uses both traditional film techniques and the conventions of the pornographic genre to combine Viola's surrogate courtship and Olivia's passionate response to the messenger.

In this production, Viola sings, as she does in Helena Modjeska's performance edition (1883), but here Viola's songs are invariably occasions for the revealing sexual fantasies of those who hear her. In effect, Wertheim replaces the stage gesture of sending and interpreting the ring with Olivia's fantasies while she listens to Viola sing. The images which dissolve into each other in this sequence are significant, not the least because Olivia's fantasy casts Cesario in the guise of a woman with long, coiffed curly hair and exposed breasts. Wertheim uses superimposed images in addition to the fantasy sequence itself in order to replace both Olivia's acknowledgment of her love at the end of 1.5 and Viola's rejection of that love when she receives the ring. After several images of Cesario on a horse, slower music replaces Viola's singing, and the film cuts to reveal Viola as a woman, nude except for her cloak. After Olivia's ardent approach establishes the lesbian nature of her desire, the camera cuts back to a longer shot from behind Viola's cloaked back, this time superimposed with an image of Cesario riding the horse. While Olivia and Viola slowly circle each other, the superimposed image persists, until Olivia once more comes into view from behind Viola's cloak. Then the superimposed image becomes Olivia, with her hair tightly covered by a black scarf and her body covered by a demure black dress. In this part of the sequence, Wertheim has superimposed images of Cesario, rejecting and riding away from Olivia, over the revelation of Cesario's sex and her circling embrace with Olivia. The film thus visually offers a lesbian subtext to the "surface" appearance of the boy rejecting the woman.

The balance of the scene makes that lesbian subtext explicit. The final images of the sequence move definitively away from classic film strategies of the dissolve and superimposed images. At first the circular camera motion provides continuity by circling Olivia and Viola, now undressed to the waist. At this point, the initial actresses are replaced by two different women who are embracing more explicitly. The abrupt shift is signaled by a minor chord and the return to Viola's voice singing the song. The change in actresses is noticeable, since not only are the blonde and brunette reversed on the screen but the camera also offers closeup shots of their faces during their embrace. The contrasts to the earlier parts of the scene underscore the poor production values evident in the abrupt musical cut and the awkward body doubling, which Linda Williams has theorized are conventions of hard-core pornography designed to imply the "reality" of the physical display.[29] The sexual aggression of the brunette "Olivia" increases while the blonde "Viola" submits. The final cut to the blonde now lying on top of the brunette's chest suggests the success of the seduction.

Among the "sexual numbers" in this film, the episode between Olivia and Viola is unique because of the care with which Wertheim establishes Cesario's resistance and Viola's complicity within Olivia's fantasy. Although the final elements of the sequence place the scene solidly as the kind of lesbian warm-up scene common in hard-core pornography, the elaborate dissolves and superimposed images of the opening offer a narrative entrance into Olivia's lesbian response to the messenger (Williams, p. 140). To the extent that Wertheim's scene starts to explore the various aspects of Olivia's desire for Cesario, this production also uses her fantasy to reveal her attraction to the messenger. However, Viola's desires are unimportant while her actions (specifically her singing) provide the background inspiration for revealing the more complex, homoerotically tinged desires of Olivia (and later Orsino).

Even though pornographic film convention ultimately recuperates Olivia's desire and Viola's imagined complicity within the dominant heterosexuality of the film text, Wertheim's *Twelfth Night* invokes homoerotic desire quite explicitly. Unlike the Lenfilm and Plowright film texts, which control Olivia's desires through idealizing her or foregrounding Viola's anxious responses, the soft-core *Twelfth Night*, because of its access to certain film conventions, willingly embraces the lesbian eroticism of Olivia's attraction to Cesario and even, like the poem "Viola and Olivia," imagines Viola's willing response.

However, Wertheim's film text's apparent openness in representing Olivia's love to be homoerotic contrasts sharply with the variety of techniques and revisions which it employs to remove absolutely any hint of male homoeroticism or indeed of any homosexual consummation of Olivia's own desires. The most noticeable revision which works to suppress love between men is, of course, the recasting of Antonio as Antonia. This alteration makes the Antonia-Sebastian association *seem* to parallel Olivia's relationship with Cesario, since both relationships offer mature, more powerful women allied with effeminate young "men." Despite the gender switch in Antonio's role and the newly created Antonia's self-evidently sexual nature, the film eschews any direct erotic encounter between Antonia and Sebastian. This is a striking omission in a film where all the other associations between male and female characters evoke erotic images. For Sebastian and Antonia, the only erotic connection is figured not in sexual attraction but in voyeurism. In a companionable drug-induced haze, both watch as a flock of sheep becomes a group of nude women walking down a hill. This odd moment allies Antonia and Sebastian, making both the bearers rather than the objects of the gaze. This position is especially important in a film text which insistently displays the female body to be looked at, especially in the brief intercut images within "normal" scenes. This voyeurism anticipates Sebastian's solitary observation of the encounter which Antonia has with another man after she parts with Sebastian in this scene.

This viewing of the female body, which recalls Orsino's dominant gaze from his opening song and from his fantasy during his second meeting with

Cesario (2.4), underscores the masculine status of Sebastian's gaze. This film
text also adopts two practical methods of invoking and maintaining the
masculinity of Sebastian, even though the role is played by the same actress
who plays Viola. First, the film text reinforces Sebastian's "maleness" by sub-
stituting a man's back for Nikki Gentile's back in Sebastian's erotic union
with Olivia. In the scene which the production offers as its version of
Olivia's proposal (4.3), inevitably in the bed rather than in the chantry, not
only is Sebastian on top, but his back is demonstrably male in its muscula-
ture and breadth of shoulder. The care which the film text takes to make this
body doubling realistic contrasts with the earlier awkward body doubling in
Olivia's fantasy with Cesario/Viola. Splicing in Sebastian's "maleness" insures that Olivia's homoerotic desires for Cesario are not realized with a Sebastian played by the same actress who plays Viola.

Second and more pervasively, the film text dubs Sebastian's lines using a
male voice.[30] As in the Plowright film text, voices register the gender differences between the twins. The male voice of Sebastian persists throughout
Wertheim's production even though the bodies inhabiting the roles apparently slip from female to male back to female with relative ease. The revelation of Viola's "true sex" in Olivia's fantasy is dependent on Viola's coin-
cident identity/image as the boy Cesario. Whereas Cesario's/Viola's singing
empowers the fantasies which transform gender or, more accurately, reveal
it, Sebastian's voice, imposed on Nikki Gentile's body, represents the aural
sign of the stability of Sebastian's sexual identity and of the production's intention to secure his masculinity despite potentially homoerotic revelations
of the "true" gender of Viola/Cesario. The voice is the promise, carried
through with the splicing of the male back in Olivia's love scene with Sebastian, that the audience may take Sebastian to be uncompromisingly male,
while Viola's gender is always compromised, in voice and in image.

This array of film texts shows that modern video editions are part of a
continuum of performance editions that both reveal and conceal issues of
gender roles and homoeroticism within *Twelfth Night*. Olivia and Viola
raise different anxieties in twentieth-century performance editions, but
the results are surprisingly similar. Twentieth-century performance editing
often idealizes Olivia through film strategies. In the BBC production, television commitment to place becomes a geography of gender which also
confines her authority even if the Folio text remains essentially uncut. The
extended abilities of the film actress, now able to play both Sebastian and
Viola, may preserve the illusion of the twins' identical appearances but ultimately prove less enabling for Viola. The productions which allow the

actress the most range for her skills ironically reinforce gender distinctions and stereotyping—in voice, in relationships, and in film images. In this feature, the films carry through the effect of stereotyping and gender constraint described by Henry Morley in Kate Terry's onstage performance of the dual role in 1865: "her Sebastian is skillfully distinguished from her Viola, by the more firm walk and tone of voice, the use of a few simple male gestures, as the folding of the hands, and by a spirited display of firmness and skill in Fence that contrasts with Viola's womanly fear in the charming scene of the mock duel."[31]

In presenting homoeroticism, the video editions make even more explicit the anxieties attendant on Antonio's love for Sebastian in the earlier texts. While nineteenth-century performance texts resorted to cutting Antonio's role to control the representation of his passion, twentieth-century film editions may cut his role, as Dexter does, or simply intercut his reaction shots to define his interest as carefully nonsexual, as Kafno does. Changing responses and awareness of homosexuality figure more directly in successive video editions; British uneasiness about homosexuality in the fifties and sixties is evident in the Dexter/Plowright 1970 revisions, while the greater openness of the eighties is apparent in the BBC *Twelfth Night*.[32] The darker version of the play produced in the 1990 RTC video edition rewrites Antonio's passion and the play's concerns in a more somber vein, possibly because of the impact of AIDS on the representations and acceptance of homoerotic desires. These video editions share with their earlier counterparts an obvious anxiety about the homoeroticism. Consequently, each production's attempt to distract or even direct attention toward Antonio's passion ultimately problematizes its own editorial stance. The BBC's *Twelfth Night* acknowledges Antonio's passion only to undermine that acceptance in a problematic exit, while the Dexter/Plowright *Twelfth Night* erases the homoerotic intimacy between Antonio and Sebastian only to resurrect it in an embrace in the final scene. The ambiguity of the RTC version both distracts from Antonio's love and foregrounds it by focusing on his paternal protectiveness.

As my analysis of these film texts illustrates, the exploration of current video editions in light of earlier performance editions has several important benefits. First the video editions illuminate the earlier texts and are illuminated by them because of issues which continue to provoke substantial changes and attention in production. Second, current video and performance editions offer us the opportunity to reassess the "normal" textual cuts and rearrangements to Shakespeare's plays, which are all too frequently dismissed as either natural directorial choices or harmless stage tradition. When these changes resurface in the very different medium of film, we must ask more forcefully what is being achieved by these variations in the texts. Third, the video editions represent an expanded and modified form of the performance edition because they increase the available modes of representing and reproducing performance.

In effect, the multiple means of reproducing performance in the twentieth century extend how sensitively performance editing can respond to cultural and social pressures. The video editions, screenplay editions, sound recordings, and whatever multimedia forms may follow require that we constantly assess and distinguish the interrelationships between performances and the material reproductions that claim performance as their source.

# Displacing and Renaming Love:
# A Lacanian Reading

isplacement has always been a concern of *Twelfth Night* critics, but usually displacing and renaming love are the popular critical pastimes. Psychoanalytic critics especially concentrate on displaced incestuous love that must be sublimated into other kinds of love or out-of-place homoerotic attraction that is in turn replaced by heterosexual union. Thomas MacCary in *Friends and Lovers* offers a typical example of the practice when he argues that *Twelfth Night* is one of several Shakespearean comedies in which the male protagonist matures by facing and replacing a series of mirrors of himself. The penultimate mirror is the transvestized female, like Viola, who is then displaced by herself in her female aspect.[1] Yet tactics of displacement and renaming extend beyond the boundaries of psychoanalytic criticism of this play. Even Stephen Greenblatt, who offers a strikingly antipsychoanalytic approach to the play and insists on Renaissance understandings of sexual identity and maturation, notices and imitates what he calls the "swerving" of the text.[2] In fact, *Twelfth Night* both expresses and implicates its audience in a symbolic order which leads inevitably to displacement and renaming, to a reiteration of the nature of the signifier.

As the performance editions insistently reorder the text and the characters in the play, *Twelfth Night*'s plot follows the itinerary of a variety of texts which rearrange characters and are themselves reordered continually. To explore this itinerary, I turn to a section in the play which has dominated both texts and performances, the scene in which Malvolio is tricked with the letter (2.5). My key to *Twelfth Night*'s treatment of text lies in the cryptic letters in Malvolio's letter: "M.O.A.I." The performance editions emphasize Malvolio's letter, both the trick played on him and the transformation of his behavior and status. The rearrangements which affect Viola and Antonio's relationship with Sebastian also streamline Malvolio's gulling. Thus, even though the performance editions curtail Malvolio's literal confinement because of the letter (4.3), their strategies actually draw attention to the initial text, "M.O.A.I.," which Malvolio must rearrange and augment in order to make the sense he wishes. These notable aspects of Malvolio's letters are repeated not just within the Folio but also throughout the performance editing of the comedy.

I propose that these letters arise from a particular discourse which speaks the characters of *Twelfth Night* and ultimately speaks the play's critics as well as the performance editions. Consequently, I am appropriating the language of place and misplace which recurs in many readings of the play as I enter into a dialogue of my own with the Folio *Twelfth Night*. It is not an original dialogue—nor can it be—since my point is that the text in its relation to signification engenders readings of place and out-of-place and creates in the performance editions a necessarily movable text. In focusing on Malvolio's letter and particularly on "M.O.A.I.," I show a shift in the reading of this particular textual crux away from short, though complicated, explanations which assert the utter clarity of rearranging these letters. In current readings, and I do not exclude my own, the letters in their "alphabetical position" are not to be tampered with; it is the *readers* who are out of place when they try to discover what these letters mean. Or perhaps we are not out of place, but merely in Malvolio's place, bringing to our reading the desire to find something of ourselves in the letters. This does not mean that we (or even Malvolio) are misreading them, but rather that we, too, are subject to the signifier, to its particular logic.

In pursuing this logic and deciphering the letters in the play, we uncover the importance and the inevitability of *Twelfth Night*'s rearrangements. In this investigation, Jacques Lacan's "Seminar on 'The Purloined Letter'" proves useful. Lacan analyzes Edgar Allan Poe's short story and discovers the signifier in its symbolic function in the movements and condition of the literal letter.[3] He suggests that the neutralized or emptied signifier, which betrays its own nature as a symbol, has no meaning in and of itself (we never learn the powerful contents of the letter), but "means" only in its function and place in a symbolic order. His analysis of the story becomes a reporting of what the letter/signifier does when it is out of its place (as it must inevitably be because of its nature as a signifier) and how it in fact controls the subjects who are possessed of it.

Lacan's reading of the particular mechanisms in Poe's story illuminates my work, especially when he reviews Sigmund Freud's work in light of Ferdinand de Saussure's linguistic theory and insists that "if what Freud discovered and rediscovers with a perpetually increasing sense of shock has a meaning, it is that the displacement of the signifier determines the subjects in their acts, in their destiny, in their refusals, in their blindness, in their end and in their fate" ("Seminar," pp. 43–44). The signifiers of dramatic texts control the characters (and actors) who speak the play's language. However, Lacan's statement is most radically true in *Twelfth Night*'s performance editions as the reordering and slippage of scenes determine characters in their actions, refusals, and so forth. In fact, the point of such alterations is in part to determine or "fix" these characters, particularly Viola and Olivia. However, the more interesting revelation is that the displacement of texts within *Twelfth Night* transverses and complicates gender in ways which have, in turn, provoked performance editions to do their own rearrangements and alterations.

Equally importantly, Lacan suggests that the subject's gender results from the relationship to the signifier. In "The Agency of the Letter in the Unconscious," Lacan tells the story of a boy and a girl sitting opposite one another in a train as it stops at the station in front of two doors to the rest rooms. Since the girl, because of her place, can only see the men's room and the boy can only see the ladies' room, an argument ensues over whether they have arrived at "Ladies" or "Gentlemen." Lacan takes this story both as evidence that the signifier "enters the signified . . . [and] raises the question of its place in reality" and as a paradigm of how the two children become gendered subjects: "For these children, Ladies and Gentlemen will henceforth be two countries toward which each of their souls will strive on divergent wings, and between which a truce will be the more impossible since they are actually the same country."[4] This achievement of gender is complicated by what Lacan sees as Freud's major revelation: the signifier which so enters and alters the signified is not fixed in relation to the signified but slips along a signifying chain.

The fact that the signifier slips, that the letter moves from one person to another, means that the gender of the subject varies depending on its relationship to the signifier. This illuminates the second major point in Lacan's reading of "The Purloined Letter." The subject who apprehends the loss of the letter (like the queen once she has lost the letter), or who sees that it is there for the taking (like the minister and Dupin before they take it), is

oriented as masculine, created as such by castration anxiety. More significantly in the "Seminar," the subject who apparently possesses the signifier
but is in fact possessed by it, "immobile in its shadow," is constituted in a
feminine position.[5] This relativity of gender in relation to the signifier/letter
operates throughout *Twelfth Night*, but most noticeably in the incident of
Malvolio's letter(s), an event which stands out both in readings and in performances of the comedy.[6]

However, a Lacanian analysis of *Twelfth Night* offers more than a new explanation of a notable textual crux. First, the pressure to interpret Malvolio's
letter(s) is related to the way other letters and supposedly clear signs of love
are exchanged in this play. As a result, tracing the itinerary of the letter
reveals how the slipping of gender affects more characters than just Viola,
offering a sophisticated understanding of Maria, whose importance is all
too frequently overlooked, and a fresh perspective on Olivia's place in the
play. Second, exploring the function of the signifier in this play also clarifies
some of the confusing aspects of the final scene, such as Viola's and Sebastian's lengthy greeting and Malvolio's intrusive, contrived reappearance. Finally, this reading leads to a reconsideration of genre in *Twelfth Night*, an
issue also raised by Joel Fineman, who suggests that *Twelfth Night*, along
with *As You Like It* and *Hamlet*, is a turning point in Shakespeare's career.[7]
While Lacan used "The Purloined Letter" to illustrate the function of the
signifier, I use Lacan's work to illuminate the way the characters and readers
of *Twelfth Night* are written by the letters they bear and the ways the play
raises the possibility of tragic as well as comic perceptions of fate.

Most importantly, however, in attending to the displacements of signifier within the playtext, I accept my own historical context, with its limitations and usefulness; I treat the Folio *Twelfth Night*, accepting the accuracy
of the 1602 date and bringing to that text(s) a contemporary critical approach based in Lacan and Jacques Derrida. In so doing, this reading also
addresses the displacements of the letter(s) in terms of folly, gender identity,
and desire, the very features which are the focus of the alterations in the
*Twelfth Night* performance editions. This results in an elaboration of my
own insistence on the slippages constituting *Twelfth Night* within multiple
texts: such slippages are not, and can never be, purely those of language and
text but will always have implications for the representation of gender and
desire in the play.

### M.O.re A.bout I.nitials

Like "The Purloined Letter," *Twelfth Night* tells the story of a signifier
which reflects its own symbolic nature. In *Twelfth Night*, it is not the letter

itself, which we hear in its entirety, but one particular signifier, "M.O.A.I.,"
which generates the symbolic order determining Malvolio's actions. This
signifier resists all interpretation, ours and Malvolio's, yet insists on interpretation as well. "M.O.A.I." is so important because it exposes how naming of
the beloved affects the actions and genders of the characters in *Twelfth Night*
and how the interpretation of that name, by Malvolio or by the readers of
Malvolio, leads to displacement and renaming.[8]

Malvolio is desperate to understand these letters because of the position
they occupy in Olivia's letter: "M.O.A.I. doth sway my life."[9] He wants the
letters to signify him: "what should that alphabetical position portend? If I
could make that resemble something in me!" (2.5.119–21). These letters are
important because of their place, but he must pull them out of place, out of
order, to recover *his* name from them. He even comments on the difficulty
of the puzzle, emphasizing the letters' resistance to his interpretation: "'M'
[for Malvolio]—But then there is no consonancy in the sequel; that suffers
under probation: 'A' should follow, but 'O' does" (2.5.130–32). To wrest the
meaning he wants, he must abandon their sequence and construe them as a
whole: "This simulation is not as the former: and yet, to crush this a little, it
would bow to me, for every one of these letters are in my name" (2.5.139).
He is finally satisfied that the letters designate him both because he wants to
occupy that position and because the rest of the letter seems more obviously
to indicate him. While Malvolio struggles in an attempt to locate himself in
the alphabetical letters which presumably refer to Olivia's beloved, Sir Toby
and Fabian are drawn into interpreting them as well. They take "O" and "I"
as Malvolio mentions them, and they, too, construe the letters to apply to
him. When Malvolio gets to "O," Fabian rather cryptically comments "And
'O' shall end, I hope" and Sir Toby responds "Ay, or I'll cudgel him, and
make him cry 'O'" (2.5.133–34). Malvolio, involved in his word, unknow-
ingly describes his own position: "And then 'I' comes behind" (2.5.135) as he
has come behind Maria to discover the letter. His unwitting construction is
followed by Fabian's reinscription of "I" in yet another order: ". . . and you
had any eye behind you, you might see more detraction at your heels than
fortunes before you" (2.5.136–38). Like Malvolio, the listeners must take the
letters out of place to fit them to his condition. The antics of Toby and
Fabian amuse us, but also show that the position of the letter determines
which of a variety of meanings the letter can convey. These letters can slip
from "I" to "eye," along different signifying chains.

The characters within the play are not the only ones drawn to interpret
these cryptic letters. As the editors of the Arden *Twelfth Night* note, a number of critics try to work out what they signify. Leslie Hotson found in the

letter the initials of the four elements: "*Mare*—Sea, *Orbis*—Earth, *Aer*—Air, and *Ignis*—Fire." To the Arden editors' objections that there are other obvious terms for water (*aqua*) and earth (*terra*), I would add that the order of the letters must, once again, be rearranged to the purpose. Isn't the conventional order of the elements earth, air, fire, and water? Hotson claims his order is "thoroughly appropriate . . . [since] woman is cold and moist, man, hot and dry; in the elements swaying Olivia, therefore, *Mare* must take first place." Yet his logic is tortured and he must invert the order of the quotation he takes from *Time's Whistle* to prove his point.[10] What is intriguing about this particular interpretation, in addition to the elaborate signifying of gender, is that it assigns to "M.O.A.I." the meaning "everything." The letters become an empty signifier into which Hotson can pour anything!

From the all-encompassing to the very specific, we move to L. S. Cox, who claims the letters are an anagram for "I am O[livia]" which, once again, forces the letters out of place to discern some significance in them. Yet another anagrammatic reading might suggest "amo I" where, suitably for my reading, the Latin statement "I love" precedes the separate English assertion of identity—"I."[11] The Arden editors, interestingly enough, identify them as "a sequence of letters expressly designed to make Malvolio interpret them as he does, thus prolonging the comic scene. Attempts to wring further meaning from them are *misplaced*" (Craik, p. 68; my emphasis). Not only do the editors identify "M.O.A.I." as a word, a sequence of letters designed to make the listener understand them as he does, but they also label attempts to discover a signified for this word as "out of place." Such efforts apparently require that the letters be *literally* misplaced to recover meaning, yet the impulse to interpret them, to attach this signifier to some specific signified, is practically irresistible.

Part of the reason surely lies in the obvious desire of both Malvolio and his dupers to attach some meaning to them. But the larger reason rests in the earlier letters which Malvolio so blithely identifies as those of his mistress: "By my life, this is my lady's hand: these be her very C's, her U's, and her T's, and thus makes she her great P's" (2.5.87–89). These four letters (not all of which occur in the letter's superscription) are readily comprehensible and reveal Malvolio's preoccupation with Olivia's sexuality. Sir Andrew even repeats them in case we did not get the joke. The very accessibility of meaning in these four letters encourages or perhaps demands that we look for the meaning of the second, more significant set of four letters. The first set of letters creates our desire to solve the next puzzle and, just as importantly, our need to distinguish ourselves from Malvolio in his self-interested and apparently misguided attempt to find the meaning. As Hotson comments,

"Clearly, this fustian riddle must have a simple solution, obvious to both audience and to all the characters but that dullard Malvolio" (p. 165). Yet the answer has been far from obvious to the many critics who have addressed the problem. The "true" meaning for which we look always seems to require the involved and elaborate rearrangements of the letters.

This impulse to pull the letters out of place has not gone unnoticed. Cynthia Lewis suggests that the way "M.O.A.I." engenders Malvolio's absurd attempts to decipher them is a model for the way the near-anagrammatic names of Olivia, Viola, Malvolio, Cesario, and Orsino tease an audience with riddling meaning. She closes her argument by insisting that the anagrammatic names "tempt us into Malvolio's *position*, where we remain until we wake up to understand that not everything in literature can be explained precisely—and not all symbols pertain directly to us or bow to our clever interpretations."[12] Lewis perceives the puzzle forcing the reader into Malvolio's position as interpreter and calls for a reordering of that reader. Stephen Booth, too, sees Malvolio as a model for the audience's response to the play but stops short of full identification: "I do not want to draw that moral because that moral does not yield itself up; it must be drawn. To draw that moral one would have to be a jackass." Like Lewis, Booth wants to have it both ways, showing Malvolio to be like the play's audience yet insisting that the audiences of the play "do not, and therefore should not, feel like fools looking at fools, or jackasses looking at jackasses."[13] Critics like Lewis and Booth tend to insist that the letters stay in place, in order; the reader's position is now suspect. What remains consistent in the slipping of this signifier along these various critical signifying chains is its pivotal importance in an interplay between what or who is in place and what or who is out of place.

My reading of these letters has the virtue of insisting that the "alphabetical position" remains in order, thwarting and engendering interpretation, as I explore and enact how this signifier generates readings in and out of place. To put it in the context of the book as a whole, I am now accepting and insisting on the Folio *Twelfth Night*'s alphabetical order as that which enables and thwarts interpretation. But, even as I resist the impulse to reorder, omit, and add (an impulse which I have documented in the performance editions), my exploration of "M.O.A.I." ultimately proposes that rearrangements, omissions, and even additions are the necessary and unavoidable condition for both this incident and, indeed, the texts of the play.

From a Lacanian perspective, I see "M.O.A.I." as the signifier of the beloved. "M.O.A.I. doth sway my life," not as an actual person, but as the signifier which occupies the position of the beloved in the lover's symbolic order. And, because of its very nature as a signifier, it slips in and out of place. The alphabetical letters represent how the literal letters in *Twelfth Night* connect sender and receiver and implicate both in their movement. In the itineraries of its letters, the play represents the strategies of movement and editing which appear throughout the performance editing of *Twelfth Night*.

Whereas the origin of Poe's letter is noticeably absent, in *Twelfth Night* we know who engineered this particular jest. It is not Olivia, but *Maria* who writes this letter and creates this signifier. Moreover, she interprets Malvolio with startling accuracy. She adopts or perhaps creates the pattern of his private fantasies, putting this signifier in the place he desires to occupy. From the moment Maria drops the letter on the stage, Malvolio reveals his private fantasy: "Calling my officers about me, in my branched velvet gown, having come from a day-bed, where I left Olivia sleeping . . . And then to have the humour of state; and after a demure travel of regard, telling them I know my place, as I would they should do theirs, to ask for my kinsman Toby" (2.5.47–49, 52–55). After letting his "tongue tang arguments of state; [putting himself] into the trick of singularity [in a branched velvet gown]," Malvolio then imagines himself being "*opposite with a kinsman*" (2.5.150–51, 149). In short, Malvolio's fantasy, which Sir Toby, Fabian, and Sir Andrew overhear, but *Maria does not*, conforms to the letter in nearly every particular—in his imagination he is already "point-device the very man" (2.5.163).

By entering Malvolio's fantasy and naming the position he wishes to occupy, Maria, or rather the letter, controls his actions, much to the delight of Sir Toby. Here at last we have an author and her work, the creation of the original letter by an agent with a clear purpose. Or do we? That letter creates Maria's fate as much as it is created by her. As Lacan notes in the "Seminar," the possession of the signifier places the subject, in this case, Maria, into a specific symbolic order. Maria's story in the comedy bears out this proposition. Sir Toby's response to the effectiveness of her trick is quite startling: "I could marry this wench for this device . . . And ask no other dowry with her but such another jest" (2.5.182, 184–85). In penning the letter, Maria has so entered the symbolic order of Malvolio's desire to marry above him that she has, in a sense, written her own desire to marry above herself.[14] Seeing Maria, rather than Malvolio or Olivia, as the true possessor of the letter, both knights respond to it and to her with the unexpected suggestion of marriage, as Sir Andrew Aguecheek eagerly seconds Toby's proposal, saying, "So could I too" (2.5.183). Indeed Sir Toby does marry her despite her lower station and her relative poverty, which would presumably be of some importance to a man who must bilk Sir Andrew for money. Fabian makes clear the reason for this marriage at the close of the play: "Maria writ / The letter, at

Sir Toby's great importance, / In recompense whereof he hath married her" (5.1.361–63).

The letter also demonstrates that Maria has entered the already existing fantasy of Olivia, who actually does woo beneath her station, sending her ring as a clear sign of her love to Cesario, ironically by way of Malvolio. The stage business frequently underscores the connection between these two events as Malvolio throws down the ring for Cesario and Maria later drops the letter for Malvolio to find. Malvolio's lines strongly suggest this action: "Come sir, you peevishly threw it to her: and her will is, it should be so returned. If it be worth stooping for, there it lies" (2.2.12–14). Most prompt-books, given such evidence in the text, insert a stage direction for Malvolio to throw down the ring. The curious thing is that Olivia does not say Cesario threw the ring at her, merely that he left it with her. The staging consequently seems an even more deliberate parallel to the scene where Maria drops the letter that is "his that finds it" (2.2.15).

Maria's identification with Olivia begins in her initiation of the jest: "I can write very like my lady your niece; on a forgotten matter we can hardly make distinction of our hands" (2.3.160–62). Indeed, the handwriting is the first proof which persuades Malvolio that the letter is from Olivia; yet more than the similarity of their hands identifies Maria with her mistress.[15] For example, Maria has exhorted Sir Toby to watch Malvolio take up the letter and "observe his construction of it" (2.3.175). Similarly, Olivia anticipates Cesario's "hard construction" of her gesture with the ring in act 3. Late in the play, she also practically quotes the letter that Maria has written when she urges Cesario: "Fear not, Cesario, take thy fortunes up, / Be that thou know'st thou art, and then thou art / As great as that thou fear'st" (5.1.146–48). The language of the two women becomes similar because the same discourse speaks through both.

By engendering Malvolio's fantasies in the letter scene, Maria creates a confusion between herself and Olivia which is evident from Malvolio's entrance: "Maria once told me she did affect me, and I have heard herself come thus near, that should she fancy, it should be one of my complexion" (2.5.23–26). The logical antecedent of Malvolio's "she" is Maria, though Malvolio actually speaks of Olivia. This conflation of the two women persists in Malvolio's letter to Olivia where, though he does not know it, "you" and "madam" apply to both women. The ambiguous "she" of Malvolio's speech marks the beginning of Maria's taking Olivia's place, becoming a desirable marriage partner and even temporarily claiming one of Olivia's suitors when Sir Andrew seconds Sir Toby's impulse to marry her. Maria occupies Olivia's place so thoroughly that the apparently clear message of love which she conveys to "M.O.A.I." is echoed in the very next scene, where Olivia draws attention to the ring which signifies her love for Cesario. Like Maria, Olivia assumes that Cesario can easily interpret the message of the ring—"To one of your receiving / Enough is shown; a cypress, not a bosom, / Hides my heart: so let me hear you speak" (3.1.122–24). She demands that Cesario acknowledge and respond to their relationship.

In linking Malvolio and Olivia, Maria's letter enters and exposes the connection which joins lover to beloved, as Maria herself enters and moves along that signifying chain from one position to the other. The sign passed from one to the other, be it a letter or a ring, establishes two positions in a symbolic order. In much the same way, Lacan notes in "The Purloined Letter" that by merely receiving the letter the queen has been implicated in a relationship with the sender. The letter controls her; she does not control the letter. The origin of the letter in Poe is uncertain and, from Lacan's perspective, irrelevant. *Twelfth Night*, by contrast, demonstrates how *both* the originator and receiver of the letter are controlled by the symbolic order which connects them. The play further suggests that this order precedes and implicates both as well as extending beyond merely Malvolio's situation.

### The Moving Signifier Writes

*Twelfth Night*'s presentation of Malvolio's letter demonstrates that the rearrangement of the letters and consequently of the text is inevitable. Equally the letter's movement from one character to the next sets each, at least temporarily, in relationship to the other and exposes both to the logic of the signifier. Neither the letter's author nor those who reiterate it, as Malvolio does on two separate occasions, constitute an authority which can stabilize the letter. Instead the subject is destabilized by participating in the signifier's movement, which places him or her in the symbolic order, an order which dictates rearrangement and slipping as its effects.

This effect of the signifier is striking in Cesario/Viola's response to receiving the ring in act 2. She may refuse the ring, but she is still controlled by its power as a signifier addressed to her and cannot refuse the position of "beloved" which it establishes. Even as she tries to reject the ring, she concurs with Olivia's story about it and reiterates Olivia's very words: "She took the ring of me, I'll none of it" (2.2.11). Like Malvolio, Cesario/Viola takes up Olivia's token and meditates on what it could mean when she presumes that she is alone. Like Malvolio, she must recognize herself as Olivia's beloved— "She loves me, sure; the cunning of her passion / Invites me in this churlish messenger" (2.2.21–22). Cesario/Viola even demonstrates how the movement of the signifier determines her own identity: "I am the man" (2.2.24). Here she/he who holds the signifier is not only controlled but gendered by it. Even as Cesario/Viola acknowledges her male identity in Olivia's signifying chain, she takes up the feminine position of immobility behind the signifier which Lacan ascribes first to the queen and later to the minister and Dupin in "The Purloined Letter." Her possession of the ring does not confer power or place her in the masculine position of fearing its loss. Rather the ring reduces her to complete powerlessness. She may appear to have it, but actually it has her.

Despite the fact that she finds herself unable to fill the position Olivia designates for her, Cesario/Viola is also incapable of denying or controlling the symbolic order the ring establishes. After receiving it from Malvolio, she admits, "O time, thou must untangle this, not I, / It is too hard a knot for me t'untie" (2.2.39–40). This pronouncement comes as something of a surprise; she is the only transvestized heroine since the very early Julia of *Two Gentlemen of Verona* to abdicate overtly the power given by her disguise and claim that she is incapable of controlling events. Yet this uncharacteristic confession of weakness makes sense in the context of others in the play who are implicated in the exchange of signifiers and who also acknowledge that some force beyond themselves controls their actions. For instance, Olivia, after sending the ring, asserts, "Fate, show thy force; ourselves we do not owe. / What is decreed, must be" (1.5.314–15). Even Malvolio, who seems capable of taking credit for everything, says, "I have limed her but it is Jove's doing" and "Jove, not I, is the doer of this" (3.4.74–75, 83–84).

This awareness not only reveals how the characteristic movement of letters or tokens in the comedy controls these characters but also signals the play's repeated movement of the signifier and the effects of that movement. The shifting of the letters in fact even precedes Maria's letter to Malvolio. Her initial jest displaces Sir Andrew's plan to duel with Malvolio and Sir Toby's encouragement: "Do't, knight. I'll write thee a challenge; or I'll deliver thy indignation to him by word of mouth" (2.3.129–31). Maria's stratagem does not foreclose the men's aggression but displaces it—to later in the play, to Viola rather than Malvolio. In a sense the letter of challenge is the inverse of the letter of love, the same letter turned inside out and readdressed as in the Poe story. As Feste puts it, "A sentence is but a chev'ril glove to a good wit—how quickly the wrong side may be turned outward" (3.1.11–13).

Even Sir Andrew expresses (or tries to express) his love for Olivia by the inverse strategy of challenging Cesario. That his logic makes sense is evident when even Orsino expresses the same kind of inversion, willing to "sacrifice the lamb that I do love, / To spite a raven's heart within a dove" (5.1.128–29). Displaced love for Olivia becomes murderous intent toward the rival; if one message cannot be delivered, the other can. This relationship between letters of challenge and letters of love in the play is underscored in Antonio, who presents his challenges to Orsino and his duel on "Sebastian's" behalf as the evidence of his willing love.

Read this way, Maria turns Toby's and Andrew's challenge to Malvolio inside out, sending in its place a letter of love to Malvolio from Olivia. Delighted and provoked by her success, Sir Toby persuades Andrew to send a letter of challenge to Cesario, turning inside out the letter of love he should be sending to Olivia. It is no surprise, then, to find out that these letters are similar in other aspects. As in the case of Malvolio's letter, the letter to Cesario arises from two sources: Sir Toby, like Maria, is the moving force behind the jest, but, whereas Maria pens her letter in Olivia's place, Sir Toby gets Sir Andrew to write the letter himself: "Why then, build me thy fortunes upon the basis of valour. Challenge me the Count's youth to fight with him" (3.2.32–34).[16] Once again we hear a letter in its entirety whose style and content "clearly" identify the sender while suggesting a somewhat mysterious addressee. Sir Andrew sends his letter to "*Youth, whatsoever thou art*" (3.4.149). Like Maria, but perhaps more obviously, Sir Andrew is controlled by his writing of the letter. Rather than sending the letter to establish a connection between himself and Cesario in the duel, Sir Andrew wants to conceal himself behind the letter, a fact which becomes apparent when the letter contradicts every challenging word it sets forth. Whereas Maria's self-concealment is a purposeful disguise, Sir Andrew's does him no good since Sir Toby, as previously promised, delivers the challenge by word of mouth and thus makes sure that the letter dictates Sir Andrew's actions.

By issuing the challenge in person, Toby rearranges it so that Cesario will take his opponent to be a serious threat. Moreover, Toby keeps the letter himself. As a result of receiving the challenge (though not the letter itself), Cesario/Viola is once again implicated in a symbolic order over which she has no control. In fact Sir Toby controls both Sir Andrew and Cesario/Viola through the means of this challenge, placing them in the feminine position of immobility behind the signifier while demanding that each "strip your sword stark naked: for meddle you must, that's certain, or forswear to wear iron about you" (3.4.254–56). Knowing their effeminacy, he challenges them to occupy the masculine position, acknowledging the potential loss of the phallus and perceiving that it is there for the taking. Ironically, but not unexpectedly, Sir Toby's actions are also determined as he, too, is feminized by possessing the signifier. The inventive Sir Toby, controlled by the letter so that he reacts only one way, challenges Sebastian and ultimately draws his own sword three times only to find himself always the victim.

The path of Andrew's letter, like that of Olivia's ring, traverses Viola/Cesario's sexually ambiguous position, overtly demanding that she occupy a masculine position. Yet while Olivia's ring leads Viola to exclaim, "I am the man," Sir Toby's challenge leads to the opposite revelation: "A little thing would make me tell them how much I lack of a man" (3.4.307–9). In both cases Cesario/Viola partakes of both the masculine and the feminine: her gender is at stake and likely to slip depending on her orientation toward the signifier. In the first instance, she holds the signifying ring, acknowledging that it determines her sex as male even while it constitutes her gender in the way Lacan describes as feminine, immobile behind the signifier as she partakes of its mystery. In the second instance, she lacks the signifier because she does not possess the letter which would give her the power to recognize the true nature of her challenger. In the face of Uncle Toby's authority and apparent possession of the signifier, she recognizes her gender in a way Lacan defines as masculine: knowing her gender because of the potential loss of what signifies her as male. This leads to a strikingly indirect acknowledgment of her sex as she acknowledges her femininity, but in peculiarly masculine terms, that is, as "lack."

Both Olivia and Sir Toby invoke Cesario's masculinity, but in different ways. As Olivia endows her with the signifier and Toby withholds it and threatens its loss, Viola, in both cases, acknowledges her "true" sex as female but in doing so shows that her gender is changeable. In both cases the signifiers which cross Cesario/Viola's path arouse intense anxiety about her gender. Within the Folio text, this anxiety appears in her own protestations; in the nineteenth-century performance editions, it surfaces in responses to her as the female husband to Olivia and the crossdressed duelist. Importantly, these situations call into question not her sexual identity but her relationship to signification. Viola's identification as the signifier of perfect womanhood in the nineteenth-century reiterates the situation which the play enacts: Viola's relationship to the signifier is constantly at risk, always implicated in her access to a secure gender and always liable to slip.

In the final scene, the problem of her gender seems to be resolved, when Orsino demands the woman's weeds which will finally signal Cesario/Viola's stable female identity. However, Viola's response brings back onstage Malvolio and his letters: "The captain that did bring me first on shore / Hath my maid's garments; he upon some action / Is now in durance, at

Malvolio's suit" (5.1.272–74). In response to Maria's letter, Malvolio's final letter demands that Olivia recognize herself as the author of his behavior: "*I have your own letter, that induced me to the semblance I put on*" (5.1.305–6). This letter also traverses Cesario/Viola's ambivalent gender since Malvolio turns out to be in possession of the necessary signifier of her stable feminine identity. It seems to me no accident that Malvolio's reiteration of his letter and Viola's insistence on her clothes are both limited in the performance editions, since both incidents reveal the transforming power of the signifier rather than the secure "natural" identifications of class and gender relations. Even as the rearrangements in the performance editions partake of the logic of the signifier of the beloved, their cuts forestall the play's foregrounding of Viola's unstable gender, revealed as an effect of the inevitable movement of the signifier.

However, Cesario/Viola's is not the only unstable gender in the text just as she is not the only one traversed by the power of the signifier. Malvolio, once in possession of the letter, is feminized in dress, as he seeks to make a fetish of himself by transforming himself into the signified of "M.O.A.I." In the "Seminar," Lacan is fairly explicit about the relationship between the feminine and the signifier: "this sign is indeed that of woman, insofar as she invests her very being therein, founding it outside the law, which subsumes her nevertheless, originarily, in the position of signifier, nay, of fetish. In order to be worthy of the power of that sign she has but to remain immobile in its shadow, thus finding . . . simulation of mastery in inactivity" (pp. 61–62). Malvolio takes on the role of fetish, investing himself in the letter and trying to simulate mastery of Olivia.

While he partakes of the feminine (and flies into what Lacan might call a "feminine rage" at the end of the play), his situation when he has the letter also partakes of a loss of the signifying phallus, but a loss which he does not apprehend. The letters "M.O.A.I." are all in his name, as he notes; what is cut out is the center of his name, those lost phallic "L"s. Nor should we forget that what Malvolio loses from his fantasy is the chance to "play with my—some rich jewel" (2.5.60–61). In possession of the letter, Malvolio is feminized, losing his masculine attributes without knowing it. Similarly, the cuts which the performance editions make feminize the text, centering both performance and editions on Viola's femininity and the transgressive womanhood of Olivia. The performance editions work to limit all the male erotic relations—Orsino's, Antonio's, and Sebastian's—in favor of concentrating the play's geography and situations around Viola and Olivia.

Like Malvolio's letter, Olivia's ring generates a series of repeated movements in the text. The ring which she sends after Cesario/Viola is not, of course, a signifier in the same way that the letter(s) are, yet Orsino's subsequent impulse to send Olivia a jewel and Olivia's own repetition of her initial gesture in person later in the play underscore the way such a token acts as the signifier of the beloved. Ironically, Olivia has "returned" the ring before Orsino sent her a jewel in his own attempt to place her as beloved: "give her this jewel; say / My love can give no place, bide no denay" (2.4.124–25). When Cesario/Viola takes the jewel to Olivia, her receipt of this token is forestalled when Olivia demands that Cesario/Viola acknowledge receiving *her* ring. This incomplete path of Orsino's jewel, like the incomplete path of Sir Andrew's letter, leaves a messenger in possession of the signifier. As Sir Toby acquires Andrew's letter and power over the two duelists and Feste acquires Malvolio's letter, Cesario/Viola collects jewels.

She receives yet another jewel in her next meeting with Olivia. In act 3, Olivia repeats in person her gesture of sending Viola the ring, saying, "Here, wear this jewel for me, 'tis my picture: / Refuse it not, it hath no tongue to vex you" (3.4.210–11). By offering the cameo, she answers Cesario's first challenge to her: "Lady, you are the cruell'st she alive / If you will lead these graces to the grave / And leave the world no copy" (1.5.244–46). Cesario asks that Olivia leave a copy of her beauty: a child. Olivia provides such a copy of beauty but in the cameo. Here she possesses and loses the power of the signifier in a way which Lacan describes as particularly feminine. She possesses and loses the "child" while appearing as the phallic mother, that is, the feminine Other in possession of the phallus. Despite her assurance that the cameo has no voice, it clearly signifies her and inscribes Viola still more thoroughly in the same symbolic order that the ring established, by offering her a "child" and reiterating the Oedipal situation.

In addition to initiating a series of repeated movements, Maria's letter and Olivia's ring both appear to be entering a set of preexisting related positions rather than creating them. Whereas Maria turns to writing the letter of love to avoid a letter of challenge and posits an existing lover/beloved relationship in her letter, Olivia "returns" a love token to Cesario/Viola, saying ". . . he left this ring behind him, / Would I or not; tell him, I'll none of it" (1.5.305–6). At one blow, she rejects the Duke's suit and binds Viola to her own, unwittingly reflecting in her own wooing both the unavoidability of the symbolic order generated by the signifier of the beloved ("Would I or not") and the beloved's attempt to reject that name as not signifying herself.

Though she does not realize it, Olivia's clear sign of love, like Maria's, is addressed to a cipher since "Cesario" is literally only a name. When she demands that he acknowledge the relationship between them established by the sending of the ring, their conversation exposes how the signifier is operating through both women:

> *Olivia.* I prithee tell me what thou think'st of me.
> *Viola.* That you do think you are not what you are.
> *Olivia.* If I think so, I think the same of you.
> *Viola.* Then think you right; I am not what I am.
>
> (3.1.140–43)

The gist of this exchange is that each is not what she is; each is, in effect, out of place. Each has the name of beloved in another's symbolic order, and, like a signifier, both is and is not what she is, wherever she might go ("Seminar," p. 39). In Cesario's case, this is patently obvious as the word, the name which exists only as a name, has been adopted into Olivia's imagined relationship to the beloved. It is clear that Viola both is and is not what she is. However, Olivia, too, has the status of a signifier in the sense that, as the beloved of Orsino, she both is and is not herself. She even wishes to replace herself with a cipher in Orsino's mind, "for his thoughts, / Would they were blanks, rather than fill'd with me" (3.1.105–6). This comment echoes Viola's story of her sister/herself whose history, as she tells Orsino, is "a blank, my lord" (2.4.111). That "blank" becomes Cesario, who subsequently remarks, "I am all the daughters of my father's house, / And all the brothers too" (2.4.121–22).

For both women, the "blanks" indicate positions to be filled. Olivia wishes to replace herself with blanks, explicitly figuring Orsino's beloved as an empty signifier. However, she also acts as he does in naming Cesario as her beloved. Viola claims her history as a blank in the role of the silent lover of Orsino, at the same time that she herself becomes the blanks in Olivia's thoughts, the empty signifier of her beloved. Each woman acts like the signifier, always holding a place which only exists because she is out of place. Together they expose the symbolic order as they slip from one position to the other and register the role of both lover and beloved as a blank, a position to be filled. The desire here is an impossible one, both within the play and within the history of *Twelfth Night*'s texts: to get the signifier to *be* the signified, to halt displacement and fix meaning. Olivia wants Cesario, like John Alden, to be the suitor whose absence she marks: "But would you undertake another suit, / I had rather hear you to solicit that / Than music from the spheres" (3.1.110–12). As in Malvolio's letter(s), the place of the beloved is held by an uninterpretable signifier, the blank which demands to be filled as Olivia solicits Cesario to complete the link between lover and beloved and reveals how her own actions are controlled by her possession of the name "beloved" for Orsino.

In her relations with Cesario, Olivia reiterates the inscription of the lover/beloved connection, which seems to originate in the prior relationship of Orsino and herself. Maria, in turn, reiterates and inscribes Malvolio in the same logic of desire. Consequently, the origins of Maria's letter (and the patterns it works out) precede the comedy in some way. The letter and letters "M.O.A.I." expose the basic conditions of the comedy's unfolding exploration of the symbolic order linking lover to beloved, the masculine (though not necessarily male) position to the feminine (though not necessarily female) position. The order overrules and interferes with the relationships in which the characters imagine they are involved. This order also creates the slippage of genders and desires which in turn produces the physical rearrangements which the performance editions enact. The letters, arising as they do from Olivia's situation as much as Malvolio's fantasies, reveal the beloved as a signifier, holding a place in a symbolic order, rather than the inevitably female position in courtship which the nineteenth century takes to be natural. The cryptic letters "M.O.A.I." make explicit the effects of naming the beloved, as the potential for loss of that signifier determines the masculine position and the immobility behind it determines the feminine. Yet the nineteenth-century performance editions can allow and even emphasize Malvolio's folly even while the itinerary of the signifier generates the blurring of gender which draws such critical and editorial attention.

### Rearranging the Beloved; Rearranging the Text

What is striking in *Twelfth Night* is not just that the signifier of the beloved possesses the characters and creates their genders but that this signifier, most noticeably in the case of "M.O.A.I.," can only designate a specific person— Malvolio—if the letters are out of place. As such, this puzzle, this symbol, stands for not just the beloved but also for the necessary rearrangement of the beloved, and that rearrangement shows the continuing itinerary of the signifier. In Cesario, there is something "out of place," "the little thing" which renders Olivia's naming him beloved subject to replacement. Only when the signifier of the beloved, the name "Cesario," is replaced by Sebastian does "Cesario" appear for what it is: a cipher which in fact has no signified. This nature of the beloved as signifier, explicit in the initials of Malvolio's letter and the name "Cesario," sways every lover's life, especially Olivia, who is, in a sense, in love with a mere name.

The displacement so obvious in the cases of Cesario and "M.O.A.I." applies as well to other lovers like Orsino who would change her whom he loves—"How will she [Olivia] love, when the rich golden shaft / Hath kill'd the flock of all affections else / That live in her" (1.1.35–37). Yet, like Olivia, he ends by replacing the signifier, literally rearranging the letters in Olivia's name, to replace Olivia with Viola as beloved. Even Viola, who never names her beloved, claims to Orsino that she is "of your complexion . . . About your years" (2.4.26, 28) and must replace "woman" with "man." The symbolic order of the play is generated by the "beloved" (a.k.a. "M.O.A.I.," blank, Cesario) as it reiterates its own nature as a signifier: it is always in place (in the symbolic order) at the same time that its only means of signifying is to be out of place (designating an absence).

Even for Antonio, the beloved is tied to an empty signifier, first when he discovers that "Roderigo" is not Sebastian's name and later when his soliloquy identifying his beloved only occurs in Sebastian's literal absence. His fullest claim to Sebastian's affections comes when the name "Sebastian" has slipped to the other twin. His response to Cesario's refusal to acknowledge she has received the money which he has given as the token of his love is as violent as Malvolio's reaction to his discovery that the itinerary of his letter of love has miscarried. He, too, is accused of madness. His gift of money, like Malvolio's letters and Olivia's ring, is implicated in an itinerary from lover to beloved, establishing both positions but ultimately revealing the inevitable reordering which the signifier occasions precisely because it cannot be anchored to a specific signified. Antonio's frustration, like Malvolio's, arises from his assumption that the token addressed to the beloved creates a stable, singular relationship rather than partaking in the unceasing movement of the signifier which alters the signified as it moves.

The beloved must be renamed in *Twelfth Night* for desire to be fulfilled, yet the closing tableau of anticipated marriages and deferred desire still represents the problem of naming the beloved and still insists on the potential for the signifier to slip. Olivia has betrothed herself to Sebastian, proposing in a speech which must suppress his name lest the impossibility of the wedding ceremony become too obvious.[17] Orsino for his part will not call Viola by her given name and claim her as his fancy's queen until she retrieves the garments which signify that she is a woman. Even Antonio, the other pursuing lover in the play, whose claim to Viola's loyalty has already gone badly awry, discovers his love thwarted by Sebastian's marriage to Olivia.

The person most visibly aware of this slipping is, of course, Malvolio, who has experienced the transformations wrought by the movement of the signifier most obviously in the play. We have seen him occupy a series of glances comparable to those Lacan discovers in Poe's short story. First as the messenger who returns Olivia's ring to Viola, casting it on the ground, Malvolio operates in the Real. He is blind to the ring's signifying address in a Symbolic order connecting lover to beloved, an order which Viola understands at a glance and in which she discovers her double in Olivia's eyes: "I am the man." Next, as he indulges his supposedly private fantasies, he discovers the letter which Maria has cast down for him to find. Now occupying Viola's place, he has the glance which sees but doesn't know that it is seen. He is involved in the Imaginary, seeing himself as he presumably appears to Olivia and trying to make himself into the coherent self presented in the letter. Malvolio does not go the step further that Viola does in acknowledging how the signifier has altered her gender and in recognizing her inscription in an order beyond her control.

His last gestures in the play, sending a letter to Olivia and returning her letter which has so changed him, shift Malvolio's place once again. He experiences the slipping of the signifier when the author of the letter changes from Olivia to Maria, and Maria, now implicated in the order connecting lover to beloved, suddenly turns out to have achieved the marriage to a social better which Malvolio anticipated. Between Maria's unexpected marriage and Feste's insistence that what goes around comes around, Malvolio is suddenly and uncomfortably aware of the Symbolic order which has controlled his actions. The signifier has slipped even while he has consistently seemed to possess it and even though he possesses the signifier of Viola's gender at the end of the play.

Although the play seems to fulfill desire in its final scenes, in fact, it does not. The attempts to make the signifier be the signified persist in the final act, when Olivia tries to force Cesario to acknowledge their marriage, when Malvolio presses his claim on Olivia, and when Antonio places his demands on Viola. All attempts fail when the signifier proves to be "what is and is not," both in place and out of place. Only the strategy of renaming and rearranging seems to complete the link between lover and beloved. Yet the signifier of the beloved retains its nature as signifier.

This quest for a stable relationship between signifier and signified produces the multiple texts of *Twelfth Night.* In the case of dramatic texts, the slipping of the signifier is always literally a fact since the language and actions of the play refer to different signifieds within each new performance. Although printing a text appears to remove the play from this inevitable sliding of the signifier, *Twelfth Night*'s texts, both within the comedy and within the performance editing tradition, reveal that their itineraries, from writer/publisher to reader, represent a sliding with significant effects. Through the historical shifts in the gender of the actor playing its roles, through the successive claims that this version presents the comedy in its purest form, these texts demonstrate that the requirements that the text be "fixed," in both senses of the word, actually create a pattern of slipping. Equally importantly, that movement is always deeply and characteristically linked to the variability of gender and desire.

For this reason, all the performance editions' efforts to fix or stabilize the gender categories in the play continue to be marked by anxieties about shifting genders, even in the recent video editions. The performance editions can edit the individual parts which contradict stable gender categories, but they cannot eliminate the movements of the material signifiers of the beloved which circulate endlessly throughout this play. This insistence of the signifier, made material as the address of letters, jewels, money, creates the beloved as a position to be filled and transforms the gender of characters who experience the movement of that signifier along the symbolic order from lover to beloved. But, as studying the editions has suggested, the shifting signifier and its engendering of character cannot be confined or fixed in the play any more than it can be fixed in the play's multiple texts. Along with the critical assessments which haunt gender in the play, the gender variability produced by the signifier in *Twelfth Night* has its analog as well in shifts of gender which have occurred on the level of performance, as first actresses rather than boys come to play Viola and Olivia and later, in the video editions, a single actress can play both the female and male twins.

The ongoing movement of the signifier through the play and its texts results in a number of marriages which are out of place. Though Malvolio, through the device of the letter, is thoroughly punished for his desire to marry out of place, the comedy ends with a striking series of such unions. Maria's marriage to Toby is perhaps the most obvious example, mitigated only somewhat by the couple's noticeable absence at the end of the comedy. But the principals of the comedy also marry out of place to the mysterious twins. Olivia remains onstage with Sebastian rather than Cesario, while Duke Orsino seems to be marrying a boy—"Cesario, come; / For so you shall be while you are a man; / But when in other habits you are seen, / Orsino's mistress, and his fancy's queen" (5.1.384–87).

The love tokens (letter or jewel) addressed to the beloved throughout this comedy establish the symbolic order linking the lover to the beloved, creating two blanks or positions to be filled. This order is curiously revealing.

The clear sign of love is directed correctly to the beloved, to that position in the symbolic order, but also incorrectly because the signifier of the beloved is out of place. Once re-placed—Sebastian for Cesario, Viola for Olivia, man for woman—the symbolic order appears complete and the slipping seems to stop. Yet Malvolio's appearance in the final scene, as he walks off with the garments signifying Viola's identity, suggests that the signifier still slips. So do the continuing attempts on the parts of readers to decipher "M.O.A.I." and the performance editions' persistent rearrangements of the play's scenes.

## Imaginary and Symbolic Fixes on the Text

If Malvolio's experience of the literal and alphabetical letters implies that the signifier will inevitably slip, there is a figure in *Twelfth Night* who appears to halt the slipping of the signifier by fixing gender and interrupting the movement of letters and tokens—Sebastian. At the moment in the play when Viola is most inscribed in the signifying orders of others, Sebastian interrupts yet another claim on her, Sir Andrew's challenge. He ends the movement of that signifier by fighting and winning against Sir Andrew and Sir Toby. When he faces Viola, two identical figures—like the two identical doors of Lacan's story—bear two different names. And Antonio asks, "How have you made division of yourself? / An apple cleft in two is not more twin / Than these two creatures" (5.1.220–22). What is remarkable here from a Lacanian perspective is that two identical objects are utterly different, especially in gender, when designated by two different signifiers, Sebastian and Viola.

But, since two identical doors are much more common than two identical people, the audience within the play focuses on the amazing likeness in the two characters, not the startling difference, as Orsino's comment indicates, "One face, one voice, one habit, and two persons!" (5.1.214). Sebastian and Viola themselves draw attention to the differences in terms of signifying, the transforming power of naming. Sebastian simply asks, "What kin are you to me? / What countryman? What name? What parentage?" (5.1.228–29). His only other effort to identify her is conditional: "Were you a woman, as the rest goes even, / I should my tears let fall upon your cheek, / And say, 'Thrice welcome, drowned Viola'" (5.1.237–39).

For her part, Viola insists on tracing the signifier of her brother which is also the signifier of her father—"Sebastian was my father; / Such a Sebastian was my brother too" (5.1.230–31). In her efforts to attach a name to the person in front of her, she turns to what signifies her father, referring to herself in the third person:

*Viola.* My father had a mole upon his brow.
*Sebastian.* And so had mine.
*Viola.* And died that day when Viola from her birth
    Had number'd thirteen years.
*Sebastian.* O, that record is lively in my soul!

                      (5.1.240–44)

Viola's elaborate verification of identity is all the more unusual given that she has suspected that her brother might be alive since she met Antonio in act 3: "O prove true, / That I, dear brother, be now ta'en for you!" (3.4.384–85).

Viola's aim here is more to place herself than to identify him. Though she acknowledges that only her "masculine usurp'd attire" keeps them from true reunion, she refuses to embrace him "till each circumstance / Of place, time, fortune, do cohere and jump / That I am Viola" (5.1.249–51). What she offers to achieve this goal is assurance of her gender as signified in her "maiden's weeds." Since her clothing has designated her as male, clothing must now restore her as female. The problem of identifying the twins comes down to gender, created in Viola's relationship to the signifier in the Folio text and reworked to suggest its "natural" inevitability in the performance editions.

Sebastian's appearance in the final scene creates a doubling which both causes the most overt slipping of the name of the beloved and seems to stop and fix the positions of lover and beloved. Because of him, Viola regains her name. As a result of attaching the specific signifier "Viola" to a specific signified, Olivia's husband slips from Cesario to Sebastian, Viola's gender slips from masculine to feminine, and Orsino's beloved slips from Olivia to Viola. Sebastian is the active force which enables the closing tableau of couples and apparently halts the slipping of the beloved.

Sebastian himself is both the most inscribed of anyone in the play and, along with Antonio, the most frequently shifted around in the performance editing. Before he meets the Illyrians, his relationship with Antonio offers an isolated and simplified version of the symbolic order connecting lover to beloved. Antonio's pursuit of the youth he loves as well as his subsequent gift of money establish him as the masculine lover and feminize Sebastian as the beloved—pursued, offered tokens of affection, and ultimately (though mistakenly) protected. This relationship gets so determinedly shifted around in the performance editions precisely because it reveals that the symbolic order connecting the positions of lover and beloved *creates* gendered roles rather than deriving from them. Sebastian's chief characteristic in this situation is his ultimate acceptance of the money, the name, and the relationship which Antonio seeks.

Once he meets the Illyrians, Sebastian discovers again and again that he is already involved with people he has never met and already implicated in a duel, a courtship, and even a marriage. The determination forced on Sebastian extends to the casting of the play: since Viola's is the principal role, a Sebastian must be cast in most cases to seem identical to her, sometimes with unfortunate results. Even if the production seeks to emphasize the *fiction* of the twinning, casting Sebastian is a function of casting Viola.

Sebastian becomes an important counterpart to Viola and Malvolio in the way he is written by the situations he encounters within the play. The difference is that Sebastian does not possess or carry the signifier; he *is* the signifier in that he stands for or takes the place of Viola. Consequently the slippage of his scenes from place to place is the result of his status and the indicator of his function as the signifier. He is at once the most active, mobile force in the comedy and the most thoroughly determined in a series of signifying orders which he enacts almost without knowing it. Whereas Viola refuses Olivia's suit as she has refused Orsino's, Sebastian simply marries Olivia when she says "would thou'dst be rul'd by me!" (4.1.63–64), with the same willingness to accept the position given him which he demonstrates in his relationship with Antonio.

Equally he resembles Malvolio in taking up the role assigned him; it is even the same role as Malvolio's. But the steward experiences the control of the letter as if "in such a dream, that when the image of it leaves him he must run mad" (2.5.193–94). Sebastian, on the other hand, seems never to leave the control of the signifier. He gets his wish: "Or I am mad, or else this is a dream: / Let fancy still my sense in Lethe steep; / If it be thus to dream, still let me sleep!" (4.1.60–62). This observation about Sebastian has implications for the relationship between genre and inscription, or fate. For Malvolio, this play is a tragedy because he recognizes that he has been controlled by the signifier. Sebastian, however, though he is equally and similarly inscribed, perceives the occurrences as comedy. Both are "written" by the name of the beloved, but their violently different responses polarize the final scene and invoke both tragedy and comedy.

It is not surprising that this analysis should ultimately arrive at the question of genre. Many striking variations in the performance editions hinge on generic differences between farce and romantic comedy. In the video editions, the contrast between light-hearted romantic comedy in the Dexter production (1970) and melancholy comedy in the RTC production (1990) could not be clearer. The question of genre also haunts Lacan's analysis of

"The Purloined Letter," although he never fully answers it. While he may deny Poe's story its literary status as Derrida suggests, he does confront the issue of genre several times in the seminar—raising the possibilities that the story is a "fable," "vaudeville," "bourgeois comedy," "tragedy," and, of course, "drama."[18]

The most crucial address to genre in Lacan's "Seminar" occurs at the very moment when he posits "The Purloined Letter" as a parable of psychoanalytic truth. He stops in the middle of this assertion to ask where in truth the interest of the story lies. Could it be that Poe's story holds a fascination because of its genre, because it is a mystery story? That Lacan stops to ask these questions is remarkable. It is as if, before he can reveal the psychoanalytic truth which generates the three scenes of the story, he must address genre and where its interests might lie. He then disposes of genre's claim on the tale by noting that "everything which warrants such mystery concerning a crime or offense—its nature and motives, instruments and execution, the procedure used to discover the author, and the means employed to convict him—is carefully eliminated here" ("Seminar," p. 33). Yet even after showing the absence of conventional features, Lacan continues to wrestle with genre. What if it is the variation on conventions which compels the reader's interest? Lacan's response to this self-imposed question is even more intriguing: "Whatever credit we may accord the conventions of a genre for provoking a specific interest in the reader, we should not forget that 'the Dupin tale'—this is the second to appear—is a prototype, and that even if the genre were established in the first, it is still a little early for the author to play on a convention."[19]

The problem of genre in Poe's story is deferred by an appeal to its originary status, but the source of the letter is of no interest. What is obscured in Lacan's reading of Poe—the issue of origins and of their relationship to genre—is explicit in *Twelfth Night*, as my first chapter suggests. Certainly *Twelfth Night*'s origin, in its date of composition, has often been marshaled as evidence of its generic position, linking the play with the melancholy of age (if written in 1614) or the onset of Shakespearean tragedy in *Hamlet* (if written in 1601). Alternatively, the play could express Shakespeare's irrepressible youthfulness (if written in 1614) or offer the best example of his high comedies (if written in 1601). The play's doubled dates, as well as its conventional features, seem to serve equally in asserting its involvement in comedy and in tragedy.

Given the ways the play calls into question the idea of origins as well as destinations, the itinerary of the signifier is figured as without beginning or end in ways that Poe's letter is not. However, despite the ongoing reiteration of the comedy's texts, each individual version does end. Moreover, genre in *Twelfth Night* is closely tied to the problem of ending, of stopping the slipping of gender, letter, beloved. Both Sebastian and Malvolio are intimately involved in the problem, and I would argue that the determination of genre depends on the symbolic order in the play, which offers double access—to Malvolio and to Sebastian.

The differences between Malvolio's perspective and Sebastian's, which finally controls the close of the comedy, are several. First Malvolio's final place in the comedy is neither as lover nor as beloved, but as someone who realizes that the letter, the signifier which he thought he possessed, in fact controls him. Like the audience, Malvolio at this point sees the symbolic order operating the play and controlling him. His ultimate vision is of his own inscription; he recoils from that revelation because he is experiencing the slipping of the signifier and must recognize that the name of the beloved, though it cannot be fixed to a signified, can nonetheless change the signified it temporarily designates.

Malvolio, in short, occupies the fourth position, half suppressed in La-can's reading: the queen's position after the letter is taken from her, the position in which Dupin imagines the minister when he discovers the loss of the letter, and even the position of Dupin after he has handed over the letter to the prefect. Each of these figures has an affinity with the mysterious originator of the letter in that each has "sent" the letter in one way or another, yet each has experienced fully the transformation occasioned by the letter's movement. Like each of these individuals, Malvolio has experienced the itinerary of the signifier and recognizes its power to transform as it traverses the signified as well as its inherent tendency to slip.

Sebastian, by contrast, recognizes the order which has controlled him but can still assume that the signifier of Olivia's beloved can truly refer to one person, himself. From Sebastian's point of view, the signifier stops here. Whereas Malvolio sees the order of the play by seeing the letter slipping away from him, Sebastian understands his inscription by seeing his double—in his twin, in Malvolio, in Orsino. It is Sebastian, not Orsino or Olivia, who explains Olivia's slip—"You would have been contracted to a maid; / Nor are you therein, by my life, deceiv'd: / You are betroth'd both to a maid and man" (5.1.259–61). Like Malvolio in the letter scene, Sebastian thinks he can be the beloved. He replaces the apparent double with himself, and he is more complete and more suitable because he is both maid and man.

Sebastian offers the alternative to seeing Malvolio as the model of the audience's inscription in the play. He suggests another way of experiencing the itinerary of the name of the beloved. In Sebastian we find a different response to the persistent interplay between being in place and being out of place which characterizes the comedy and which I have explored in terms of "M.O.A.I." We can dream either like Malvolio, wishing to force the signifier to *be* the signified, or like Sebastian, recognizing, accepting, and even enjoying our inscription in the text's meditation on naming the object of desire. The text's inevitable reordering functions similarly, encouraging us to insist that the text can be fixed and authentic or allowing us to experience the dizzying slippages which make multiple texts of apparently single ones.

Malvolio's perspective is tragic as he perceives the control of the signifier and the ways he has been written because he has access, for the moment, to the Symbolic order of the play. Sebastian's view of that same inscription is comic because he perceives it in terms of the Imaginary. He believes he can not only achieve the wholeness of his double—he has already surpassed that wholeness. Sebastian's introduction of this possibility, inherent in the Imaginary, is enough to avert Orsino's potentially violent rejection of Viola and Olivia's disappointment. With access to the Imaginary and mirror images, the slipping of the beloved, otherwise figured as betrayal and changeability, offers wholeness and completion and produces comic closure.

What *Twelfth Night* shows again and again is that the signifier slips and, with it, the clothing, the status, even the gender of those who possess it, lose it, or seek to repossess it. While Malvolio has the most thorough access to this order and his response indicates that he sees the play as tragic, his reappearance, ironically, encourages audiences and critics alike to occupy the Imaginary and see the play as Sebastian does—as a comedy. We see in Malvolio our reflected image as interpreters and rearrangers of the play. Moreover, as Viola is a double that Sebastian feels he can easily surpass in completeness, Malvolio seems a double that we can easily surpass. Malvolio, whose intrusion in the scene and possession of Viola's "woman's weeds" forcibly recall the movement of the letters and resulting instability of gender, experiences his inscription as tragic while encouraging an audience's experience of comic inscription. The doubled perspectives offered by Malvolio and Sebastian mark *Twelfth Night* as a turning point between comedy and tragedy, somewhere between folly (*moria*) and fate (*moira*).

Despite my emphasis on the historicity of *Twelfth Night*'s texts—or perhaps because of it—I find this Lacanian reading of the play peculiarly revealing. To me, the slippages of scenes and lines in the performance texts which I have been studying are not, as they were for the nineteenth century, necessary amendments to perfect what Shakespeare left imperfect. I see in that revealing sliding of character and text the historical realization of the impulse to keep the beloved, to fix gender securely, to stop the slippery text from sliding again. I see traces only apparent because they are under erasure; I study editorial variations of *Twelfth Night* only visible when comparing a range of copies which enact varying repetitions of the text as, indeed, the play itself does. The greater the effort to fix gender and to name the beloved, the more obvious the reworking of the text. Like the histories of the performance editions, the careers of these objects in the play prove that, even when made material, the signifier moves and, having moved, moves us.

# "What's in a Name?";
# Or What Do We Talk about
# When We Talk about
# *Twelfth Night*?

I began this study with a deconstructive move of denying any original or singular identity for *Twelfth Night*, despite the fact that we have only one early text in the Folio. Because of the array of texts that follow and potentially precede that text, we cannot stabilize the text so that it yields a fixed order or content that sets the standard for all subsequent reproductions. Now, by the end of this study, I have multiplied the texts into dozens of performance editions, none of which has any necessary or exclusive right to be called the definitive *Twelfth Night*. Instead we are faced with a long history of variable though related texts. But if there is no origin, then what exactly is being repeated and revised in the histories of these textual incarnations? The question remains—what then is the work called *Twelfth Night* that appears in so many forms?

In order to find an answer to these questions, let us return to Jerome McGann's definitions of the three key terms: the text, the play, and the work. The text is the material event or object. The play is "the locus of a specific process of production (or reproduction) and consumption." And the work is "the global set of all the texts and poems which have emerged in the literary production and reproduction processes."[1] Historically all three are interrelated and contingent on each other. Consequently, we tend to give the play an abstract or reified identity that exceeds its specific manifestations. We look at the physical texts, which often vary significantly, and assume that they conserve an "essential" *Twelfth Night*. However, although these three categories of text, play, and work are mutually constitutive, each concept has its own distinct features.

The apparent result of these distinctions is to simplify and specify the text, the object which we can create, read, interpret, edit, buy, sell, or even destroy. We can even turn the text into another object, such as a door stop or a support for a short table leg. Anchored in its physical form and historical context, the text emerges in its reproduction and changes within the histories of different editorial traditions. However, we purchase such accessibility to the text in all its material glory and historical specificity only by positing its interactions with other less readily and intuitively available categories, the play and the work.

The ground of the triad seems to be the play, as a location where both the individual text and the collective work occur. But the play is an abstraction and consequently only discoverable through them. I envision the play as the center of an irregular shape, an outline traced by texts and other reproductions. Although clearly encompassed by the work, that center is also only definable by triangulation, by the projection of where it might be based on the texts marking its surrounding margins. Moreover, as the texts that make up that outline change, the play as center becomes a moving target.

To put it another way, the play does not and cannot exist without at least one event, one performance or one text. Moreover, if the play is reproduced in only one text or a very limited number of texts and never generates an array of texts and plays, the "work" is limited and in turn the play possesses less potential for textual reproductions. Sometimes it even turns out to be just an aspect of another play's (or poem's or novel's) work. For example, Charles Burnaby's *Love Betray'd* (1703), published only briefly in the eighteenth century and unsuccessful on stage, is nonetheless sufficiently connected to *Twelfth Night* to be treated as a tangential element of that work.[2] Yet *Love Betray'd* has no textual or performative descendants. The play can only fully become a "locus" of production if such production takes place, reproducing the play and constituting it through multiple texts. The characterization of this "locus" is problematic, dependent entirely on what does and does not count as part of the work.

On the surface, the "work" as the "global set" of all texts and plays reproducing the play has itself an appealing determinacy—after all, we are now, in the main, talking about many texts. The problem, of course, is the nature of that global set. Whereas it is relatively easy to achieve agreement about what an individual material text is, we have difficulty in determining what constitutes the global set of texts and plays/novels/stories/poems which are produced and reproduced under the name of *Twelfth Night*. The complexity of the work becomes apparent because studying it raises the difficult issue of what is inside and what is outside the work; in a very real sense, creating the boundaries creates the work. Even when we carefully define boundaries, by singling out performance editions for example, we find that the work proves fluid when new reproductions push our limits. Although the individual text can demonstrate a similar permeability of boundaries, as chapter 1 suggests, an array of texts exposes such problems of the work most drastically.

Even though McGann's definition of the work limits the texts and plays involved by specifying the "*literary* production and reproduction" [my emphasis], that description causes its own problems. Since McGann's perspective is avowedly that of a scholarly editor, the literary production of *Twelfth Night* could be confined to the series of scholarly reproductions of the text or even further restricted to the first Folio text(s), as Warren and others might argue. A brief examination of the first copies illustrates that limiting the play to that text (or the texts) in fact seriously curtails the play as a source of literary reproduction and consumption. By returning to the original, we would posit the work in its endless variations as merely a function of its first text. This proposition unconscionably limits a specific play like *Twelfth Night*, especially since many of these other versions are reproduced under circumstances which often suggest no connection to the Folio text but instead relate to other versions. Even so, this view of the work requires some examination.

The *Twelfth Night* in the 1623 Folio is not the first play Shakespeare writes about the confusions of separated twins; it is not even the first of his plays to present a girl disguised as her lover's page, forced to woo another on his behalf. Both *The Comedy of Errors* and *Two Gentlemen of Verona* precede *Twelfth Night* in the Shakespearean canon (as far as we can now determine) and offer prior versions of the later comedy's concerns and situations. In fact, in some ways these two comedies explore salient features of *Twelfth Night* more completely. *The Comedy of Errors* carries through the mistaking of one twin for the other in much more elaborate complications than the later comedy exploits. *Two Gentlemen of Verona* includes an even more detailed representation of the sufferings of the girl disguised as her lover's page. Julia's function as Proteus's surrogate suitor to Silvia allows her to reimagine herself back into her own history as eloquently as Viola does in her patient speeches to Orsino. Moreover, Julia's identity is finally revealed in her moment of greatest emotional anguish: she faints when Valentine volunteers to surrender Silvia to Proteus. All in all, Julia's sufferings as the disguised page rival Viola's in intensity and expression. Why then are we not including

*Twelfth Night* in the work called *Two Gentlemen of Verona* or the work called *The Comedy of Errors*?

Perhaps the answer lies in those features which distinguish *Twelfth Night* from the earlier plays. *Twelfth Night* stands apart from the other two plays both because it blends the farce of twins and the love of the crossdressed girl for her master and because it represents as a crucial element of both plots the heterosexual and homoerotic desires which arise from the gender confusion of identical twins of different sexes. Moreover, *Twelfth Night* weaves these two threads together with two others: the letter jest and the below-stairs conflicts of Sir Toby and Sir Andrew. These distinctive features, taken up by the many texts of the comedy, set those texts in contrast to other Shakespearean plays.

Nonetheless, we *could* treat *Twelfth Night* as one of the plays reproducing the situations of the earlier plays and thus as part of their works, especially if we were confining our attentions only to the very early texts. In fact, the first comment that we have on *Twelfth Night*, John Manningham's diary entry, describes the play as a version of three earlier plays, *The Comedy of Errors*, *Menechmi*, and *Gl'Ingannati* even though he also notes the pleasing addition of Malvolio's gulling, which remains a distinctive attribute of the play in its multiple texts. When Manningham identifies the performance as "very like" other plays, reproducing their characteristics, he also raises the issue of the texts which precede even Shakespeare's earlier efforts.

Those sources reveal that two of the defining features of play—the interplay of desire and double plots of farce and romantic comedy—do not originate with *Twelfth Night*. If anything, *Gl'Ingannati* presents the desires aroused by the twins more emphatically. Lelia's [Viola's] nurse worries about her sleeping alone in Flamminio's [Orsino's] antechamber, asking "What if, some night, seized with the accursed temptation, he called you in to sleep with him, what would you do?"[3] Though Lelia responds that she will worry about that when it happens, the potential of same-sex desire is articulated early in the text in Flamminio's predicted seduction of his boy page. Heterosexual desire in *Gl'Ingannati* is, in contrast, vividly realized rather than merely anticipated, first in the descriptions of Isabella's [Olivia's] and Fabrizio's [Sebastian's] mutual embraces when locked in together and later when the daughter of Lelia's nurse "naively describes the sounds she hears coming from the bedroom where Flamminio and Lelia are together."[4] *Gl'Ingannati* strongly represents both the anticipation and the enactments of the twins' desirability, explicitly staging the sexual confusions that Shakespeare's comedy only suggests.

The other source that Bullough cites, Barnabe Riche's *Apollonius and Silla*, is similarly explicit about Julina's [Olivia's] desire for Silla [Viola] and the consummation of that desire with Silvio, her brother. In fact, Julina becomes pregnant and challenges Silla as the father of her child so that Silla must take her aside to prove that she is actually a woman: "with all loosing his garmentes doune to his stomacke, shewed Julina his breastes and pretie teates" (Bullough, p. 361). The sexually explicit quality of both these sources anticipates the 1972 soft-core *Twelfth Night*, whose revelation of Viola's femininity is a similar exposure of her chest. Yet we are not watching a soft-core *Apollonius and Silla*. If *Twelfth Night* reproduces the situations, characters, and slippages of *Gl'Ingannati*, *Laelia*, or *Apollonius and Silla*, then why do we consider them *Twelfth Night*'s sources? Why isn't *Twelfth Night* an adaptation of one or all?

True, *Twelfth Night* differs from its sources in significant ways. The homoerotic elements of Flamminio's potential desire for his page and Julina's headlong pursuit of the girl Silla (dressed as Silvio) are present in these sources, but they are either deferred (a problem which Lelia will deal with later) or displaced (Julina's offer of love to Silla is consummated with her brother, Silvio). *Twelfth Night* omits the explicit heterosexual encounters of the sources, thus concentrating on the possibilities of homoerotic desire which the aggressively heterosexual encounters of the sources defuse. Though Bullough attributes to Shakespeare's greater discretion his unwillingness to include the bawdy descriptions of Flamminio and Lelia or the pregnancy of Julina, Shakespeare does include the near-rape of Silvia in *Two Gentlemen of Verona*. And later plays, like *Measure for Measure* and *All's Well*, do not flinch from pregnancy or the implication of sexuality consummated through disguise. The effect of this deferral of desire in *Twelfth Night* is to shift the emphasis of the action from heterosexual union to homosexual as well as heterosexual possibilities. Once again, the entanglements of gender and the displacements of desire are the distinguishing features of *Twelfth Night*, even though representations of such desires also appear in the sources.

Although Shakespeare's play has some distinct differences from these earlier versions—most notably the trick played on Malvolio with its own pattern of displacements—the question remains: what gives *Twelfth Night* or any other Shakespearean play its status as a work and consequently subordinates even texts and performances which *precede* the Folio or quarto? It is more than just a matter of personal perspective. Even if I were writing a book about *Apollonius and Silla* and tried to present *Twelfth Night* as an aspect of that play, the shift in my point of view would not endow Riche's tale with the same status as a work. The reasons that persuade us to focus on

*Twelfth Night*, or any other canonical creation, rather than on its sources as the work lie in the history of the play's reproductions as texts and as performances. Not only the aggregate cultural authority invested in Shakespeare as author, but, more specifically, the play's continual reconstructions have established *Twelfth Night*'s apparent identity. The comedy is singled out here precisely because it generates a historical array of texts. That textual history is the necessary condition which establishes and characterizes the play as a site of "literary" reproduction and consumption.

Equally importantly, as this study has demonstrated, there are a great many more material events and texts connected to *Twelfth Night* than simply the first copies or even the scholarly reproductions of the play. For example, would performances constitute "literary" productions or are only printed texts "literary"? Does the work include concordances, variorum editions, electronic texts and their data-searching capabilities? To extend the category of literary production just a bit, couldn't critical reworkings of the play be included among its literary productions? In other words, why couldn't this book be one of the texts of *Twelfth Night*? All of these examples have some specific claim to being part of the *literary* production of *Twelfth Night* while also challenging and redefining the work in the context of its reproductions.

There are also numerous other *Twelfth Night* texts whose status as "literary" productions is even less secure. Most notably, this study as a whole has argued that performance editions are an important part of the work *Twelfth Night* because they function within a tradition of performance editing shared by the Folio texts. That array of editions tests the boundaries of what the play might be; their variations from the Folio represent a blend of enactments on the stage and on the page which nonetheless participate in the nineteenth-century play *Twelfth Night*. Obviously, I would argue that these texts are also a part of the work and thus determinant of the play.

However, the performance editions are only a small segment of the texts representing *Twelfth Night* in the late eighteenth and early nineteenth centuries. Surely the work could also include the other types of texts mentioned in chapter 2, the breviates, the reading editions, and the expurgated texts in addition to scholarly and performance texts. These texts and their intertextual influences establish both the conditions and purposes of reproducing *Twelfth Night*. By defining the play as a site of cultural production and consumption, this investigation thus discovers *Twelfth Night* as a play specifically within the history of its textual and theatrical reproductions.

Since even McGann allows that the work could include other artistic creations as well as texts which reproduce *Twelfth Night*, then a play like

Charles Burnaby's *Love Betray'd*, with its Restoration comedy skew on the action of Shakespeare's comedy, is also part of the work, one avenue available for tracing our way to that elusive locus *Twelfth Night*. If we include such adaptations, we must at least acknowledge the various reworkings of *Twelfth Night* in other genres: as story in the Lambs' *Tales from Shakespeare*; as poem in "Viola and Olivia"; as novella in Mary Cowden Clarke's *The Girlhood of Shakespeare's Heroines*.[5]

Whereas McGann's view *seems* to assume that the poem as work will inevitably include only poems and texts of poems, the different genres in which *Twelfth Night* is reproduced—and we might easily see film as just such an alternative genre—demonstrate that drama unsettles any use of genre as a mechanism for limiting the work. The pressure of conventional narrative coherence contributes to the nineteenth-century scenic rearrangements which promote sequential action and climax rather than the interrupted action of the Folio. Even some specific narrative strategies, like the Lambs' introduction of both twins' shipwrecks at the beginning of the tale and Mary Cowden Clarke's inventions of the prehistories of Viola and Olivia to serve as exempla of proper behavior for young women, have clear analogs in the stage representations of both shipwrecks in the opening (as in Daly's production) and the persistent editing of the female roles throughout the period.[6] Moreover, *Twelfth Night*'s rendering in poetry, both as excerpts of texts of collected passages and in the rhymed paraphrases of Samuel Ferguson's breviate, underscores the fact that poetry is already an aspect of Shakespeare's dramas. Thus distinguishing the two genres is difficult, if not impossible. The revisionist poetry of Antonio's pardon is actually interpolated into the performance editions, while "Viola and Olivia" exposes the nineteenth-century preoccupation with female friendship which influences dramatic presentations of these two characters. These texts of *Twelfth Night*, arising in different genres and reproducing varied elements of the play, not only interact in ways which significantly affect each other, but also participate in the work as much as the dramatic texts of the play do. They reveal that limiting the work according to genre denies *Twelfth Night*'s involvement in the narration of a story and in the use of poetry and song. To put it another way, confining the work to dramatic texts contradicts the sheer variety of ways in which the play is reproducible, ways which demonstrate the interrelatedness of genres inherent in drama.

My close attention to the nineteenth-century texts also leads me to insist that the work encompasses visual as well as verbal renderings of the play. One early-nineteenth-century text, *The Spirit of the Plays of Shakspeare*, drawn and engraved by Frank Howard, offers excerpts of *Twelfth Night*'s text only as definition for the sequence of engraved images of the play which is the main purpose of the volume.[7] The large number of nineteenth-century engravings of Olivia unveiling for Viola in 1.5 identify that moment as a defining one in the play in much the same way that the inevitable excerpting of Viola's "Patience on a monument" speech singles out those verses as the play's revelation of maiden modesty. Both offer a shorthand invocation of the play which is nonetheless tied to its more conventional textual productions, not the least because both engravings of Olivia unveiling and lines of Viola's speech often appear in the context of more "worklike" texts. Like the elimination of generic variety, the omission of the visual representation contradicts the basic fact that *all* texts are visual constructions in addition to verbal ones. Even the earliest Folios offer the engraved image of Shakespeare and decorative engraved borders marking the beginning and end of individual plays.

At our historical distance from these reproductions of *Twelfth Night*, their pertinence in the context which produces scholarly and performance editions of the nineteenth century is clear enough. In fact, chapters 3 and 4 draw upon many early Victorian aspects of the work not only to analyze the historicity of these texts but also to suggest the significance of the play *Twelfth Night* as a medium for nineteenth-century constructions of female roles and desire. Reproduction and consumption of the literary work is not ideologically—or historically—neutral. This fact produces distinctive problems when we approach the work in our time.

Because twentieth-century video editions of the play are connected to the early performance editions, I have argued for including them in the work. However, such contemporary reproductions of *Twelfth Night* challenge the category of the work more viscerally. Our current perception of the play is not so directly intruded upon or violated by earlier abbreviated or adapted texts; at the remove of time, we can accept those texts as partial revelations of what *Twelfth Night* does in a particular society at a given historical moment. In the same way, the nonscholarly textual and visual productions of *any* literary text would reveal how that play, poem, novel, short story, etc., was specifically constituted as a historical production within the context of available publishers, forms, materials, and social and cultural requirements. More to the point, this book insists that these "marginal" texts unveil not only how the historical and social contexts reproduce *Twelfth Night*, but also how those revelations pertain to our contexts.

Without the comfortable cushion of time distancing us from such texts, we face texts and films that are actively circulating now. We respond much more ambivalently to our own culture's reproductions of the play because those texts participate in the work *now* and, at least potentially, challenge our identification of the play as a recognizable and familiar cultural icon, with a given identity. Nonetheless, we *should* study those texts, including the multiple film versions, in order to understand how the play is now constituted. The "quality" of the production is all but irrelevant; its purposes, its relations to earlier texts and productions, and its participation (successful or not) in our particular historical moment mark the historical shifts in how we define the identity of the play.

The work, in my view, includes contemporary texts and films not because they offer "authentic" Shakespeare or an "authentic" *Twelfth Night* but because they enact the current possibilities for reproducing Shakespeare's plays and thus represent points of access to that elusive object/concept "the play." The qualities which distinguish current reproductions from the earlier texts examined here suggest that, while most of these texts/productions offer an ongoing self-identification as *Twelfth Night*, the changing possibilities for reproduction reveal that the play is an evolving set of conditions for representation and that those representations function within changing constructions of gender and sexual desire. We recognize *Twelfth Night* as a play and insist on its "identity" from our embeddedness in the current work, yet our view of it is influenced by the homoeroticism which it displays to us and its presentation of women wooing. Our "global set of texts" includes not only the imagined "original" texts (especially if we are literary scholars) but also current representations that reflect contemporary issues of sexuality and gender. This set will also ultimately encompass new reproductions of the play in new forms.

For example, the latest form of this evolution extends the work into the realm of computer reproduction: *Shakespeare's Twelfth Night, Or What You Will* in its CD-ROM hypertext edition.[8] Actually, the title overstates *Twelfth Night's* role on the CD: the comedy and its glossary are only two sections in comparison to several other segments devoted to "Shakespeare's Life and Times," "Elizabethan Theatre," "Elizabethan History," and the "Theatre of Memory." In fact the animated performances, aural narrations, and music which the program promises appear in other sections of the program but not in the *Twelfth Night* section. *Twelfth Night* occupies a three-window screen with an array of character icons along the top, allowing the reader access to the play's text in several ways. By selecting a character, the viewer observes a description of that character and a list of scenes in which he or she appears with a brief statement of their content. By selecting an act and scene, the viewer can read a scene synopsis in the lateral midscreen section and, in the lower righthand quarter of the screen, scroll through the text of the scene.

All underlined items can be selected for glossary entries, further character information, or other scenes.

For example, the description of act 2, scene 1 dominates the top half of the screen (except for the character icons) and announces: "*Sebastian* makes his appearance in this scene. He has been saved from drowning by a sea-captain, Antonio, with whom he exchanges elaborate expressions of friendship. The audience is informed of who Sebastian is in relation to *Viola* (*Cesario*) and thus the scene mainly moves the plot forward." This summary frames Antonio's adoration as "elaborate expressions of friendship." The closest the hypertext edition comes to acknowledging Antonio's love is one sentence in the commentary on act 3, scene 3—"Once again Antonio and Sebastian exchange words of friendship, particularly Antonio who is risking his life by staying in Illyria." Although the text screen shows all of Antonio's lines stating his love, the summary which hovers over the comparatively small text in the lower quarter of the screen is notably silent about Antonio's adoration and the homoeroticism of his language.[9] Even more telling, Antonio does not count as a character whose progress through the play merits any attention. On the main screen, he appears only under "Other Characters"; the program offers no access to any description of his role or any list of the scenes in which he participates.

As this brief description of the *Twelfth Night* hypertext suggests, this new electronic reproduction of the play has enormous capacity for linking text, image, and performance, in effect producing a *Twelfth Night* text which *is* a performance. More to the point, this "performing text" offers the Folio order and text as only one option among multiple possibilities available to the viewer who could "perform" this *Twelfth Night* in any scenic order desired. This multiplicity nonetheless offers its own hierarchies and its biases. By enabling the viewer to track Viola, Feste, and Orsino through the play, but denying access to Antonio's role, the hypertext *Twelfth Night* imposes a view of the play even though its form suggests multiple possibilities for reordering and accessing the play's text.[10] The presentation, availability, and multiple forms of *Twelfth Night*, like the hypertext edition, underscore our historical situation at the juncture of multiple means of reproduction: video, print, and hypertext/computer.

Nonetheless, I can easily imagine objections to numbering the CD-ROM or video versions of *Twelfth Night* in the work. Yet I would even include modern crib sheets like Cliffs Notes and *Shakespeare Made Easy* or *Twelfth Night by William Shakespeare: The Cartoon Shakespeare Series*. Some of these even include the full Folio text (the cartoon *Twelfth Night* guarantees it!).[11] Although some might lament, "But these are not *Twelfth Night*!" (or, just as revealingly, "That is not Shakespeare," as if the author were somehow inherent in the words which are produced and reproduced), their rejection actually *proves* that these reproductions participate in the work. The dismissal of these versions, either because of their audiences or because of their failure to be faithful to the "original," actually registers a perception of the play. *Twelfth Night* has a recognizable identity partially because of the reproductions which challenge that identity.

A particular text's claim to the signifier, to the name *Twelfth Night*, inevitably calls the play into question. Ron Wertheim's soft-core film examined in chapter 5 has only the loosest connections to the Folio text, yet, by claiming that title, the film announces itself as a reproduction of Shakespeare's comedy. However unacceptable a reproduction some might find it to be, that video edition counts as part of the work and contributes to the evolving play. The fact that some would accept these texts as part of the work and others would deny them merely proves how thoroughly the play inheres within the work (that is, the collection of texts which reproduce the play). Defending the boundaries against encroachers is an essential part of securing an identity for *Twelfth Night*.

The textual productions of *Twelfth Night* take on a bewildering range of forms, yet all of these physical enactments participate in the work and are pertinent to discovering what the play might be and how it might function within its cultural context. In fact theatrical productions, as realizations of *Twelfth Night*, would also fit as "texts" in this sense. Any close consideration of the array of texts and performances which could be included in this work soon reveals that to study the "global set" of texts and "plays" associated with a given Shakespearean play is virtually impossible without choosing a corner, setting boundaries around the kinds of texts under exploration, and, for scholarly explorations, justifying those choices using current academic logic. Establishing those boundaries can fix *Twelfth Night* solely as a literary work, limit its genre to theatre, or even circumscribe the time frame of its reproduction as a work. Such investigations will find what they are looking for— *Twelfth Night* as a scholarly text embedded in literary practices leading up to the facsimile, *Twelfth Night* as a dramatic construction recreated and created through performance, *Twelfth Night*'s sixteenth-century or nineteenth-century or twentieth-century identity as fashioned in the texts and artistic renderings of the period of choice. By contrasting these configurations of the work, we can test the work's boundaries in order to underscore the significance of deciding what may and may not be encompassed there.

So what is *Twelfth Night*? It is a play, of course. However, our understanding of what that play is depends entirely on our perceptions of the work—the texts, films, images, jokes, or performances we include and exclude from that category. Even if we fail to make permanent, stable sense of the fantastic alterations of size, shape, order, and character which we meet when rifling through the current work *Twelfth Night*, we cannot, as I have shown, blithely single out the Folio, as the beginning of the proliferating work, and assume the trajectory revealing the play can be recovered by choosing one text. Our confident knowledge of what *Twelfth Night* is, like our recognition of the familiar identity of all literary creations, actually derives from our perception of the array of texts that we accept and reject as part of its work. Only by exploring the boundaries we have constructed to limit the work and moving beyond them to study those texts which exceed and transgress our careful categories will we ever understand how and why we construct identities for literary creations. And even then, as *Twelfth Night* assures us, those identities will slip.

# Notes

### Introduction

1. William Shakspeare, *Twelfth Night, or What You Will* (London: Cumberland, 1830). All references to editions appear as parenthetical citations to edition title and page number within the body of the chapter. Unless otherwise indicated, these are all editions of *Twelfth Night*, and their full bibliographical notation and abbreviated name appear in the bibliography of performance editions.

2. Because these published texts present the specifics of performance, I prefer to call them performance editions as opposed to "acting texts" as they are occasionally named.

3. See William Shakespeare, *The Complete Oxford Shakespeare*, ed. Stanley Wells and Gary Taylor (London: Oxford University Press, 1983).

4. Gary Taylor, *Reinventing Shakespeare: A Cultural History from the Restoration to the Present* (Oxford: Oxford University Press, 1989).

5. John P. Genest, *Some Account of the English Stage from the Restoration in 1660 to 1830*, vol. 5 (Bath: H. E. Carrington, 1832), p. 439.

6. William P. Halstead, *Shakespeare as Spoken*, vols. 13 and 14 (Ann Arbor: University of Michigan Press, 1989).

7. Charles Shattuck, *John Philip Kemble Promptbooks: The Folger Facsimiles* (Charlottesville: University Press of Virginia, 1974).

8. Arthur Quiller-Couch and John Dover Wilson (eds.), "The Copy for the Text of 1623," in *Twelfth Night, or What You Will* (London: Cambridge Univer-

sity Press, 1930). See also Gary Taylor and John Jowett, *Shakespeare Reshaped: 1606–1623* (Oxford: Clarendon Press, 1993).

9. My information about the staging of the play in this period comes largely from *The London Stage: 1660–1800*, ed. C. B. Hogan. et al. (Carbondale: Southern Illinois University, 1960–68). Genest, in *Some Account of the English Stage*, indicates pretty explicitly that Bell's text comes from Garrick's revival.

10. See Stephen Urkowitz, *Shakespeare's Revision of "King Lear"* (Princeton: Princeton University Press, 1980), Random Cloud [Randall MacLeod], "'The very names of persons': Editing and the Invention of Dramatick Character," and Stephen Orgel, "What Is a Text?" in *Staging the Renaissance: Reinterpretations of Elizabethan and Jacobean Drama*, ed. David Scott Kasdan and Peter Stallybrass (London: Routledge, 1991).

11. Margreta de Grazia, *Shakespeare Verbatim: The Reproduction of Authenticity and the 1790 Apparatus* (Oxford: Clarendon Press, 1991); Taylor, *Reinventing Shakespeare*.

12. See Keir Elam, *The Semiotics of Drama* (London: Methuen, 1980).

13. Marco De Marinis, *The Semiotics of Performance*, trans. Aine O'Healy (Bloomington: Indiana University Press, 1993), pp. 47–70.

14. Stephen Greenblatt, "Fiction and Friction," in *Shakespearean Negotiations: The Circulation of Social Energy in Renaissance England* (Berkeley: University of California, 1988), pp. 82–92.

15. Charles Dickens, *The Life and Adventures of Nicholas Nickleby*, ed. Michael Slater (New York: Penguin Books, 1982). Slater mentions only in passing that the book was first published in nineteen monthly parts between March 1838 and September 1839 (p. 35).

### 1. Double Dating

1. William Shakespeare, *Twelfth Night: The Arden Shakespeare*, ed. J. M. Lothian and T. W. Craik (New York: Methuen, 1975), act 2, scene 1, lines 18–20. All further references to the play by act, scene, and line (rather than edition name and date) refer to the Arden edition and appear in the body of the chapter.

2. Olivia's emotional turmoils are also marked by time as a clock inexplicably strikes in the middle of her confession of love for Cesario and she responds, "The clock upbraids me with the waste of time" (3.1.132).

3. J. Dennis Huston, "'When I Came to Man's Estate': *Twelfth Night* and Problems of Identity," *Modern Language Quarterly* 33 (1972): 274.

4. J. Dover Wilson (ed., with Arthur Quiller-Couch), *Twelfth Night, or What You Will* (Cambridge: Cambridge University Press, 1930), p. 163, n. 93.

5. Oscar Wilde, *The Importance of Being Earnest*, in *Complete Works of Oscar Wilde* (New York: Harper and Row, Publishers, 1989), p. 363.

6. Horace Howard Furness, Introduction to *The New Variorum Shakespeare: "Twelfth Night"* (New York: American Scholars Publications, 1966), p. viii. Tyrwhitt's contribution to the scholarly production of Shakespeare's works in the eighteenth century has recently received more formal recognition in Arthur Sherbo's *Shakespeare's Midwives: Some Neglected Shakespeareans* (Newark: University of Delaware Press, 1992).

7. Edmond Malone, "An Attempt to Ascertain the Order in Which the Plays Attributed to Shakspeare Were Written," in *The Works of William Shakspeare*, vol. 1, ed. George Steevens and Samuel Johnson (London: Bathurst, 1778), pp. 269–71. Malone did change his mind and in a later edition gave the date as 1607. I provide the full text of these titles, but regularize the capitalization in both chapters and the bibliography of performance editions.

8. Joseph Graves, *The Life of William Shakespeare: Collected and Arranged from Numerous Rare and Authentic Documents. Containing Every Fact of Importance from the Birth of This Eminent Poet to the Close of His Brilliant Career. To Which Are Added His Last Will and Testament* (London: Printed and Published by J. Duncombe, n.d.), p. 10.

9. Charles Symmons, "The Life of Shakspeare," bound up in *The Complete Works of Shakspeare* (Leipzig: Baumgartner, 1837), p. ix.

10. *The Dramatic Souvenir: Being Literary and Graphical Illustrations of SHAKESPEARE and Other Celebrated English Dramatists* (London: Charles Tilt, Fleet Street, 1833), p. 26.

11. John William Cole's annotated Shakespeariana is part of the Folger Shakespeare Library's Shakespeare Miscellany (verso to page 68).

12. J. P. Collier, *The History of English Dramatic Poetry to the Time of Shakspeare*, vol. 1 (London: John Murray, 1831), pp. 327–28.

13. William Shakespeare, *Twelfth Night: Chambers's Household Shakespeare* (London and Edinburgh: Printed by William and Robert Chambers, n.d. [1840]).

14. Jorge Luis Borges, "Pierre Menard, Author of *Don Quixote*," in *Ficciones*, trans. Anthony Bonner, ed. Anthony Kerrigan (New York: Grove Press, 1962), p. 48.

15. See Leslie Hotson, *The First Night of Twelfth Night* (London: Rupert Hart-Davis, 1954).

16. Gary Taylor, *Reinventing Shakespeare: A Cultural History from the Restoration to the Present* (Oxford: Oxford University Press, 1989), pp. 171–72.

17. Margreta de Grazia, *Shakespeare Verbatim: The Reproduction of Authenticity and the 1790 Apparatus* (Oxford: Clarendon Press, 1991).

18. William Shakespeare, *The Tragedy of King Lear*, in *The Complete Oxford Shakespeare*, vol. 3, ed. Stanley Wells and Gary Taylor (Oxford: Oxford University Press, 1987), act 3, scene 2, lines 74–77.

19. See Karen Greif, "A Star Is Born: Feste on the Modern Stage," *Shakespeare Quarterly* 39 (1988): 61–78.

20. *Leigh Hunt's Dramatic Criticism: 1808–1831*, ed. Lawrence Huston Houtchens and Carolyn Washburn Houtchens (New York: Columbia University Press, 1949), p. 231.

21. Leonard F. Manheim, "The Mythical Joys of Shakespeare: Or, What You *Will*," in *The Design Within: Psychoanalytic Approaches to Shakespeare*, ed. M. D. Faber (New York: Science House, 1970).

22. W. Thomas MacCary, *Friends and Lovers: The Phenomenology of Desire in Shakespeare's Comedies* (New York: Columbia University Press, 1985), p. 190.

23. Joel Fineman, "Fratricide and Cuckoldry: Shakespeare's Doubles," in *Representing Shakespeare: New Psychoanalytic Essays*, ed. Murray Schwartz and Coppélia Kahn (New York: Columbia University Press, 1980), pp. 70–109.

24. C. L. Barber and Richard Wheeler, *The Whole Journey: Shakespeare's Power of Development* (Berkeley: University of California Press, 1986).

25. Matthew Wikander, "Secret as Maidenhead: The Profession of the Boy-Actress in *Twelfth Night*," *Comparative Drama* 20 (1986): 349–63.

26. Jacques Derrida, "Living On," in *Deconstruction and Criticism*, ed. Harold Bloom et al. (New York: Seabury Press, 1979), p. 84.

27. Jerome McGann, *The Textual Condition* (Princeton: Princeton University Press, 1991), pp. 9–11.

28. Derrida associates this kind of coincidence with the study of borders in Blanchot's narrative where "the edge of the set [ensemble] is a fold [*pli*] in the set." The fold he discovers, the invaginated structure he describes, where the "inverted reapplication of the outer edge to the inside of a form where the outside then opens a pocket," offers the text as Kleinian bottle, where the outside somehow becomes an inside (Derrida, "Living On," p. 96).

## 2. Performance Editions and the Quest for the Original *Twelfth Night*

1. Gary Taylor and Michael Warren (eds.), *The Division of the Kingdoms: Shakespeare's Two Versions of "Lear"* (New York: Oxford University Press, 1983).

2. I use the term "stable" in the same sense that Jerome McGann does in *The Textual Condition* (Princeton: Princeton University Press, 1991), that is, uncomplicated in its textual transmission and therefore well established and not variable.

3. Barry Adams, "Orsino and the Spirit of Love: Text, Syntax, and Sense in *Twelfth Night*, I,i,1–15," *Shakespeare Quarterly* 29 (1978): 52–59.

4. See my introduction in *Twelfe Night, or what you will (F 1623)* (Hertfordshire: Prentice-Hall International, 1995), pp. 23–24.

5. Robert Turner, "The Text of *Twelfth Night*," *Shakespeare Quarterly* 26 (1975): 137.

6. Fredson Bowers, *On Editing Shakespeare* (Charlottesville: University Press of Virginia, 1966), p. 9.

7. See Jonathan Goldberg, "Textual Properties," *Shakespeare Quarterly* 37 (1986): 214.

8. Fredson Bowers, "A Search for Authority: The Investigation of Shakespeare's Printed Texts," in *Print and Culture in the Renaissance*, ed. Gerald P. Tyson and Sylvia Wagonheim (Newark: University of Delaware Press, 1986), p. 32.

9. Michael Warren, "Textual Problems, Editorial Assertions in Editing Shakespeare," in *Textual Criticism and Literary Interpretation*, ed. Jerome McGann (Chicago: University of Chicago Press, 1985), p. 35.

10. Grace Ioppolo, *Revising Shakespeare* (Cambridge, Mass.: Harvard University Press, 1991).

11. Margreta de Grazia and Peter Stallybrass also explore the absence of an authorizing original in "The Materiality of the Shakespearean Text," *Shakespeare Quarterly* 44 (1993): 255–83.

12. As McGann frames these in *The Textual Condition*: "The 'text' is the literary product conceived as a purely lexical event; the 'poem' is the locus of a specific process of production (or reproduction) and consumption; and the 'work' comprehends the global set of all the texts and poems which have emerged in the literary production and reproduction processes" (pp. 31–32).

13. Harry Berger explores this proximity in terms of the creation of the reader as imaginary and imagining audience in *Imaginary Audition: Shakespeare on Stage and Page* (Berkeley: University of Calfornia Press, 1989).

14. See Taylor and Warren, *The Division of the Kingdoms*, where almost half the essays particularly focus on theatrical revision, and Stephen Urkowitz's *Shakespeare's Revision of "King Lear"* (Princeton: Princeton University Press, 1980).

15. William Shakespeare, *The Complete Oxford Shakespeare*, ed. Stanley Wells and Gary Taylor (London: Oxford University Press, 1987).

16. John P. Genest, *Some Account of the English Stage from the Restoration in 1660 to 1830*, vol. 5 (Bath: H. E. Carrington, 1832), p. 439.

17. In fact, William P. Halstead lays the groundwork for such an exploration in *Shakespeare as Spoken* (Ann Arbor: University of Michigan Press, 1979–), a work which collates the cuts and other alterations in more than 5,000 promptbooks for Shakespeare's plays. Much of my information has been cross-referenced with vol. 4 (1983) of this work.

18. See Jacques Derrida, "Structure, Sign, and Play in the Discourse of the Human Sciences," in *The Structuralist Controversy: The Languages of Criticism and the Sciences of Man*, ed. Richard Macksey and Eugenio Donato (Baltimore: Johns Hopkins University Press, 1972), pp. 247–65.

19. For a full discussion of the histories of scholarly texts, see Gary Taylor,

*Reinventing Shakespeare* (Oxford: Oxford University Press, 1989). As Margreta de Grazia argues in *Shakespeare Verbatim: The Reproduction of Authenticity and the 1790 Apparatus* (Oxford: Clarendon Press, 1991), Malone's work inaugurates a new interest in Shakespeare's authentic texts.

20. As in the introduction, references to specific editions appear in the body of the chapter and use abbreviations listed in the bibliography of performance editions, which also includes the full bibliographical references.

21. Samuel Ferguson, *Shakespearean Breviates: An Adjustment of Twenty-four of the Longer Plays of Shakespeare to Convenient Reading Limits* (London: G. Bell and Sons, 1882), p. 11.

22. Hazlitt's predominant interest in Shakespeare's poetry is evident throughout his *Characters of Shakspeare's Plays* (New York: Wiley and Putnam, 1845, first published 1817). In *Coleridge's Criticism of Shakespeare* (Detroit: Wayne State University Press, 1989), R. A. Foakes, in his editorial introduction, acknowledges that Coleridge is more preoccupied with the reading audience than the stage, but does note his interest in the general matter of dramatic illusion (p. 5).

23. Charles and Mary Lamb, *Tales from Shakespeare for the Use of Young Persons* (New York: Houghton Mifflin, 1894, first published in 1807).

24. See Stephen Orgel, "The Authentic Shakespeare," *Representations* 21 (1988): 1–26.

25. For a discussion of how Jonson's 1616 *Folio* affected the bibliographic ego and the presentation of publication, see Joseph Lowenstein, "The Script in the Marketplace," in *Representing the Renaissance*, ed. Stephen Greenblatt (Berkeley: University of California Press, 1988), pp. 265–78. Stephen Orgel has also discussed the issue in "What Is a Text?" in *Staging the Renaissance: Reinterpretations of Elizabethan and Jacobean Drama*, ed. David Scott Kasdan and Peter Stallybrass (New York: Routledge, 1991), pp. 83–87.

26. Shirley Strum Kenny, "The Publication of Plays," in *The London Theatre World: 1660–1800*, ed. Robert D. Hume (Carbondale: Southern Illinois University Press, 1980), pp. 313–15.

27. See Ioppolo, *Revising Shakespeare*, and Earnest A. J. Honigmann, "Shakespeare as Reviser," in *Textual Criticism and Literary Interpretation*, ed. Jerome McGann (Chicago: University of Chicago Press, 1985), pp. 1–22.

28. See Timothy Murray, "From Foul Sheets to Legitimate Model: Anti-Theatre, Text, Ben Jonson," *New Literary History* 14 (1983): 641–64. See also his book *Theatrical Legitimation: Allegories of Genius in Seventeenth-Century England and France* (New York: Oxford University Press, 1987).

29. See Alvin Kernan, *Print Technology, Letters, and Samuel Johnson* (Princeton: Princeton University Press, 1987), and for much fuller detail Elizabeth Eisenstein, *The Printing Press as an Agent of Social Change* (Cambridge: Cambridge University Press, 1979).

30. *Stockdale's Shakspeare* (London: Stockdale, 1784), p. A2.

31. As quoted in Roger Manvell's *Elizabeth Inchbald: England's Principal Woman Dramatist and Independent Woman of Letters in 18th Century England: A Biographical Study* (Lanham, Md.: University Press of America, 1987), p. 128.

32. S. R. Littlewood, *Elizabeth Inchbald and Her Circle: The Life Story of a Charming Woman (1733–1821)* (London: Daniel O'Connor, 1921), p. 104.

33. James Boaden, *Memoirs of the Life of John Philip Kemble, Esq.*, vol. 2 (London: Longman, 1825), p. 2.

34. Lists of *Dramatis Personae* for Shakespeare begin, in most cases, with Rowe's 1709 scholarly edition (Stallybrass and de Grazia, "The Materiality of the Shakespearean Text," p. 267).

35. When referring to Kemble's 1815 edition of *Twelfth Night*, I indicate Kemble, rather than *A Select British Theatre*, in the reference note.

36. Charles Shattuck himself suggests that these editions are "in effect the promptbook" in his introduction to *John Philip Kemble Promptbooks: The Folger Facsimiles* (Charlottesville: University of Virginia Press, 1976), p. xiv.

37. Winifred H. Friedman, *Boydell's Shakespeare Gallery* (New York: Garland, 1976), p. 3.

38. Jonathan Bate, *Shakespearean Constitutions: Politics, Theatre, Criticism 1730–1830* (Oxford: Clarendon Press, 1989).

39. Samuel Phelps, in his 1840 promptbook which uses the Kemble text, restores much of the Folio text that was commonly cut from the performance editions and in general aims to return the text to its Folio version.

40. Samuel Johnson, *Johnson on Shakespeare* (London: Oxford University Press, 1929), p. 93. His comments were first published in his 1765 edition of Shakespeare's works, issued in a second edition by George Steevens in 1773.

41. Edward Tomarken, in *Samuel Johnson on Shakespeare: The Discipline of Criticism* (Athens: University of Georgia Press, 1991), devotes an entire chapter to "History of Criticism in *Twelfth Night*" (pp. 51–70).

42. Fredson Bowers, "The Problem of Variant Forme in a Facsimile Edition," *Library*, 5th series, vol. 7 (1952): 262.

43. *Shakespeare's Plays in Quarto: A Facsimile Edition of Copies Primarily from the Henry J. Huntington Library*, ed. Michael J. B. Allen and Kenneth Muir (Berkeley: University of California Press, 1981), p. 662.

### 3. Rearranging the Texts from Bell to Lacy and Beyond

1. As in previous chapters, the full bibliographical references are available in the bibliography of performance editions; within the chapter, first references offer name and date, but subsequent references include only the name of the edition, unless date is required by context. I extend the editions I consider to

include some American editions, since by the nineteenth century theatrical productions have become international properties.

2. In studying the variations, I not only examine the texts themselves but also refer to William P. Halstead's *Shakespeare as Spoken*, vol. 4 (Ann Arbor: University of Michigan Press, 1983).

3. To make these rearrangements obvious, my references to the scenes describe their principal action, followed by the Folio act and scene designation, so that I might refer to Viola's first appearance (1.2) as preceding Orsino's lament for Olivia (1.1).

4. See Ralph Berry, "The Season of *Twelfth Night*," *New York Literary Forum* (1978): 139–50.

5. John Weaver argues that the Folio defuses Viola's anxiety before we witness it, in "The Other Twin: Sebastian's Relationship to Viola and the Theme of *Twelfth Night*," in *Essays in Honor of Esmond Linworth Marilla* (Baton Rouge: Louisiana State University Press, 1970), pp. 89–100.

6. Randall MacLeod, "UnEditing Shakespeare," *SubStance* 33–34 (1982): 26–55. My scene designations, like my "generic" quotations, come from *Twelfth Night: The Arden Shakespeare*, ed. J. M. Lothian and T. W. Craik (London: Routledge, 1975, rpt. 1988).

7. Charles Shattuck, *John Philip Kemble Promptbooks: The Folger Facsimiles*, vol. 1 (Charlottesville: University Press of Virginia, 1974), p. xiv.

8. Karen Greif, "A Star Is Born: Feste on the Modern Stage," *Shakespeare Quarterly* 39 (1988): 62.

9. Brian Vickers, "The Emergence of Character Criticism, 1774–1800," *Shakespeare Survey* 34 (1981): 11–21.

10. Thomas Whatley, *Remarks on Some of the Characters of Shakspeare*, ed. Richard Whatley (London: B. Fellows, 1839), pp. 21–22.

11. John Philip Kemble, *Macbeth and King Richard II: An Essay* (London: John Murray, 1817), p. 6.

12. John Philip Kemble, "Some Thoughts on Macbeth and Richard III" (London: T. and J. Egerton, 1786), p. 3. The 1817 version has slight changes in language.

13. My information on benefit performances, the dates of their occurrence, and the roles of those benefited comes from two principal sources. *The London Stage: 1600–1800*, ed. C. B. Hogan et al. (Carbondale: Southern Illinois University Press, 1960–68) offers an exhaustive catalog of performances, cast lists, profits, and, of course, benefits. John Genest's *Some Account of the English Stage from the Restoration in 1660 to 1830*, vol. 5 (Bath: H. E. Carrington, 1832), though less complete, gives information on the benefits of the period not covered by *The London Stage*.

14. See G. W. Stone, "The Benefit Performance," in *The London Stage: 1747–76*, vol. 4 (Carbondale: Southern Illinois University, 1968), pp. ci–cvii.

15. Alan Sinfield, "When Is a Character Not a Character? Desdemona, Olivia, Lady Macbeth, and Subjectivity," in *Faultlines: Cultural Materialism and the Politics of Dissident Reading* (Berkeley: University of California Press, 1992), pp. 52–79.

16. William Hazlitt vigorously asserted that Shakespeare's particular skill was the creation of distinctive individuals, in *Characters of Shakspeare's Plays* (New York: Wiley and Putnam, 1845), pp. xix–xxii.

17. Sandra Billington, *A Social History of the Fool* (New York: St. Martin's Press, 1984), pp. 81–98.

18. *Leigh Hunt's Dramatic Criticism: 1808–1831*, ed. Lawrence Huston Houtchens and Carolyn Washburn Houtchens (New York: Columbia University Press, 1949), p. 231.

19. The promptbook in question, TN 17 at the Folger Shakespeare Library, is tentatively dated at 1820, which makes it very possible that it records some version of Reynolds's operatic *Twelfth Night*.

20. Since both the earlier part of this speech and the later close with thanks to Jove, Malvolio's soliloquy might be the sort of extended speech that Grace Ioppolo argues could contain two versions of the same material, both included rather than presented as alternatives (*Revising Shakespeare* [Cambridge, Mass.: Harvard University Press, 1991], p. 95).

21. John Ruskin, "Of Queens' Gardens," in *Sesame and Lilies: Two Lectures by John Ruskin* (New York: Charles E. Merrill and Co., 1891, rpt. 1972), pp. 117–21.

22. William Winter, introduction to *Twelfth Night*, printed by Augustine Daly, 1893, p. 6.

23. The omission of Viola's challenge to Olivia's beauty underscores her virtue in ways which Leigh Hunt describes: "there is something extremely touching and gratifying, not only in viewing the disinterestedness with which she [Viola] pleads his cause to Olivia, but still more so in anticipating the amends she is to make him for the latter's disdain" (p. 42).

24. John Potter, *Theatrical Review*, December 1771 (on the production of *Twelfth Night* at Drury Lane, 1771), p. 277.

25. Alan Sinfield makes much of Olivia's loss of authority in this sequence, noting her offer to pay for both weddings as acquiescence to Orsino as a kinsman ("When Is a Character Not a Character?" p. 72).

26. Hazlitt finds that "the great and secret charm of *Twelfth Night* is the character of Viola," principally because of her confession of her love (*Characters of Shakespeare's Plays*, p. 166).

27. See also Jean Marsden's "'Modesty Unshackled': Dorothy Jordan and the Dangers of Cross-dressing," *Studies in Eighteenth-Century Culture* 22 (1992): 21–35.

28. Elizabeth Howe, *The First English Actresses* (Oxford: Oxford University Press, 1992), and Michael Baker, *The Rise of the Victorian Actor* (Totowa, N.J.: Rowen and Littlefield, 1978). In *Actresses as Working Women: Social Identity in Victorian Culture* (New York: Routledge, 1992), Tracy Davis discusses the financial benefits of such displays (112–14).

29. Kristina Straub views the controversy over the reputation and person of the eighteenth-century transvestite actress as evidence that these figures were "a site of ideological contradiction in the emergence of dominant notions of gender and sexuality in the eighteenth century" (*Sexual Suspects: Eighteenth Century Players and Sexual Ideology* [Princeton: Princeton University Press, 1992], p. 89).

30. Mrs. [Elizabeth] Griffith, *The Morality of Shakespeare's Plays Illustrated* (London, 1772), p. 121.

31. The second edition of *Inchbald's British Theatre*, published in 1810, actually claims Kemble as the editor, but the earlier text offers different cuts and revisions.

32. Calvert was definitely influenced by Phelps, since Phelps played in Calvert's revivals of Shakespeare at the Princess Theatre in Manchester (Richard Foulkes, *The Calverts: Actors of Some Importance* [Oxford: Alden Press, 1992], p. 57).

33. For a very persuasive argument that playtexts must have been cut in performance even in the Renaissance, see Stephen Orgel, "Acting Scripts, Performing Texts," in *Crisis in Editing: Texts of the English Renaissance*, ed. Randall MacLeod (New York: AMS Press, 1994), pp. 251–94.

### 4. Textual Perversity in Illyria

1. Margreta de Grazia and Peter Stallybrass, "The Materiality of the Shakespearean Text," *Shakespeare Quarterly* 44 (1993): 270–72.

2. Once again, all references to editions appear as parenthetical citations to edition title and page number within the body of the chapter. Unless otherwise indicated, these are all editions of *Twelfth Night*, and their full bibliographical notation and abbreviated name appear in the bibliography of performance editions. In addition to the popular published shift of the scene to follow 2.5, the other two positions which 3.3 occupies in printed editions are after 2.3 in Augustine Daly's edition (1893) and after 3.1 in Henry Irving's edition (1884). In production, as indicated by promptbooks, William Burton (1852) moved 3.3 to follow 2.3, Winthrop Ames in 1906 and E. H. Sothern and Julia Marlowe in

1905 both moved the scene to follow 1.5 (possibly because they also moved his first scene to the beginning of the play). Henry Jewett in 1915 moved it to follow 2.4.

3. Joseph Pequigney, "The Two Antonios and Same-Sex Love in *Twelfth Night* and *The Merchant of Venice*," *English Literary Renaissance* 22 (Spring 1992): 201–21; Bruce R. Smith, *Homosexuality in Shakespeare's England* (Chicago: Chicago University Press, 1991); and Valerie Traub, *Desire and Anxiety: Circulations of Sexuality in Shakespearean Drama* (New York: Routledge, 1992).

4. For a full discussion of homosocial desire, see Eve Sedgwick's *Between Men: English Literature and Male Homosocial Desire* (New York: Columbia University Press, 1985).

5. Stephen Greenblatt, "Fiction and Friction," in *Shakespearean Negotiations: The Circulation of Social Energy in Renaissance England* (Berkeley: University of California Press, 1988), pp. 82–92.

6. Of Antonio's 107 lines, 19 (17.7 percent) are typically cut.

7. Interestingly, Lowndes (1791), which is the first to cut this speech, removes the first two lines underlined here *and* is the only text to cut Antonio's "desire more sharp than filed steel."

8. See Camille Slights, "The Principle of Recompense in *Twelfth Night*," *Modern Language Review* 77 (1982): 537–46.

9. Randolph Trumbach, "The Birth of the Queen: Sodomy and the Emergence of Gender Equality in Modern Culture," in *Hidden from History: Reclaiming the Gay and Lesbian Past*, ed. Martin Duberman, Martha Vincinus, and George Chauncey (New York: Penguin, 1989), pp. 129–40.

10. Joseph Donohue, "Women in the Victorian Theatre: Images, Illusions, Realities," in *Gender in Performance: The Presentation of Difference in the Performing Arts*, ed. Laurence Senelick (Hanover, N.H.: University Press of New England, 1992), p. 118.

11. For a fuller discussion of the pardon's treatment in promptbooks, see my essay "Antonio's Pardon," *Shakespeare Quarterly* 45 (1994): 9–15.

12. Jane Gallop, *Reading Lacan* (Ithaca: Cornell University Press, 1985), pp. 41–42.

13. Alan Bray, *Homosexuality in Renaissance England* (London: Gay Men's Press, 1982).

14. See also Jonathan Goldberg's *Sodometries: Renaissance Texts/Modern Sexualities* (Stanford: Stanford University Press, 1992).

15. Alan Bray, "Homosexuality and the Signs of Male Friendship in Elizabethan England," *History Workshop: A Journal of Socialist and Feminist Historians* 29 (1990): 1–19.

16. For an opposing viewpoint, see Janet Adelman, "Male Bonding in Shake-

speare's Comedies," in *Shakespeare's "rough magic": Renaissance Essays in Honor of C. L. Barber*, ed. Peter Erickson and Coppélia Kahn (Newark: University of Delaware Press, 1985), esp. p. 89.

17. Louis Crompton, *Byron and Greek Love: Homophobia in Nineteenth-Century England* (Berkeley: University of California Press, 1985), p. 16.

18. Charles Cowden Clarke, *Shakespeare-Characters; Chiefly Those Subordinate* (London: Smith, Elder and Company, 1863), p. 197.

19. [Mrs. M. L. Elliott], *Shakspeare's Garden of Girls* (London: Remington and Company, 1885), p. 215.

20. Arthur Symons, introduction and notes to *Twelfth Night*, in *The Henry Irving Shakespeare*, ed. Henry Irving and Frank Marshall, vol. 4 (London: Blackie and Son, 1888), p. 355.

21. Orsino generally loses 48 of his 219 lines, or 22 percent of his part.

22. See Randolph Trumbach's assertion that the category of female homosexuality was developing in this period ("London Sapphists: From Three Sexes to Four Genders in the Making of Modern Culture," in *Body Guards: The Cultural Poetics of Gender Ambiguity* [New York: Routledge, 1991], p. 134).

23. John Lucas Tupper, "Viola and Olivia," in *Art and Poetry: Being Thoughts towards Nature Conducted Principally by Artists*, no. 4 (London: Dickinson and Company, 1850), p. 145. William Rossetti identifies both poet and engraver (preface to *The Germ: Thoughts towards Nature in Poetry, Literature, and Art*: Facsimile Reprint of the Literary Organ of the Pre-Raphaelite Brotherhood, published in 1850 [London: Elliott Stock, 1901], p. 25).

24. Barbara Arnett Melchiori, "Undercurrents in Victorian Illustrations of Shakespeare," in *Images of Shakespeare: Proceedings of the Third Congress of the International Shakespeare Association*, ed. Werner Habicht, D. J. Palmer, and Roger Pringle (Newark: University of Delaware Press, 1988), p. 128.

25. Lillian Faderman, *Surpassing the Love of Men: Romantic Friendship and Love between Women from the Renaissance to the Present* (New York: William Morrow and Company, 1981). See also Martha Vicinus, "'They Wonder to Which Sex I Belong': The Historical Roots of Modern Lesbian Identity," *Feminist Studies* 18:3 (1992): 467–98.

26. Lisa Moore, "'Something More Tender Still Than Friendship': Romantic Friendship in Early-Nineteenth-Century England," *Feminist Studies* 18:3 (1992): 499–520.

27. "Memoir of Miss Ann Maria Tree," *Oxberry's Dramatic Biography*, vol. 3 (London: G. Virtue, 1825), p. 205.

28. William Winter, *Shakespeare on Stage*, second series (New York: Moffat, Yard and Company, 1915), pp. 80–82.

29. Anna Jameson, *Characteristics of Women, Moral, Poetical and Historical*, vol. 1, 2nd ed. (London: Saunders and Otley, 1833), p. 243.

30. Louis Lewes, "Twelfth Night—Viola—Olivia," in *The Women of Shakespeare*, trans. Helen Zimmern (London: Hodd, Hodder Bros., 1895), p. 228.

31. Stephen J. Meany, *The Women of Shakspeare: A Paper* (Liverpool: D. Marples, 1859), p. 35.

32. In his influential critique of the comedy, Samuel Johnson singles out Viola's aggressive pursuit of Orsino as unmaidenly, especially in a plan taken up just after her brother's apparent death.

33. Henry Fielding's *The Female Husband* (London, 1746) indicates eighteenth-century awareness and vilification of this figure.

34. Charles Knight, *Studies of Shakspere* (London: Charles Knight, Fleet Street, 1849), p. 313.

35. Henry Hudson, *Shakespeare: His Life, Art, and Characters*, 4th ed. (Boston: Ginn, 1895, copyright 1872), p. 365.

36. Jonathan Dollimore, *Sexual Dissidence: Augustine to Wilde, Freud to Foucault* (Oxford: Clarendon Press, 1991).

### 5. The Video Editions

1. See Dennis Kennedy, *Harley Granville-Barker and the Dream of Theatre* (Princeton: Princeton University Press, 1985), pp. 136–47.

2. William Shakespeare, *Othello*, as arranged for the stage by J. Forbes-Robertson and presented at the Lyric Theatre on Monday, December 15, 1902 (London: Nassau Press, 1902), and William Shakespeare, *The Tempest*, as arranged for the stage by Herbert Beerbohm Tree (London: J. Miles, 1904).

3. Of course, Samuel French remains in business today, but mostly publishes Shakespearean performance editions long after the production, if at all.

4. *The Works of William Shakespeare: The Henry Irving Shakespeare* (London: Blackie, 1888–90), and Harley Granville-Barker, *More Prefaces to Shakespeare*, ed. Edward M. Moore (Princeton: Princeton University Press, 1974), pp. 8–9.

5. William Winter, *Shakespeare on Stage*, first and second series (New York: Moffat, Yard and Company, 1915).

6. William Shakespeare, *Twelfth Night* (London: Folio Society, 1966).

7. Charles Ede, foreword to *Introductions to Shakespeare* (London: Michael Joseph, 1978), p. 10.

8. George Cukor, "Directing *Romeo and Juliet*," in William Shakespeare, *Romeo and Juliet: A Motion Picture Edition, Illustrated with Photographs* (New York: Random House, 1936), p. 247.

9. Kenneth Branagh, introduction to *Much Ado about Nothing, by William Shakespeare, Screenplay, Introduction and Notes on the Making of the Movie by Kenneth Branagh* (New York: W. W. Norton and Company, 1993), p. xvi.

10. William Shakespeare, *The BBC TV Shakespeare: Twelfth Night*, ed. John

Wilder (London: BBC, 1979), p. 29. The *Animated Twelfth Night* was released simultaneously with William Shakespeare, *Twelfth Night*, abridged by Leon Garfield, illustrated by Ksenia Prytkova (New York: Alfred Knopf, 1993).

11. *The Mercury Shakespeare: The Merchant of Venice, Twelfth Night, Julius Caesar*, ed. Orson Welles and Roger Hill (New York: Harper and Brothers, 1934, rpt. 1939), p. 15.

12. See, for example, William Shakespeare, *Twelfth Night*, prod. Caedman (New York: Shakespeare Recording Society, 1961).

13. John Collick, *Shakespeare, Cinema, and Society* (New York: Manchester University Press, 1989), p. 33.

14. *Hamlet*, dir. Laurence Olivier (London: Two Cities Production, 1948); *Macbeth*, dir. Roman Polanski (New York: Playboy Productions, 1970); *The BBC Shakespeare Plays*, prod. Cedric Messina (London: BBC Productions, 1980).

15. For evidence of the availability of these video editions, see Kenneth Rothwell's and Annette Melzer's bibliography of Shakespearean films, *Shakespeare on Screen: An International Filmography and Videography* (New York: Neal Schuman, 1990).

16. David Bordwell and Kristin Thompson, *Film Art: An Introduction* (Reading, Mass.: Addison-Wesley Publishing Company, 1979), p. 153.

17. Lorne Buchman analyzes mise-en-scène in Shakespearean film extensively in *Still in Movement: Shakespeare on Screen* (New York: Oxford University Press, 1991), pp. 33–51.

18. *Twelfth Night: or, What You Will*, dir. Charles Kent (Vitagraph, 1910), *Dvenadtsataia noch'*, dir. Y. Frid (Leningrad: Lenfilm Productions, 1955), *Twelfth Night*, dir. John Dexter (London: John Dexter Productions, 1970, first aired 1968), *William Shakespeare's Twelfth Night*, dir. Ron Wertheim (n.p.: AJB, Films, 1972), *Twelfth Night; Or What You Will*, dir. John Gorrie (London: BBC Shakespeare Plays, 1980), *Twelfth Night*, dir. Paul Kafno (London: RTC Productions, 1990), and *Twelfth Night: Shakespeare—The Animated Tales*, dir. Maria Muat (Moscow and Cardiff: Shakespeare Animated Films Limited, Christmas Films, and Soyuzmultfilm, 1992). Of these films, Wertheim's *Twelfth Night* is sometimes listed according to its re-release date on Showtime in 1988 and again in 1991. However, the Showtime scheduling department gives the film's date as 1972, which makes the most sense given content and language.

19. See A. Nicholas Vardac, *Stage to Screen* (New York: Benjamin Blom, 1968), especially pp. 89–135.

20. Richard Stites, *Russian Popular Culture* (London: Cambridge University Press, 1992), pp. 123–48.

21. "Screening Shakespeare," *Leningrad Pravda* (October 21, 1955): 4. I would like to acknowledge the help of Mary Ann Ryshina, who translated this article

from Russian for me, and Sheila McCarthy, who helped me find the bibliographical reference. For a further discussion of this film and its relationship with the Soviet film of *Othello* also produced in this period, see my "Filming Shakespeare in a Cultural Thaw: Soviet Appropriations of Shakespearean Treacheries, 1955–56," *Textual Practice* 9.2 (Summer 1995): 325–47.

22. I have cross-referenced the quotations from the film with act, scene, and line numbers from *Twelfth Night: The Arden Shakespeare*, ed. J. M. Lothian and T. W. Craik (New York: Methuen, 1975).

23. Kaja Silverman, *The Acoustic Mirror: The Female Voice in Psychoanalysis and Cinema* (Bloomington: Indiana University Press, 1988), pp. 46–56.

24. Susan Willis, *The BBC Shakespeare Plays: Making the Televised Canon* (Chapel Hill: University of North Carolina Press, 1991), pp. 85–86.

25. John Gorrie, as quoted by Harry Fenwick, "The Production," in *The BBC TV Shakespeare: Twelfth Night* (London: BBC, 1979), p. 20.

26. As Cedric Messina, the series producer, puts it, "It may be Illyria, but it's English through and through" (BBC *Twelfth Night*, p. 20).

27. See Simon Karlinski's "Russia's Gay Literature and Culture: The Impact of the October Revolution," in *Hidden from History: Reclaiming the Gay and Lesbian Past*, ed. Martin Duberman et al. (New York: Penguin Books, 1990), pp. 347–64.

28. Laura Mulvey, "Visual Pleasure and Narrative Cinema," in *Feminism and Film Theory*, ed. Constance Penley (New York: Routledge, Chapman and Hall, 1988), pp. 57–68. For a critique of Mulvey's reading, see Mary Ann Doane, *Femmes Fatales: Feminism, Film Theory, Psychoanalysis* (New York: Routledge, 1991), esp. pp. 17–43.

29. Linda Williams, *Hard Core: Power, Pleasure and "the frenzy of the visible"* (Berkeley: University of California Press, 1989), pp. 123–25.

30. In a similar way, the boy-actresses' voices, together with the clothes, were the major signals of gender on the Renaissance stage, as Kate McLuskie notes in "The Act, the Role, and the Actor: Boy-Actresses on the Elizabethan Stage," *New Theatre Quarterly* 3 (1987): 120–30.

31. Henry Morley, *The Journal of a London Playgoer* (London: Leichester University Press, 1974), p. 308.

32. As David Greenblatt notes, in *The Construction of Homosexuality* (Chicago: University of Chicago Press, 1988), there was a major policing of homosexuals in the 1950s in Great Britain, followed by increasing prosecutions on charges of indecency after decriminalization.

## 6. Displacing and Renaming Love: A Lacanian Reading

1. See Thomas MacCary, *Friends and Lovers: The Phenomenology of Desire in Shakespearean Comedy* (New York: Columbia University Press, 1985), and

Barbara Freedman, "Separation and Fusion in *Twelfth Night*," in *Psychoanalytic Approaches to Literature and Film*, ed. Maurice Charney and Joseph Reppen (Rutherford, N.J.: Farleigh Dickinson University Press, 1987), pp. 96–119.

2. Stephen Greenblatt, "Fiction and Friction," in *Shakespearean Negotiations: The Circulation of Social Energy in Renaissance England* (Berkeley: University of California Press, 1988), pp. 82–92.

3. Jacques Lacan, "Seminar on 'The Purloined Letter,'" trans. Jeffrey Mehlman in *The Purloined Poe: Lacan, Derrida, and Psychoanalytic Reading* (Baltimore: Johns Hopkins University Press, 1988), pp. 28–54.

4. Jacques Lacan, "The Agency of the Letter in the Unconscious," in *Ecrits: A Selection*, trans. Alan Sheridan (New York: W. W. Norton and Co., 1977), p. 152.

5. See Lacan, *Ecrits: A Selection*, especially "The Signification of the Phallus" (pp. 281–91).

6. See chapter 1 for commentary on John Manningham's diary, mentioning Malvolio.

7. Joel Fineman, "Fratricide and Cuckoldry: Shakespeare's Doubles," in *Representing Shakespeare: New Psychoanalytic Essays*, ed. Murray Schwartz and Coppélia Kahn (Baltimore: Johns Hopkins University Press, 1980), pp. 70–109.

8. In Lacan's terms, "M.O.A.I." could be seen as the signifier of the effects of signification. Lacan's term for this signifier of the total effects of the signified is, of course, the phallus. See also Jonathan Goldberg, "Textual Properties," *Shakespeare Quarterly* 37 (1986): 213–17.

9. William Shakespeare, *Twelfth Night: The Arden Shakespeare*, ed. J. M. Lothian and T. W. Craik (New York: Methuen, 1975), act 2, scene 5, line 109. All further references to the play in this chapter refer to this text.

10. The quotation from *Time's Whistle* as Hotson notes it is "Fire hot and dry, air moist and hot we call / Sea cold and moist, earth dry and cold withal" (*The First Night of "Twelfth Night"* [London: Hart-Davis, 1955], p. 166).

11. L. S. Cox, "The Riddle in *Twelfth Night*," *Shakespeare Quarterly* 13 (1962): 360. Stephen Melville pointed out this particular anagrammatic possibility.

12. Cynthia Lewis, "'The Fustian Riddle'?: Anagrammatic Names in *Twelfth Night*," *English Language Notes* 22.4 (1985): 36 (my emphasis).

13. Stephen Booth, "*Twelfth Night*: 1.1: Malvolio as Audience," in *Shakespeare's "rough magic": Renaissance Essays in Honor of C. L. Barber*, ed. Peter Erickson and Coppélia Kahn (Newark: University of Delaware Press, 1985), pp. 166–67.

14. For further class and gender implications of the marriage of Maria (and of Olivia), see Cristina Malcolmson, "'What You Will': Social Mobility and Gender in *Twelfth Night*," in *The Matter of Difference: Materialist Feminist Criticism*

*of Shakespeare*, ed. Valerie Wayne (Ithaca: Cornell University Press, 1991), pp. 29–58.

15. See Jonathan Goldberg, *Writing Matter: From the Hands of the English Renaissance* (Stanford: Stanford University Press, 1990), for a full discussion of the significance of handwriting and training in the skill in the Renaissance. Maria's "identical hand" with Olivia denotes, in part, her status in the household.

16. The confusion of pronouns so evident in Malvolio's "she did affect me" recurs; this time Sir Toby could be confusing himself with the other participant implicated in the duel, the Count's youth, and calling for Sir Andrew to write a challenge to him.

17. As Craik notes, "Olivia must not use the name Cesario in this scene, as she did in IV.i.49, or the audience's attention will be drawn to the impossibility of keeping up the mistake of identity throughout the ceremony" (p. 130).

18. See Jacques Derrida, "The Purveyor of Truth," in *The Purloined Poe: Lacan, Derrida, and Psychoanalytic Reading*, pp. 173–212.

19. Actually this is the third story to appear; the narrator actually mentions the other two in the first paragraphs of "The Purloined Letter."

### 7. "What's in a Name?"; Or What Do We Talk about When We Talk about *Twelfth Night*?

1. Jerome McGann, *The Textual Condition* (Princeton: Princeton University Press, 1991), pp. 31–32.

2. Charles Burnaby, *Love Betray'd* (London, 1703). William Halstead includes *Love Betray'd* in his list of texts but declines to catalog its changes with the other performance editions and promptbooks because it does not include more than 50 lines (*Shakespeare as Spoken*, vol. 4 [Ann Arbor: University of Michigan Press, 1983], p. 280b).

3. Geoffrey Bullough, *Narrative and Dramatic Sources of Shakespeare, Vol. 2—the Comedies* (New York: Columbia University Press, 1958), p. 297.

4. Bullough coyly paraphrases rather than translating this indelicate speech (p. 338).

5. Charles and Mary Lamb, *Tales from Shakespeare* (New York: Houghton Mifflin, 1894, first published 1807); "Viola and Olivia," in *Art and Poetry: Being Thoughts towards Nature Conducted Principally by Artists*, no. 4 (London: Dickinson and Company, 1850), p. 145; Mary Cowden Clarke, *The Girlhood of Shakespeare's Heroines in a Series of Tales* (New York: A. C. Armstrong and Son, 1891; first published as a set of fifteen novelettes between 1850 and 1852).

6. See George C. Gross, "Mary Cowden Clarke: 'The Girlhood of Shakespeare's Heroines' and the Sex Education of Victorian Women,'" *Victorian Studies* 16 (1976): 37–58.

7. *The Spirit of the Plays of Shakspeare*, drawn and engraved by Frank Howard, vol. 1 (London: Cadell, 1833).

8. *Shakespeare's Twelfth Night, Or What You Will*, directed by Graham Howard, software design and programming by Rob Bevan, and research and design by Andrew Child and Kavita Sharma, copyright 1991.

9. This coyness about homosexual desire extends to other parts of the CD-ROM program, possibly in response to the presumed student audience. Certainly the silence on such matters also appears in the discussion of Shakespeare's contemporaries. Although both Francis Bacon and Christopher Marlowe are given commentaries and lengthy aural descriptions, not a word surfaces about Marlowe's heretical homoeroticism or Bacon's legal difficulties over his relationships with his male servants.

10. For more on hypertext and literary canons, see Jay David Bolter's "Literature in the Electronic Writing Space," in *Literacy Online: The Promise (and Peril) of Reading and Writing with Computers*, ed. Myron C. Tuman (Pittsburgh: University of Pittsburgh Press, 1992).

11. *Complete Study Edition: Twelfth Night*, ed. Sidney Lamb (Lincoln, Neb.: Cliffs Notes, 1967); *Twelfth Night, or What You Will: Shakespeare Made Easy*, edited and rendered into modern English by Alan Durband (Woodbury, N.Y.: Barron's Educational Series, 1985); and *Twelfth Night by William Shakespeare: The Cartoon Shakespeare Series—The Complete Text of Shakespeare's Plays in Illustrated Form*, illustrated by John H. Howard (Montreal: Eden Press, 1985) all offer the full "original" text of the comedy.

# Bibliography of *Twelfth Night* Performance Editions

Entries are listed chronologically and followed by the reference name used in the book.

*Twelfth Night, or What You Will*, as they are now performed at the Theatres Royal in London. In *Bell's Edition of Shakspeare's Plays*, vol. 5. London: Printed for John Bell near Exeter Exchange in the Strand, and C. Etherington at York, 1774. (Bell)

*Twelfth Night; Or What You Will*, By William Shakspeare—as it is acted at the Theatres-Royal in Drury Lane and Covent Garden. London: Harrison and Wenman, 1779. (Wenman)

*Twelfth Night; Or What You Will* (London: Bathurst, 1786). (Bathurst)

*Twelfth Night; Or, What You Will*, A Comedy by William Shakspeare. London: Randall, 1787. (Randall)

*Twelfth Night; Or What You Will*: A Comedy by William Shakspeare. Printed conformable to the Representation at the Theatre Royale Drury-Lane—under the inspection of James Wrighten, Prompter. London: Lowndes, 1791. (Lowndes)

*Twelfth Night; Or What You Will*: A Comedy, in five acts. Written by William Shakespeare. As performed at the Theatre in Boston, with notes critical and illustrative. Boston: Printed for David West and John West, n.d. [1794]. (West)

*Twelfth Night; Or What You Will*, a comedy in five acts, by William Shakspeare. As performed at the Theatres Royal, Drury Lane and Covent Garden.

Printed under the authority of the managers from the prompt book. With remarks by Mrs. Inchbald. In *Inchbald's British Theatre*, vol. 5. London: Longman, Hurst, Rees, and Orm, 1808. (Inchbald)

*Shakspeare's Twelfth Night; Or What You Will.* A comedy, revised by J. P.
Kemble; and now published as it is acted at the Theatre Royal in Convent
Garden. London: Printed for the theatre, 1810. (Kemble 1810)

*Shakspeare's Twelfth Night; Or, What You Will*: A comedy, revised by J. P.
Kemble; and now published as it is performed at the Theatres Royal. In *A Se-
lect British Theatre*, vol. 1. London: Printed for John Miller, 25 Bow Street,
Convent Garden and sold in the theatres, 1815. (Kemble)

*A Select British Theatre*; containing all the plays formerly adapted to the stage by
Mr. Kemble; revised by him, with additional alterations, in eight volumes.
London: John Miller, Convent Garden, 1815. (*Select*)

*Twelfth Night; Or, What You Will*, A comedy; by William Shakspeare. with
prefatory remarks. The only edition which is faithfully marked with the stage
business and stage directions, as it is performed at the Theatres Royal. By
W. Oxberry, Comedian. In *Oxberry's New English Drama*, vol. 12. London:
Simpkin, 1821. (Oxberry)

*Twelfth Night, or, What You Will*: A Comedy, In Five Acts, by William
Shakspere. Printed from the Acting Copy, with remarks Biographical and
critical, By D. ——G. In *Cumberland's British Theatre*, vol. 11. London:
Cooke, n.d. [1830] (dated following Halstead). (Cumberland)

*Twelfth Night, Or, What You Will*, by William Shakespeare in *French's Standard
Drama*; New York: Samuel French, 1847. (French)

*Twelfth Night; Or What You Will*, by William Shakespeare; Burton's Theatre
Edition. New York: Taylor, n.d. [1852]. (Taylor)

*Twelfth Night, or What You Will: A Comedy in Five Acts.* By William Shakespeare. In *Lacy's Acting Plays*, vol. 36. London: T. H. Lacy, n.d. [1855]. (Lacy)

Shakespere's Comedy of *Twelfth Night*, arranged for representation in five acts
by Charles Calvert—produced under his direction at Prince's Theatre Manchester, Sept. 1873; Manchester: Alex. Ireland & Co, Pall Mall. (Calvert)

*Twelfth Night*, A Comedy in five acts, by William Shakespeare, the Memorial
Theatre Edition—meant for reading aloud, ed. by C. E. Flower. London:
Samuel French, n.d. [1882]. (*Memorial Theatre*)

*Twelfth Night*: A Comedy in Five Acts by William Shakespeare, as performed
by Madame Modjeska (Countess Bozenta). Indianapolis: Hasselman Journal
Co., Stereotypers, Printers and Binders, 1883. (Modjeska)

*Twelfth Night; Or What You Will*, A Comedy in Five Acts, by William Shakespeare, as arranged for the stage by Henry Irving, and presented at the
Lyceum Theatre, July 8, 1884, London: Chiswick Press, 1884. (Irving)

*Twelfth Night; Or What You Will*, by William Shakespeare. Privately printed for Augustine Daly, 1893. (Daly)

*Twelfth Night*, Souvenir of the comedy produced at Her Majesty's Theatre, by Henry Beerbohm Tree, February 5, 1901. London: Hentschel, 1901. (Tree)

*Twelfth Night: An Acting Edition.* London: William Heineman, 1912. (Granville-Barker)

*Twelfth Night; Or, What You Will*, by William Shakespeare. *Mercury Shakespeare*, Orson Wells and Roger Hill. New York: Harper, 1934. (*Mercury Twelfth Night*)

*Twelfth Night; Or What You Will*, by William Shakespeare. *Globe Theatre Version*, Thomas Wood Stevens. New York: French, n.d. [1937]. (Globe Theatre)

### Video Editions

*Twelfth Night: or, What You Will.* Dir. Charles Kent. Vitagraph, 1910. (Vitagraph *Twelfth Night*)

*Dvenadtsataia noch'.* Dir. Y. Frid. Leningrad: Lenfilm Productions, 1955. (Lenfilm *Twelfth Night*)

*Twelfth Night.* Dir. John Dexter. London: John Dexter Productions, 1970. (Dexter/Plowright *Twelfth Night*)

*William Shakespeare's Twelfth Night.* Dir. Ron Wertheim. n.p.: AJB, Films, 1972. (Wertheim's *Twelfth Night*)

*Twelfth Night; Or What You Will.* Dir. John Gorrie. London: BBC Shakespeare Plays, 1980. (BBC *Twelfth Night*)

*Twelfth Night.* Dir. Paul Kafno. London: RTC Productions, 1990. (RTC *Twelfth Night*)

*Twelfth Night: Shakespeare—The Animated Tales.* Dir. Maria Muat. Moscow and Cardiff: Shakespeare Animated Films Limited, Christmas Films, and Soyuzmultfilm, 1992. (*Animated Twelfth Night*)

# Index

Goldberg, Jonathan, 18, 181 n. 7, 187
  n. 14, 192 n. 8, 193 n. 15
Goodall, Charlotte (as Viola), 55
Gorrie, John, 119–20, 123, 190 n. 18,
  191 n. 25
Granville-Barker, Harley, 105–06, 189
  n. 4
Graves, Joseph, 5–6, 9, 179 n. 8
Greenblatt, David, 191 n. 32
Greenblatt, Stephen, xvi, 80, 92, 137,
  178 n. 14, 187 n. 5, 192 n. 2
Greif, Karen, 51, 180 n. 19, 184 n. 8
Griffith, Elizabeth, 73, 186 n. 130
Gross, George C., 193 n. 6

Hall, Peter, 106
Halstead, William P., *Shakespeare
  as Spoken*, xii–xiii, 35, 177 n. 6,
  181 n. 17, 184 n. 2, 193 n. 2
*Hamlet*, 8, 11, 16, 109, 114, 140, 160, 190
Harper, Elizabeth (as Olivia), 55
Hazlitt, William, 23, 182 n. 22, 185
  n. 16
Heminge, John, xvi, 25, 27–28, 35
*Henry VI*, 5
Heterosexuality, 72, 80, 86–87,
  91–92, 104, 121, 126, 133, 137,
  167–68
Hogan, C. B., *The London Stage*, 178
  n. 9, 184 n. 13
Homoeroticism, xiv, 11, 78–104 pas-
  sim, 113–14, 119, 121, 123–25, 128,
  131, 133–35, 137, 167–68, 172–73
Homosexuality, 87–89, 124–25, 133,
  135, 168
Honigmann, Earnest A. J., 182 n. 27
Hotson, Leslie, 8, 141–43, 179 n. 15,
  192 n. 10
Howard, Frank, *The Spirit of the Plays
  of Shakspeare*, 170, 194 n. 7
Howe, Elizabeth, 72, 186 n. 28

Hudson, Henry, 103, 189 n. 35
Hunt, Leigh, dramatic criticism,
  9, 12, 58, 60, 72, 98, 180 n. 20,
  185 n. 18
Huston, J. Dennis, 2, 11, 178 n. 3

Illustrations. *See* Performance editions
Inchbald, Elizabeth: as critic, xi, 41,
  54, 56, 63, 104; as editor, 32,
  34–39, 41–42, 54, 56, 63–64, 183
  n. 31, 183 n. 32
*Inchbald's British Theatre*, 16, 30, 31,
  34, 49, 57, 65, 67, 70, 74–75, 186
  n. 31
Introductions. *See* Performance
  editions
Ioppolo, Grace, 19, 181 n. 10, 182
  n. 27, 185 n. 20
Irving, Henry, 76, 94, 105–06, 111,
  186 n. 2, 188 n. 20, 189 n. 4

Jaggard, William, 18, 26, 35
Jameson, Anna, 99–100, 102, 188 n.
  29
Jessica, 100
Jewett, Henry, 186 n. 2
Johnson, Samuel, 22, 42, 183 n. 40,
  189 n. 39
Jonson, Ben, xvi, 25, 35, 182 n. 25
Jordon, Dora, 41, 186 n. 28
Jowett, John, 178 n. 8
Julia, 100
*Julius Caesar*, 34

Kafno, Paul, 113–15, 118, 121–22, 135,
  190 n. 18
Karlinski, Simon, 191 n. 21
Kean, Charles, 102
Kemble, John Philip: as actor, 38; as
  editor, xii–xv, 15, 26, 28–32,
  34–39, 41–51, 56–57, 59, 60,